RETHINKING READINESS

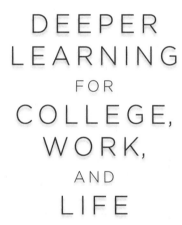

DEEPER LEARNING FOR COLLEGE, WORK, AND LIFE

EDITED BY

RAFAEL HELLER
REBECCA E. WOLFE
ADRIA STEINBERG

HARVARD EDUCATION PRESS
CAMBRIDGE, MASSACHUSETTS

Paperback ISBN 978-1-68253-052-8
Library Edition ISBN 978-1-68253-053-5

Library of Congress Cataloging-in-Publication Data

Names: Heller, Rafael, editor. | Wolfe, Rebecca E., editor. | Steinberg, Adria, editor.
Title: Rethinking readiness : deeper learning for college, work, and life / edited by Rafael Heller, Rebecca E. Wolfe, Adria Steinberg.
Description: Cambridge, Massachusetts : Harvard Education Press, [2017] | Includes bibliographical references and index.
Identifiers: LCCN 2016053466| ISBN 9781682530528 (pbk.) | ISBN 9781682530535 (library edition)
Subjects: LCSH: Student-centered learning—United States. | Experiential learning—United States. | High school teaching—United States. | Career education—United States. | Educational change—United States. | Education, Secondary—Aims and objectives—United States.
Classification: LCC LB1027.23 .R46 2017 | DDC 371.39/4—dc23
LC record available at https://lccn.loc.gov/2016053466

Published by Harvard Education Press,
an imprint of the Harvard Education Publishing Group

Harvard Education Press
8 Story Street
Cambridge, MA 02138

Cover Design: Endpaper Studio
Cover Image: iStock/© ma_rish

The typefaces used in this book are Minion and Gotham.

CONTENTS

FOREWORD

What does it mean for young people to be truly well prepared for college, careers, and civic life? What can the nation's secondary schools do to ensure that all students—regardless of their race or ethnicity, cultural or linguistic heritage, or economic background—have meaningful opportunities to succeed in the twenty-first century? And what will it take to remodel a public school system that was designed for the industrial age?

Over the last few decades, educational policy makers have tended to respond to these complex, many-sided questions by giving a one-dimensional answer: students from all backgrounds will succeed if schools do more to support proficiency in basic academic content.

In 2010, the Hewlett Foundation asked leading education researchers, practitioners, and other experts to reconsider this assumption in light of the latest research into learning, brain science, adolescent development, college access and success, and the changing nature of the American workplace. What we learned, and what the National Research Council has validated, was that students need a combination of cognitive, interpersonal, and intrapersonal competencies, and they must be able to use their knowledge and skills to solve novel problems.[1]

More specifically, essential goals for cognitive development include:

- *Mastery of core academic content.* Students build their academic foundation in subjects like reading, writing, mathematics, and science. They understand key principles and procedures, recall facts, use the correct disciplinary language, and draw on their knowledge to complete new tasks.

- *Critical thinking and problem solving.* Students think critically, analytically, and creatively. They know how to find, evaluate, and synthesize information to construct arguments. They can design their own solutions to complex problems.

In addition, students must be able to interact with others, building interpersonal competencies, including:

- *Collaboration.* Students work well in teams. They communicate and understand multiple points of view and they know how to cooperate to achieve a shared goal.
- *Effective communication.* Students communicate effectively in writing and oral presentations. They structure information in meaningful ways, listen to and give feedback, and construct messages for particular audiences.

Finally, students must be able to engage in self-management through intrapersonal competencies:

- *Learning how to learn.* Students develop an ability to direct their own learning. They set goals, monitor their own progress, and reflect on their own strengths and areas for improvement. They learn to see setbacks as opportunities for feedback and growth. Students who learn through self-direction are more adaptive than their peers.
- *Academic or learning mind-sets.* Students have a strong belief in themselves and believe they belong in school. They trust their own abilities and believe their hard work will pay off, so they persist to overcome obstacles. They also learn from and support each other. They see the relevance of their schoolwork to the real world and their own future success.

We call this collection of six competencies "deeper learning," and we believe that they must be included in any contemporary definition of what it means for our students to be well prepared for the challenges they will face in the real world.

The term *deeper learning* pertains to educational outcomes—what students need to know and be able to do by their high school graduation.

However, we do not assume there is a single best way to improve secondary education to deliver on these outcomes. We trust that high schools need to explore and pursue effective approaches to help their students gain proficiency in the deeper learning competencies, and we assume that schools will need to continue to improve by learning what works.

But while we do not advocate for any particular school intervention, we know that policy makers and others will have important questions about how to promote and measure deeper learning. So, over the last several years, our goal has been to invite an open-ended, evidence-based conversation among all the key stakeholders.

To inform that conversation, we invited Jobs for the Future to develop a series of white papers—focusing on the issues that policy makers told us were their highest priorities—that have now been revised, edited, and collected in this volume. If we accept that deeper learning outcomes matter for students and, therefore, that schools should focus on deeper learning, *then* what? What should this mean for policy, practice, and school improvement? What are the implications for every aspect of secondary education, including teaching, curricula, assessment, and leadership? How can focusing on deeper learning ensure more equitable approaches and outcomes in education? And what new opportunities to pursue deeper learning have been made possible by the Every Student Succeeds Act?

The resulting work, conducted by some of the nation's leading experts, is impressive, providing readers with important background on the research that informs the goals of deeper learning, the challenges that schools must confront in order to teach to those goals, and the benefits that will accrue when they are successful in doing so. I am thankful for the rigorous and disciplined approach that Jobs for the Future took to assemble this book. My hope is that as this collection helps us begin to answer the aforementioned questions, we will be in a better position to prepare all of our children for the complex world they will inherit.

Barbara Chow
Education Program Director
The William and Flora Hewlett Foundation

ACKNOWLEDGMENTS

The Jobs for the Future team is grateful to the many people who supported and guided the development of the Deeper Learning Research Series as it became a book. First and foremost, we deeply appreciate the researchers, educators, and writers whose papers are the core of this book. Their passion for identifying, examining, and seeking new ways to pursue deeper learning outcomes for all young people is the soul of this work. We also acknowledge the many researchers, practitioners, policy makers, and philanthropists who joined the authors at JFF's national meeting "Turning the Corner: Toward a New Policy Agenda for College, Career, and Civic Readiness" in late 2015 to discuss next steps for the deeper learning movement on the eve of the Every Student Succeeds Act. The thought-provoking conversations helped shape a set of priorities outlined in our 2016 brief, "Advancing Deeper Learning Under ESSA," an early version of this book's concluding chapter. We are indebted to Carol Gerwin of JFF's communications team for her superb editorial guidance, and we owe many thanks also to our JFF colleagues Sophie Besl, Eugenie Inniss, Sarah Hatton, and Karyl Levinson, and to proofreader Alex Johnson and graphic designer Jenna Rodrigues. We are grateful to Marc Chun and Chris Shearer, our program officers at the William and Flora Hewlett Foundation, and to Barbara Chow, the education program director, for their enthusiasm for this project. (Please note, however, that the opinions expressed in this book are those of the authors and do not necessarily reflect the views of the Hewlett Foundation.) Finally, we thank Nancy Walser of the Harvard Education Press for her patience, good humor, and thoughtful advice.

—Rafael Heller, Rebecca E. Wolfe, and Adria Steinberg

Introduction

Rafael Heller, Rebecca E. Wolfe,
and Adria Steinberg

AS WE WRITE THESE WORDS, in the fall of 2016, educational policy makers in every part of the country are thumbing through the pages of the 2015 Every Student Succeeds Act (ESSA), poring over the related regulations issued by the U.S. Department of Education, and struggling to determine what it all means for the future of public schooling in their own states, districts, and towns.

ESSA makes a few things abundantly clear: to receive federal funding under the law, states must continue to abide by certain ground rules carried over from No Child Left Behind (NCLB) that aim to push school systems to provide all children with equitable opportunities to learn. For instance, states must hold all of their students to the same academic standards; test all students against those standards every year in grades 3 through 8 and once in high school; disaggregate and report the test results by race, income, disability status, and other variables; and take action to improve their lowest-performing schools.

On balance, though, ESSA is designed not to tell states what to do but, rather, to get the federal government to back off previous attempts to do so. For example, the new law doesn't tell states how to hold schools accountable for low test scores, what tests to use, what criteria they should use to identify their lowest-performing schools, or what they should do to fix those schools. In fact, ESSA's congressional sponsors have expressly prohibited the U.S. Department of Education from trying to compel states to adopt specific policies or practices.

Hence the dilemma that local policy makers now face: After spending so many years trying to comply with a federal agenda for school improvement—focusing on standards setting, test-based accountability, teacher evaluation, and a handful of other strategies—are state superintendents, governors, legislators, school leaders, and others prepared to grab the wheel and pursue an agenda of their own? Given the opportunity to chart a new course for K–12 education, how in the world should they proceed?

In 2014, more than a year before ESSA was passed, Jobs for the Future, a national nonprofit that works to expand college and career success and build a more highly skilled workforce, commissioned a series of white papers by some of the nation's most well-respected educational researchers. Looking beyond NCLB, we asked them what it would mean for the public schools (high schools in particular) to embrace a truly ambitious and equitable mission. Rather than continuing to attach so much importance to student scores on shallow tests of reading and math, what if they were to set their sights on much worthier goals, such as the kinds of "deeper learning" that Barbara Chow describes in her foreword?

That is, what if education policy makers and practitioners were to agree that by the time young people complete high school, they should have a truly well-rounded set of knowledge and skills, including not just a solid grasp of academic content but also the ability to reflect on and direct their own learning, the ability to communicate effectively in diverse contexts, the confidence to debate competing views, and other capacities needed to be responsible classmates, coworkers, and citizens? And if schools were to place greater emphasis on such goals, then what kinds of school reforms would be most useful to consider?

These questions strike us as even more urgent and timely today, now that Congress has reined in the federal government's influence over educational decision making at the state and local levels. Critics have described ESSA as a purely negative piece of legislation, one that dismantles NCLB's theory of change (especially the idea that strict accountability systems will create powerful incentives for schools to improve) but offers no new theory in its place. However, that makes it all the more important to share the kinds of research findings, recommendations, and principles that are discussed in the following chapters (which have been edited and revised from the original papers for this collection). If it will be up to state and local leaders to decide how best to proceed under ESSA—without having a theory of change imposed on them—then it will be critical for them to understand that today's young people require much deeper and more powerful educational experiences than NCLB was designed to provide.

READINESS REDEFINED

In recent years, it has become a truism to say that, in the twenty-first century, the United States can no longer afford to maintain a twentieth-century school system, one that permits legions of students (mainly from low-income and/or minority backgrounds) to leave high school without a diploma or to graduate with only basic academic knowledge and skills. Once upon a time, young people could find a job and perhaps even make a good living in a factory or on a construction site, without higher education. But today, as policy makers are fond of saying, the goal of K–12 education must be to prepare every student to succeed in college *and* careers (which now require at least a year or two of postsecondary education) so they can at least support themselves and their families, if not live comfortably.

So what does that entail, precisely?

The phrase *college and career readiness* has become so familiar that it may strike some readers as a well-worn cliché. However, it is a relatively new term, and its meaning has evolved quite a lot over a short period of time. When it first came into popular usage roughly a decade ago, it was associated almost entirely with students' *academic* preparation, having to do with their high school course taking, the rigor of the curriculum, and the alignment of twelfth-grade exit standards to the academic demands of first-year college courses. Even as recently as 2010, the authors of the Common Core State Standards equated the mastery of rigorous academic standards (at least in English language arts and mathematics) with becoming "ready for success" in college and the workforce.[1]

Today, however, that understanding of what it means to be prepared for life after high school seems quaint—not because it is wrong so much as because it is *incomplete*.

For one thing, educational policy makers have become increasingly aware of research findings that show that students' performance in college has to do with much more than just their academic preparation. As David Conley describes in chapter 9, he and other researchers have found that while high school students' content knowledge and academic skills (such as the ability to organize new information, come up with interesting research questions, and grasp the fine points of an argument) certainly contribute to later success in college courses, so do a host of other capacities (such as goal setting, time management, and a willingness to consider new ideas), along with their knowledge of college planning, financing, campus norms, and the like.[2]

At the same time, policy makers have become increasingly familiar with similar findings from the research into career development. Beginning in the 1990s with the case for "soft skills" and codified more recently in the business-led twenty-first-century skills movement, workforce readiness has been redefined to include much more than just academic and technical preparation. For example, data collected over the past two decades from studies of U.S. workplaces and from large-scale surveys of employers point to a fast-growing need for workers who possess skills such as the ability to communicate and collaborate with diverse colleagues, solve complex problems, and adapt to changing contexts.[3]

Moreover, recent research in educational psychology has generated a wealth of important findings about the inter- and intrapersonal dimensions of learning (sometimes described as noncognitive or metacognitive skills, or social and emotional learning), calling attention to critical topics that were often absent from policy discussions during the NCLB era. Today, growing numbers of educators, policy makers, and researchers are steering discussions about school reform toward issues such as student motivation and engagement, the social environment of schools and classrooms, the effects of stress and bullying on adolescent development, the nature of productive persistence and academic mind-set, and the ability to apply knowledge and skills to real-world problems, among many others.[4]

Finally, and perhaps most important, it has become increasingly clear that millions of the nation's young people are facing challenges that cannot be addressed simply by raising academic standards and holding teachers and schools accountable for test scores and graduation rates. To be sure, many of NCLB's supporters conceived of the act as a civil rights bill, and it can still be argued that test-based accountability has a role to play in the larger effort to push schools to provide all children with meaningful opportunities to learn. However, gaps in Americans' income and wealth have only widened in recent years, with dire consequences for children growing up in poverty. Further, not only did most states cut per-pupil funding during and after the Great Recession, but researchers continue to find that, in many parts of the country, important educational resources are being distributed inequitably, resulting in starkly different learning environments for youth from different backgrounds. And at the same time, resource disparities are exacerbated by ongoing patterns of racial bias in decisions about school suspensions, referrals to special education, selection for gifted and talented programs, and other areas. In short, the present moment demands more serious and creative investments in supporting the nation's most vulnerable children (as Pedro Noguera, Linda Darling-Hammond, and Diane Friedlaender argue in chapter 4), such as efforts to create and fund new school and community services in distressed neighborhoods, monitor and address civil rights violations in public education, and ensure that basic skills instruction does not crowd out opportunities to learn higher-order skills and advanced content.[5]

THE IMPLICATIONS FOR SECONDARY SCHOOLING

In an earlier collection, *Anytime, Anywhere: Student-Centered Learning for Schools and Teachers* (published by Harvard Education Press in 2013), we focused on recent research into cognition, learning, youth development, and school improvement. Note, though, that we did not offer a prescriptive agenda for school reform. We are leery of reformers' past efforts to find, as the historian David Tyack put it, "one best system" for educating children.[6] But we do find strong evidence to suggest that most schools should do far more to support certain kinds of intellectual, social, and emotional development.

Specifically, we argue in *Anytime, Anywhere* that public education ought to provide adolescents with ample opportunities to (1) participate in ambitious and rigorous instruction tailored to their individual needs and interests; (2) advance to the next level, course, or grade based on demonstrations of their skills and content knowledge; (3) learn outside of the school building and the typical school day; and (4) take an active role in defining their own educational pathways.

The present volume comes at these issues from a somewhat different angle. Rather than focusing on research-based teaching practices (i.e., the *means* of supporting adolescents' developmental needs), we begin with a focus on the *ends* of secondary education. If college and career readiness (and civic readiness, we add) require students not just to master academic standards but to develop a more comprehensive set of intellectual, personal, and relational skills—that is, to learn deeply—then what does this mean for educational policy making? And how might this lead school reformers to rethink their priorities and turn their attention from a one-dimensional focus on standards and accountability to a deeper look at everything from improving teacher education and professional development to investing in college and career advising, student health services, bilingual education, work-based learning, school integration, support for students with disabilities, early college and dual-enrollment programs, community engagement, civic learning, and on and on?

We have organized this book into three broad themes:

1. *The purposes and goals of secondary education.* We begin with an overview chapter by Jal Mehta and Sarah Fine that explains how deeper learning fits into the historical trajectory of secondary schooling in the United States and why it could represent a truly new agenda for school reform, focusing simultaneously on educational excellence and equity. In chapter 2, Nancy Hoffman looks at deeper learning through its connection to career readiness, arguing that work-based education provides unique opportunities to learn deeply. And in chapter 3, Peter Levine and Kei Kawashima-Ginsberg explore the intersection of civic readiness and deeper learning, demonstrating the essential role of deeper learning in our democracy.

2. *Access and opportunity.* In chapter 4, Pedro Noguera, Linda Darling-Hammond, and Diane Friedlaender ask what can be done to ensure that all students, regardless of their family income or racial/ethnic background, have meaningful opportunities to learn deeply. In chapter 5, Sharon Vaughn, Louis Danielson, Rebecca Zumeta Edmonds, and Lynn Holdheide look specifically at the supports and instructional strategies needed to help students with disabilities to learn deeply. And in chapter 6, Patricia Gándara focuses on English language learners and immigrant students, discussing both the hurdles they must overcome to learn deeply and the advantages that they bring to the table.

3. *School improvement for deeper learning.* To help students develop a combination of academic, interpersonal, and intrapersonal competencies, what must teachers know and be able to do, asks Magdalene Lampert in chapter 7—and how can they pull it off day after day in their classrooms? In chapter 8, Meredith Honig and Lydia Rainey examine what school system leaders can do to create the conditions under which such teaching and learning are possible. And in chapter 9, David Conley discusses the kinds of assessments that will be needed to guide teachers and students toward deeper learning outcomes.

We close, in chapter 10, with a review of policy principles and priorities to consider in the ESSA era, including recommendations offered by the authors of the preceding chapters and suggestions made by dozens of other researchers, practitioners, and policy experts that we have consulted with over the last two years.

We anticipate that this book will be of great interest not only to policy makers and advocates, but also to teachers, school and district administrators, journalists, university faculty members, and graduate students. While all of the chapters are strongly grounded in academic research, they are written in a nonacademic and highly accessible style, meant to offer readers a broad introduction to the given topic, highlight the most critical debates in the field, and provoke further discussion.

Finally, please note that this collection is not meant to promote "deeper learning" as a brand name or to advocate for a specific school model or policy initiative. As we referenced earlier, others may prefer to frame the discussion in terms of "social and emotional learning," "twenty-first century skills," "metacognitive learning," or other terminology. Rather than insisting that any one label is best, our goal is to encourage truly open-ended debate about the larger and more important question: If college, career, and civic readiness require more than just higher academic standards and tougher accountability—the focus of most education policy making over the last few decades—then what are the implications for schools, educators, and students?

Numerous examples of high-quality teaching practices, curricular materials, and other resources for student-centered teaching and learning are available (free of charge) at http://studentsatthecenterhub.org.

PART ONE

The Purposes and Goals of Secondary Education

1

$$\sim\!\sim\!\sim$$

How We Got Here

The Imperative for Deeper Learning

Jal Mehta and Sarah Fine

SUCCESSFULLY NAVIGATING twenty-first-century adult life requires far more than basic academic knowledge and skills. On the personal front, adults need to be able to navigate among plural identities, to confront complex ethical questions, and to make informed decisions in the face of uncertainty.[1] On the civic front, they need to be able to articulate and advocate for their perspectives, to engage in productive dialogue across ideological divides, and to decide among imperfect options.[2] On the professional front, they need to be able to tackle open-ended problems in critical, creative, and collaborative ways and to engage in ongoing learning that allows them to adapt to the needs of a rapidly changing job market.[3]

As the nation's one truly "common" institution, public schools play a critical role in helping students to build the capacities that will allow them to thrive as adults. Unfortunately, however, a large body of evidence suggests that the current system falls short of preparing most (or even many) students for the realities depicted above. A rich literature describes the dominance of low-cognitive-demand tasks as a mainstay of American public education.[4] High schools in particular tend to ask only the most capable students to engage in ambitious thinking; students in lower tracks and in higher-poverty schools are least challenged.[5] On international tests, American fifteen-year-olds from all but the top quartile of socioeconomic status fall behind on problems that require higher-order skills.[6]

The annual High School Survey of Student Engagement reveals, year after year, that almost three-quarters of adolescents find their classes to be lacking in challenge, authenticity, or relevance.[7] Overall, as Vito Perrone once argued: "Large numbers of students are not receiving an education of power and consequence—one that allows them to be critical thinkers, problem posers, and problem solvers who are able to work through complexity, beyond the routine, and live productively in this rapidly changing world."[8]

In the years immediately following the passage of the No Child Left Behind Act in 2001, the misalignment between what schools were teaching and the realities of modern life was rarely a theme of public debates about education reform. Instead, reflecting the priorities of the test-based accountability movement, the emphasis was on providing a system-wide guarantee of basic literacy and numeracy—a return to the "three Rs" with an intensified focus on serving students from all backgrounds.

By the time the decade came to a close, however, a growing number of Americans had begun to voice their concerns about the limitations posed by focusing exclusively on preparing students for tests of basic ability. Propelled in part by the work of forward-looking business groups and foundations, including Cisco and Hewlett-Packard, many of these actors framed their aspirations for schools using the language of twenty-first-century skills—a term that refers to competencies such as creativity, problem solving, and collaboration.[9] Around the same time, a number of district and school leaders began referring to "the new three Rs'" of school reform: rigor, relevance, and relationships. And the sector's growing commitment to moving beyond the basics was reinforced by the widespread adoption of the Common Core State Standards, which (while embroiled in an ongoing controversy about federal involvement in local educational decisions) place an unprecedented emphasis on critical thinking.

Skeptics who take the long view might dismiss this recent change of focus as just another swing of the pendulum in an endlessly repeating pattern of ideological shifts. And it is certainly true that American school reform efforts have tended to cycle back and forth between "basic" and "higher-order" goals.[10] In the 1960s, for example, educators and policy makers talked a great deal about the importance of fostering curiosity and creativity through student-centered instructional practices—only to change their tune as "back to the basics" once again became the mantra in the 1970s.

Nevertheless, we see reasons to be hopeful that the nation's schools will embrace the more ambitious goals that have been collected under the umbrella term *deeper learning.*

For one thing, recent calls for deeper learning have been infused with the equity-focused ideals of the No Child Left Behind era. Today, large and growing numbers of education reformers express the conviction that students from all backgrounds are capable of engaging in critical and creative thinking, and that the schools have a moral imperative to teach those skills to all children. In the past, those who argued for deep learning tended to focus mainly on cultivating the best and the brightest so that the United States could retain its global edge with respect to creativity, entrepreneurship, and scientific innovation. And in fact, the vast majority of schools (and tracks within schools) that emphasized critical problem solving, student self-direction, and creative thinking catered to children from wealthy families.[11] Against this backdrop, the current rhetoric of "deeper learning for all" is a striking new development, quite different from the pendulum swings of the past.

However, an even more powerful reason to believe that deeper learning is more than a passing fad lies in the rapid and irreversible transformations to the landscape of modern life. Even to those who are not involved in the work of school reform, it is clear that when today's kindergartners finish high school, they will graduate into a world that is dramatically more complex than the one they currently inhabit. By the same token, it is also clear that the traditional textbook-based curriculum is becoming less and less relevant to young people's lives. Already, digital technologies have made self-directed learning opportunities so accessible that some educators are predicting the death of the brick-and-mortar school.[12] Many remain optimistic about the future of formal learning environments, but they agree that if schools are to retain any semblance of utility, they must reorient their work around the goal of preparing students to navigate a complex and uncertain future; to do otherwise is to doom themselves to obsolescence.[13]

Thus, while in previous eras it might have been possible to construe deeper learning as an optional supplement to the core work of schools, it is becoming hard to see it as anything less than the central imperative around which the entire K–12 system must reorganize itself.

In this chapter, we will explore some of the key questions that follow from this observation. First, we will examine the various terms, definitions, and strands of research that are associated with deeper learning, and we will show how the current movement for deeper learning fits into the broader historical arc of American school reform. Second, we will draw on the results of our own multiyear research project to discuss where and in what ways deeper learning is (and isn't) happening in contemporary American high schools. Finally, we will discuss the conditions that would need to be in place to move "deeper learning for all" from aspiration to reality.

WHAT IS DEEPER LEARNING? RESEARCH AND HISTORICAL CONTEXT

To begin at the beginning: What does it mean to understand something deeply?

There is no consensus on exactly how best to define deeper learning. According to one prominent definition, for example, deeper learning refers to the mastery of core academic content, as well as critical thinking and problem solving, collaboration, communication, self-directed learning, and the development of an academic mind-set.[14] As Barbara Chow explains in the foreword, these six priorities are drawn from a wealth of research, conducted over more than two decades, into the specific knowledge and skills needed to succeed in college, careers, and adult life.

However, many cognitive scientists define deeper learning more narrowly, focusing especially on the ability to transfer knowledge.[15] That is, knowledge becomes deep when you can use it not only to address a problem in the context in which it has been taught, but also to understand or explain something in a different, but related, context. For example, a shallow understanding of cell biology might enable one to label a cell's parts; a deep understanding would enable one to grasp how a cell's components function together as a system, and thus what might be expected to happen if a particular component were damaged.

Much of the recent research in the cognitive tradition—which associates deeper learning with the ability to transfer knowledge and skills to new contexts—draws its inspiration from earlier research on expertise. People who are widely seen as experts, studies have shown, tend to notice details that are not apparent to nonexperts because they have developed cognitive schemas that help them understand the domain. That is, they have become familiar with the field's individual parts and the ways in which those parts connect to a larger whole, which also allows them to zero in on those pieces that don't fit.[16] That is why, for example, expert teachers are able to assess students' thinking, spot their misunderstandings, and adjust their lessons midstream to help them, while novice teachers tend to proceed mechanically through the lesson they have prepared, unable to stop and explain how the material connects to what students already know.[17] In other words, experts are able to see both the forest and the trees.

Similarly, while critics sometimes deride deeper learning as just the latest attempt to favor "skills" over "content" (or "concepts" over "facts"), research shows this to be a false dichotomy: people who possess expertise in a domain tend to demonstrate a command of both skills and content. The ability to offer a historical interpretation of the causes of the French Revolution, for example, requires both a detailed knowledge of the key players and events *and* an ability to draw inferences, construct historical arguments, and use evidence to support one's point.

Further, the development of expertise also depends upon emotional involvement. In the most powerful educational settings, the "cold" cognitive dimensions of learning tend to be married to "warmer" qualities such as passion, interest, and active engagement—qualities that enliven the classroom and push students to learn more and build expertise. (By contrast, studies show that in most schools, the longer students attend, the lower their levels of reported engagement.[18]) From this vantage point, efforts to promote deeper learning must focus not just on building cognitive schemas and teaching both skills and content but also on issues of *motivation*.

A number of researchers have made a point of asking experts how they went from their very first experiences to becoming deeply knowledgeable and skilled in their domains.[19] The general pattern is that people initially become interested in a field by playing around in it (e.g., splashing in a pool or experimenting with a musical instrument); then they begin to engage in deliberate practice under the supervision of a coach or someone with more experience in the domain; their identities gradually shift to reflect their participation in the domain (from "I'm someone who swims" to "I'm a swimmer"); they continue to practice; and then eventually "play" and "creation" reemerge, this time in a much more complex way. We might describe this process as a kind of spiral, in which one returns again and again to the same activities, but each time in a more sophisticated way.[20]

This account of how individuals become deep learners is complemented by work that emphasizes the role that communities can play in this process. To that end, psychological researchers Lave and Wenger suggest that much of the most powerful learning takes place in communities of practice; these are fields (like midwifery, sculpting, butchering, and many others) in which one begins as a "legitimate peripheral participant" (e.g., an assistant to a midwife) and through the process of observation, modeling, and emulation, is gradually apprenticed into the knowledge and skills of the domain.[21]

Researchers Allan Collins, John Seely Brown, and Susan E. Newman have applied similar insights to more classically academic subjects in their argument for "cognitive apprenticeship," in which skilled readers, writers, and mathematicians gradually induct less expert members into their crafts.[22] Such a process brings together many elements that are hypothesized to be important for deep learning: the field sets a standard for what good work looks like; there is a significant role for coaching, modeling, and feedback; the desire to do what leading practitioners do provides direction and motivation; and the task is grounded in a human activity that has intrinsic value. The image of moving from a "peripheral participant" to a more central one is also consistent with the language of increasing "depth"; from this perspective, deepening one's learning in a given domain happens in part by becoming enmeshed in a domain-specific community, which links one's individual growth with one's social position. It also suggests a shift in role from passive observer to active participant.

Our Own Perspective: A Focus on Mastery, Identity, and Creativity

Our perspective on deeper learning is informed by all of these strands of research, as well as by our own extensive and systematic observations of classrooms that explicitly pursue deeper learning. We found that while their stated goals varied somewhat (to promote disciplinary understanding, or interdisciplinary problem solving, or experiential learning, and so on), these classrooms tended to have quite similar qualities as well. Most important, they were environments where the challenge of working at the edge of their knowledge and skills led students to become deeply absorbed, and where learning involved grappling with uncertainty, ambiguity, and the real possibility of failure. The motivation to persevere through such obstacles was rooted in the intellectual vitality that characterized these classrooms as a whole—an intangible quality that infused the work with meaning and momentum.

Pulling these strands together, we suggest that deeper learning often emerges at the intersection of the following three elements: mastery, identity, and creativity. If the goal is for students to develop the range of competencies that the William and Flora Hewlett Foundation has identified—understanding of core academic content, critical thinking, collaboration, communication, self-directed learning, and an academic mind-set—then schools must address all three of these fundamental needs.

Mastery captures the dimensions of deeper learning that are tied to knowledge of substantive content, transfer, pattern recognition and expertise, and understanding the structure of a field or discipline. Identity captures the way in which deeper learning generally is driven by intrinsic motivation, how it is fueled by learners' perceptions about the relevance of the content, and by the way that learning deepens as it becomes a more core part of the self. Creativity captures the shift from receiving the accumulated knowledge of a subject or domain to being able to act or make something within the field; taking this step builds upon understanding a domain (e.g., analyzing how a play is written) and incorporates it into a creative act (e.g., writing an original play).

Seen this way, aspirations for deeper learning pose a serious challenge to schools as we know them. At minimum, they suggest the importance of a long-called-for but thus far unachieved increase in the cognitive demand of the tasks that most students, particularly high-poverty students, are asked to complete. From this vantage point, the kind of rigor present in the Common Core and related state standards and assessments is a critical step for realizing deeper learning because those standards call for fewer topics, more depth in each topic, and more opportunities to integrate knowledge and make conceptual connections than previously has been the case.

More radically, some advocates of deeper learning are questioning many of the industrial-age structures that organize today's classrooms. From this perspective, a commitment to deeper learning would entail a shift from discipline-specific, age-graded classrooms based on Carnegie units and seat time toward a system that is more interdisciplinary, problem based, and organized around demonstrations of mastery. Metaphors of coach and producer would replace teacher and student, and there would be many opportunities for young people to join communities of practice, which can gradually induct them into more sophisticated levels of work.

Clearly, a serious commitment to deeper learning would require a significant departure from current practice, and particularly from the practices that tend to characterize instruction in schools and classrooms serving disadvantaged and minority students.

Learning from the Past

The history of deep learning is one of powerful intellectual backing but limited real-world impact. Despite major pendulum swings of "policy talk," the majority of American schools have changed slowly, fitfully, and, in many cases, not at all. It is a history that modern deeper learning advocates should understand if they want their efforts to be more successful than those of their predecessors.[23]

Deeper learning has had no shortage of prominent intellectual supporters. From Socrates in Classical Greece, to Rousseau in Napoleonic Europe, to Bronson Alcott in nineteenth-century America, educators and philosophers have long insisted that powerful learning hinges on the facilitation of ongoing inquiry rather than the delivery of static knowledge. However, the evidence suggests that schooling in the early United States was on the whole a rote activity, focused more on teaching children the "three Rs" and on socializing them to be productive citizens than on cultivating creativity or independent thought.[24]

As the system of publicly funded, publicly provisioned, coeducational "common" schools came to encompass the secondary grades in the early twentieth century, the landscape shifted—but not in the direction of deeper learning. To the contrary, accounts of a prototypical Midwestern public high school suggest that instruction in the core academic subjects was focused largely on the development of rote knowledge and basic skills.[25] Not coincidentally, this period of time is the same one that cemented the core organizational "efficiencies" that have persisted through to the present: age-graded classrooms, the division of the curriculum into discrete academic subjects, and teacher-centered pedagogy, which requires students to master knowledge and skills in lockstep.[26]

To the new class of bureaucrats whose job it was to run America's burgeoning city school systems, these practices were the latest in industrial-inspired design, drawing on the popular principles of "scientific management" in order to streamline the process of providing a full twelve years of education to the country's youth.[27] To others, however, these practices were troublingly misguided. Foremost among these voices of dissent was philosopher John Dewey, who insisted that the existing model of schooling all but guaranteed that the learning process would be devoid of meaning and depth. Rather than modeling themselves after contemporary factories, he argued, schools—including high schools—should look backward, emulating the values of agrarian households by adopting an interdisciplinary, hands-on, collaborative curriculum that, drawing on Swiss education reformer Johann Heinrich Pestalozzi, engaged the head, hands, and heart in equal measure.[28]

Dewey's ideas had a profound influence on the aspirations of reform-minded contemporaries and many who followed.[29] Rejecting the efficiency model of schooling, they strived instead to enact a more "progressive" approach to education—at first, well outside the mainstream. By 1920, they banded together to form the Progressive Education Association, whose first act was to develop and widely circulate its seven core principles, including "Interest, the motive of all work" and "The teacher a guide, not a task-master." Posing a clear challenge to the norms of the day, these principles together asserted that the role of schools was to foster individual growth rather than to cultivate mastery of predetermined content.

Over the next several decades, members of the Progressive Education Association (PEA) experimented with putting their beliefs into action. The result was extraordinary education in some small private schools, which drew upon the social and cultural capital of their students, paired with highly skilled teachers, to produce creative and individualized education that retained significant academic content. In the larger sphere of public schools, however, a bastardized vision of progressive education emerged. Vocational and "life adjustment education"—nonacademic courses in fields like shop and home economics intended to prepare non-college-going students for life after high school—sacrificed academic content in their search for relevance.

By the end of World War II, most high schools across the country had adopted elements of educational progressivism, at least at eye level. (To enable collaborative work, desks were no longer nailed to the floor.) To support students in "adjusting" to the nonacademic dimensions of life, high schools offered an array of vocational classes along with an expanded program of elective courses. Finally, in formal recognition that academic learning is informed by social and emotional development, many schools added social workers to their payrolls.[30] None of these changes represented the more radical of the PEA's propositions, however, and few had the kind of impact that reformers hoped. In many cases, teachers assimilated discrete elements such as group work and tangible "props" into their pedagogical repertoires, but continued on the whole to be "knowledge-centered," "subject-centered," and "teacher-centered" in their teaching.[31]

In other cases, teachers tried to institute more substantive changes but did so with limited success. In the 1960s, for example, curriculum reforms created opportunities for "guided inquiry." The aspiration was decidedly "deeper": teachers would facilitate while students engaged in exploration of open-ended problems, constructing deep understandings of academic concepts. However, in the absence of rich content knowledge, ongoing professional development, and broader changes in school culture, most teachers were unable to realize the aspirations of the program's designers.[32]

The third quarter of the twentieth century saw yet another swing of the ideological pendulum, with an increasing number of educators urging the field to reject what they saw as the academic vapidity of progressive education. If America wanted to maintain its economic dominance, they argued, its schools needed to get "back to basics" by focusing on providing students with a consistent baseline of skills and knowledge. Such calls waxed and waned throughout the 1960s and 1970s, but they grew exponentially louder with the publication of *A Nation at Risk* in 1983, which suggested that American high school students lagged far behind their international peers.[33] This report prompted a renewed emphasis on core content knowledge, sowing the seeds of the modern accountability movement. Although traces of progressivism could still be seen in widespread classroom practices such as group work, the dominant policy logic once again favored the development of baseline literacy and numeracy.[34] The passage of No Child Left Behind in 2001 inscribed this vision into federal law, and it remained the dominant thrust up until the recent emergence of the Common Core, a growing push for twenty-first-century skills, and the passage of the Every Student Succeeds Act in 2015.

Finally, this history also underscores perhaps the most important reason there has not been more deep learning in American schools: limited public demand for it. The qualities associated with deep learning—critical thinking, grappling with nuance and complexity, questioning authority, and embracing intellectual questions—are not ones that are widely embraced by the American people.[35] For example, the 1960s National Science Foundation curriculum, Man: A Course of Study (MACOS), which invited students to study another culture as part of an anthropological examination of what it means to be human, died at the hands of a fundamentalist backlash.[36] And MACOS is just one example among many of the ways in which efforts to have students ask difficult questions have been rebuffed by a more conservative electorate.

Toward an Equitable Approach to Deeper Learning

Throughout this history, the dividing lines of race and class have played a critical role in determining who has had access to deeper learning experiences. Faced with massive immigration and a rapidly growing high school population at the beginning of the twentieth century, reformers built a school system that created different pathways for students of different abilities and/or family backgrounds. Emboldened by the then new science of intelligence testing, these reformers created an explicitly differentiated school system that funneled more advantaged students into fairly rigorous academic tracks and poorer and working-class students into much less academically demanding tracks.

In the second half of the twentieth century, these inequalities were exacerbated by the growth of residential segregation and the deindustrialization of cities, developments that led to increasing disparities between city and suburban schools.[37] The result, according to both quantitative evidence and closely observed ethnographies of classrooms, is that schools and tracks that serve upper-middle-class students more frequently feature interactions where students are given ample opportunities to express their thinking and grapple with complex or open-ended questions, whereas schools or classes serving working-class or high-poverty students tend to be dominated by teacher talk and to feature worksheets and other low-level tasks.[38]

It is perhaps not surprising that the examples we do have of deeper learning—some private schools, Advanced Placement, International Baccalaureate, and some honors track classes in large comprehensive high schools, exam schools, and magnet schools—tend to involve niches of interested students, supportive parents, and teachers who are willing and able to teach in such environments.[39]

Thus, while the overall enthusiasm for progressive or inquiry-oriented education has waxed and waned across decades, to the degree that it has been taken up, it has frequently been for the most advantaged students. As the following sections argue, expanding these niches to the whole will require a seismic shift.

WHERE CAN WE FIND DEEPER LEARNING? MAPPING THE CONTEMPORARY LANDSCAPE

In 2011, the two of us set out to "map the landscape" of nonelite public high schools that are enacting deeper learning for all of their students.[40] Our plan was to use our professional networks to identify a range of such places and then to immerse ourselves in them, studying their work using ethnographic methods and emerging with sparkling case studies to inspire and guide others in the field.

When we described the work to others, we referred to it as an antidote to the often negative portrayals of schools, calling it by turns the "good schools beyond test scores" project and the "varieties of excellent schooling" project.[41] Twelve months later found us in a very different state of mind. As planned, we had solicited names of leading nonelite high schools from an array of stakeholders in the field: teachers, parents, school and district leaders, policy makers, foundation heads, and researchers. We made plans to visit and study teaching and learning practices at thirty of those schools, focusing on the ones that were recommended most consistently. We spent thousands of hours at those schools, shadowing students through their days and conducting structured observations in their classrooms. And at school after school, we found startling gaps between aspirations and realities.

Most classrooms were spaces to passively sit and listen. Most academic work consisted of tasks that asked students to recall or minimally apply what they had been told. Even in schools that actively were striving to organize instruction around authentic tasks, when we asked students about the purpose of what they were doing, the most common responses were "I dunno—the teacher told us to" and "I guess it might help me in college." We had hoped to be inspired, but instead we felt profoundly disheartened. Perhaps we should not have been surprised. Even at these recommended schools, what we saw was consistent with the history described above, as well as with qualitative accounts of secondary schools in the 1980s and more recent quantitative assessments of classroom practice.[42]

More Deeper Learning in Individual Classrooms Than in Whole Schools

A central part of the problem, we came to think, was that schools on the whole do not have the mechanisms to translate their espoused values to their enacted practices. This underscores one of the key findings that emerged from our project: it is not simply the "containers" of the work that allow a given school to translate its aspirations into consistently powerful teaching and learning. Just as two teachers teaching the same curriculum to the same level of students in the context of the same school community can diverge dramatically in their instructional prowess, so too can schools pursuing similar goals using similar theories of action part ways in terms of the quality and consistency of the learning they produce.

This holds true even for schools whose structures reflect a particularly innovative or student-centered vision. Our work suggests that it is by creating dense and mutually supportive connections among elements such as curriculum, assessment, pedagogy, school culture, and teacher learning, rather than by merely adopting a promising framework, that some such schools are able to make headway while others struggle to create any kind of consistent depth from classroom to classroom.[43]

This is not to say that we did not encounter any deep learning. To the contrary, even in the schools that had made the least amount of headway as whole institutions, we found individual classrooms that were joyful, engaging, and/or intellectually rich places to teach and learn. In a few cases, we found entire departments and programs that consistently embodied some or all of these qualities. And, among the thirty schools that we visited, we did encounter a few that were moving toward the consistent depth that we sought at the outset—though even those were still somewhat uneven from classroom to classroom.

Finally, it is worth noting that, while the main focus of our work was on high schools, we visited a handful of elementary schools as well, and on the whole they embodied many more of the qualities to which deeper learning advocates aspire: a commitment to leveraging students' natural curiosities into learning, an emphasis on active thinking and reasoning, and an overall sense of warmth. Certainly, deep learning was not present in every classroom, but the structures and values characterizing elementary schools and elementary school teaching tended to be more promising than those of their secondary counterparts.[44]

Three Ways That Schools Approach Deeper Learning

As we tried to come to terms with what we were seeing, the stance of the project began to shift. By synthesizing the glimmers and glimpses of deep learning that we encountered in the field with the existing research literature, we identified the elements of the deeper learning triangle described above: mastery, identity, and creativity. A large number of such schools, we realized, can be clustered into rough groups that share a set of underlying values as well as a theory of action about how these values can be instantiated through organizational structures and classroom pedagogy.

For example, a number of the schools and school models participating in the Hewlett Foundation's deeper learning network—which facilitates knowledge sharing among high schools that have embraced a common set of deeper learning goals—share an aspiration to support students in developing the kinds of general competencies that Wagner describes as the "seven survival skills" necessary for the twenty-first century.[45] These schools, which include those in the High Tech High and Envision Schools networks, emphasize the development of original work through engagement in interdisciplinary, collaborative, real-world-aligned projects—a model that often entails block scheduling, cross-subject teaching, and the use of performance- or portfolio-based assessments. We see these schools as sitting closer to the creativity node of the deeper learning triangle with respect to their aspirations.

A second group of schools sits much closer to the mastery node of the triangle, organizing themselves around the goal of supporting students in developing deep knowledge, skills, and competencies within the traditional academic disciplines. These schools, which include some that have adopted the Advanced Placement program, some that have adopted the International Baccalaureate program, and a few that have developed their own inquiry-based approaches, aspire to help students learn to do what Perkins calls "playing the whole game" of the traditional academic disciplines. This means not just superficially learning about historical events, for example, but also emulating the processes of historical inquiry through analyzing primary sources, debating competing interpretations, and conducting original research.[46] Schools that are organized around the International Baccalaureate program are even trying to go one step further, striving to help students understand how the core epistemologies (e.g., "ways of knowing") of each discipline compare to and differ from others.

A third group, which notably includes schools in the Big Picture Learning network and the NYC iSchool, focuses more on the identity node of the deeper learning triangle, striving to help students develop a stronger sense of themselves as learners, citizens, and soon-to-be professionals by offering them ongoing opportunities to learn from out-of-school mentors and extensive choices in terms of their in-school course of study. These schools tend to bank heavily on structures that support individualized pathways toward graduation: online courses, student-chosen internships, elective courses, and "looping" advisories.

Of course, to describe schools by their central tendencies ignores that a number of schools aspire to multiple priorities. Schools in the Expeditionary Learning network, for example, aim to involve each element of the deeper learning triangle in relatively equal measure. Likewise, many of the schools described as solidly at one or the other node of the triangle have programs that suggest plural priorities; High Tech High, for example, has an internship program intended to support eleventh graders in exploring possible professional identities, and International Baccalaureate schools require seniors to write an extended essay that reflects their personal interests.

Overall, though, we were struck by the difficulty of finding the sweet spot. Looking across these schools was like looking at a microcosm of the historical debates between progressive and traditional forms of education. The schools that were more progressive, in a Deweyan sense, often struggled to ensure that students consistently mastered basic academic content, whereas the more traditionally academic schools struggled to make their material authentic and connected to students' interests.

Bad News, Good News

The bad news coming out of our study, then, is that the field is not as far along as some accounts might suggest when it comes to enacting deeper learning at the whole-school level. The good news is that such learning is happening somewhere in virtually every school that we visited—including schools that were heavily focused on standardized testing and schools that had made no commitments to deeper learning whatsoever. This became a predictable dimension of our work: we knew that if we shadowed a given student over the course of a six-period day, we inevitably would encounter one or perhaps two standout practitioners who had figured out how to infuse their classrooms with rigor and vitality.

This finding is consistent with the Gates Foundation Measures of Effective Teaching project, which estimates that one out of every five classrooms features at least a moderate amount of critical and/or creative thinking.[47]

This statistic can be seen as disheartening—only one in five!—but it also can be construed as a source for hope. After all, if there are 3.7 million teachers working in the U.S. public schools, it means that more than seven hundred thousand have some degree of capacity around teaching for deeper learning.

The outlook gets brighter still if we widen the lens a bit to include elective classes and extracurricular activities. At a number of schools we visited, the deepest learning seemed to be concentrated in these so-called "peripheral" contexts. Spanning the gamut from visual art and film scoring to theater and Model United Nations, such contexts often harness the power of an apprenticeship model, in which real-world domains of professional practice provide standards for good work, teachers model expertise and conviction, and students gradually are inducted into more complex aspects of the work. This constellation of qualities infuses the learning with depth, meaning, and a palpable sense of momentum—the very qualities that are often lacking from mainstream academic classes.

While we recognize that electives and extracurriculars are structurally "special"—students self-select them based on interest and/or ability; there are rarely external pressures for specific content coverage or assessments—we also think that there is something powerful to be learned from them about how to engage adolescents in deep learning.[48] By extension, we believe that a critical question moving forward is how schools might be able to infuse more of what happens at their "peripheries" into their core programs of academic study.

THE NATURE OF THE CHALLENGE: CONSTRAINTS AND OMISSIONS

Why is deeper learning so rare in contemporary schools? Our observations have led us to think that a number of powerful and interconnected forces mediate against teaching for deep learning in secondary schools. Most readily apparent are the forces that manifest as constraints—the barriers that have received widespread treatment in the research literature and popular press and which practitioners name as reasons that they and their colleagues find it difficult to make deeper learning a core goal of their work.

These constraints are real and important, and, in aggregate, they pose a significant obstacle to making progress at scale. Equally important, however, are the forces that can best be described as omissions—structures, processes, and institutions that could help to support the growth and spread of deeper learning in secondary schools, but which remain largely absent from the sector. Seen as a whole, these constraints and omissions paint a fairly bleak picture with respect to the conditions for making headway toward deeper learning in secondary schools. To build on the strand of optimism from the previous section, however, this picture also suggests that there are many promising levers that might help to open up the grip of the status quo.

The Structural "Grammar" of Secondary Schools

Starting at the school level, barriers are readily apparent: engaging students in sustained, authentic, high-cognitive-demand tasks requires structures and supports that many high school teachers simply do not have. Compared to their elementary school counterparts, they teach many more students in total and see each student for far fewer hours each day, making it difficult to build relationships and to create opportunities for sustained inquiry. As one eleventh-grade science teacher ruefully reported, "Forty-seven minutes is just enough time to get the kids really interested and engaged in whatever you want them to be learning, and then the bell rings and you have to start pretty much from scratch the next day."

The convention of allocating each block to a separate subject area—a core piece of the typical "grammar" of American secondary schools—can compound this sense of fragmentation, limiting opportunities to support students in drawing connections and transferring knowledge across disciplines.[49] Large classes and high teacher loads (the number of students a teacher has across their classes) also work against more individualized attention and high levels of teacher feedback to student work.

Beyond this, at a more subtle level, high schools also seem to reflect the profound dis-ease that characterizes our society's stance toward adolescents. Teenagers are expected to sit for hour after hour passively listening and following directions, but they are seldom engaged in tasks that involve real choice and latitude—perhaps in part because doing so would involve ceding some of the rigid control that often characterizes teacher-student relationships in secondary schools, especially secondary schools serving poor and/or minority populations.[50]

Another major structural constraint—the one most frequently cited by teachers themselves—is the pressure for content coverage associated with external assessments such as state tests, SAT Subject Tests, and even some Advanced Placement exams. This pressure has amplified in recent years, accruing particular urgency in low-performing schools where administrators worry about making Adequate Yearly Progress as measured by state standardized tests, as well as in upper-middle-class schools where students are competing for acceptance to top-tier colleges. More broadly, however, they are part of a long-standing cultural tradition that emphasizes coverage of disciplinary content as the central value of secondary schooling. This coverage comes at the expense of the more in-depth investigations that would permit genuine understanding.[51]

The Status Quo of Teaching Practice

Nevertheless, a large body of evidence affirms that secondary teachers continue to rely heavily on lectures, textbook-based teaching, and other forms of direct instruction as a means to "efficiently" cover material.[52] The presence of these traditions and pressures is certainly a key reason so few teachers even venture to try reorganizing their practice around deeper learning goals. An equally powerful reason, however, is the absence of processes that could help them to do so.

Essentially, the status quo of teacher practice is the product of a vicious cycle that has yet to be disrupted and reversed at any kind of scale. The realities that we described earlier in this chapter mean that during their own experiences in high school, teachers were unlikely to have experienced much deep learning, especially in their core academic classes. Similarly, the widely acknowledged weakness and incoherence of American teacher preparation programs means that, as preservice professionals, teachers were unlikely to have learned anything substantive about teaching for deep learning.[53]

While we saw some progress in breaking down the norms of isolation that historically have plagued teaching as a profession, we did not see much evidence that the growth of professional learning communities and other forms of teacher collaboration was oriented toward increasing rigor or depth of instruction.[54] On the whole, we observed that even if teachers yearn to infuse their classrooms with greater vitality and depth (a sentiment shared by many we interviewed), they lack rich models for what this might look like and what it might take to achieve—and so they default to teaching in the ways that they themselves were taught.

It is not just individual schools that lack processes by which teachers can learn from and participate in the development of a rich and evolving knowledge base about deeper practice—it is the system as a whole. Unlike most countries whose students score at the top of the Program for International Student Assessment distribution, the United States has a fragmented system that fails to attract and retain high-performing teaching candidates, rarely capitalizes on the potential synergy between research and practice, and lacks strong mechanisms for capturing, vetting, and disseminating usable knowledge.[55]

The Goals of American Education

At the root of the problem lies a constellation of deeply value-ridden arguments about the means and ends of schooling—arguments that a few individual schools, networks, and/or districts have managed to solve through inspired leadership and bold actions, but which thwart the system as a whole from building the kind of infrastructure needed to make headway toward deeper learning at scale.[56] As a result, some of the most intractable and high-leverage problems of practice—for example, the question of how to engage low-performing students in deeper learning while simultaneously helping them to build foundational skills—remain unaddressed in any kind of systematic way.

It is not a stretch to imagine the interconnected web of constraints and absences that mediate against the spread of deeper learning as an impenetrably dense and thorny thicket. In one sense, this is profoundly disheartening—for example, to think along these lines is to acknowledge that simply removing constraints such as fragmented scheduling and high-stakes testing would by no means be sufficient to guarantee significant changes in the status quo.

From another perspective, however, the interconnected nature of the barriers to deeper learning can be seen as a boon. After all, making significant headway on any one of them will necessarily involve the others. We saw examples of this on a small scale in some of the schools that we visited: once educators arrived at clear and shared agreements about the kind of teaching and learning that they were aiming to produce, they were able to make strategic choices about how to use space, time, and personnel; to decide which external pressures to downplay or resist; to begin developing the kind of materials and processes that would support teachers in learning and growing; to build a usable and continually evolving knowledge base of best practices; to curate examples of excellent work that helped students and parents to understand the nature of the school's vision and standards; and, throughout, to develop an organizational culture that reinforced all of these things.[57]

BUILDING A SYSTEM TO SUPPORT DEEPER LEARNING

To provide all children with real opportunities to learn deeply, educators will need to overhaul the industrial-age architecture of public schooling that they inherited from the early twentieth century. Precisely what will this entail? That question lies mostly outside the scope of this chapter, but we would like to close by offering some brief highlights, at least, of the multiple and interrelated changes that will be required—and which are explored from various perspectives and in considerable detail in other chapters in this volume.

First and foremost, educators will need to ask more of their students, giving them assignments that are much more cognitively challenging and personally engaging than is the norm today. It is worth noting that the Common Core State Standards were meant to provide an impetus for such a shift (though, as we write this, it is unclear how widely they will be implemented). Indeed, research into the two main Common Core–aligned assessments has found that, on the whole, they are significantly more challenging than previous state tests, calling upon students to show greater command of disciplinary content and skills.[58]

However, increasing disciplinary rigor represents only one way to engage students in more challenging and meaningful work. Many deeper learning advocates have focused instead on making fundamental changes to the academic curriculum, particularly at the secondary level, with the goal of moving away from disciplinary silos and toward more integrated, problem-based coursework. According to this perspective, preparation for college, careers, and civic life has to do not with the mastery of individual disciplines so much as the ability to work across them, confronting the messiness and complexity of real-world problems.

Of course, changing the curriculum in these ways also implies significant changes to the social organization of schools and the policies that govern them. For example—as Nancy Hoffman discusses in chapter 2, and as Peter Levine and Kei Kawashima-Ginsberg discuss in chapter 3—problem- and project-based instruction often blurs the boundaries between the campus and the real world, with students venturing out into the workplace and the community for internships, service learning, and other kinds of hands-on learning opportunities. And teachers often bring in outside experts to share their work, participate in events, serve as judges for presentations, and so on.

Further, these kinds of instruction have major implications for the structure of the school day and the academic year. Problem- and project-based approaches tend to favor longer class periods (and fewer subjects per day), giving students the time they need to go through the process of grappling with difficult questions, experiencing dead ends, and eventually finding workable approaches. (It is hard to imagine that, if we were starting from scratch and aiming for deeper learning, we would choose to divide the school day into six or seven fifty-minute periods, each for a distinct subject). In turn, this poses a serious challenge to the long-standing use of the Carnegie Unit as our chief measure of student progress. Indeed, many educators are now experimenting with more flexible ways of offering credit for integrated problem- or project-based work, rather than requiring students to complete a fixed number of instructional hours in each disciplinary subject.

But if deeper learning requires major changes in curriculum, scheduling, and school organization, it requires equally dramatic changes in teacher practice, with implications for every part of the teacher development pipeline. For example, the selection of new teachers will need to become more stringent, ensuring that novice educators have high levels of academic preparation and content knowledge. Teacher education will need to provide many more opportunities to see what ambitious instruction looks like up close and to *un*learn the sorts of rote, shallow practices that dominate most classrooms today.[59] And, perhaps most important, the profession of teaching itself will need to be restructured, allowing for teachers to grow and extend their practice throughout their careers.[60] As Magdalene Lampert describes in chapter 7, "ambitious teaching" for deeper learning requires knowledge and skills that have always been quite rare among the nation's educators, and few educators have seen examples of such instruction in their own academic lives. Thus, teachers themselves will need frequent opportunities to learn deeply, joining with colleagues to participate in the kinds of intellectually challenging and highly engaging projects, discussions, and activities that they will be asked to replicate in their own classrooms.[61]

By extension, deeper learning will require major changes in school and district leadership, as well. If teachers are to rethink old modes of instruction, and if they are to attempt to teach in more ambitious ways, they will need active support from principals, superintendents, and other administrators. Notably—as Meredith Honig and Lydia Rainey argue in chapter 8—this will require a major change for school systems, with district offices shifting from an emphasis on bureaucratic compliance to a focus on creating the conditions under which local educators can provide deeper teaching.

So too does it require a shift away from the recent emphasis on test-based school accountability and teacher evaluation, which have subverted the goals of deeper learning in at least three ways: by focusing narrowly on performance on state-administered tests in reading and math; by placing the onus of improvement on individual teachers rather than on schools as whole organizations; and by discouraging the kinds of creativity and experimentation needed to teach in ambitious ways. As David Conley argues in chapter 9, the pursuit of deeper learning calls for an entirely different approach to assessment, one that doesn't ignore the importance of school accountability but that places greater emphasis on the use of performance tasks, school quality reviews, student self-assessments, and other means of providing actionable information to students and educators.[62]

An Adaptive Challenge

The leadership expert Ronald Heifetz famously distinguished between "technical" challenges, which are problems that can be solved using existing knowledge, and "adaptive" challenges that require substantial new learning and reevaluation of existing commitments.[63] While this distinction is now so frequently invoked as to be a cliché, in this case it really does apply. Building a system that would support deeper learning for all would be an adaptive challenge in many respects.

First, it would extend to all students what historically has been reserved for a relatively small minority. As the history outlined here shows, to the degree that we have had success in producing deep learning, it has come in pockets for advantaged or highly motivated students and self-selected teachers. Deeper learning also entails a kind of education that most parents have not experienced and that many might not value—one that teaches students how to question assumptions, think independently, and ask hard questions about social, political, and ethical issues. Thus, at the most fundamental level, "deeper learning for all" is a challenge that has not been attempted in this country. Further, at a time of vast and growing income and wealth inequality, coupled with unprecedented levels of residential and educational segregation and an increasingly polarized electorate, an equity agenda becomes all the more important. As Pedro Noguera and colleagues argue in chapter 4, Sharon Vaughn and colleagues in chapter 5, and Patricia Gándara in chapter 6, advocates will have to be especially steadfast in their commitment to providing all children, and not just the privileged few, with meaningful opportunities to learn deeply.

Adaptive learning also entails loss; people have to give up some of what they value and know in order to make room for something new; teachers will need to reimagine how they teach; education schools will need to fight university imperatives that pull them away from practice and become more focused on carefully guiding their charges toward deeper learning; K–12 schools will need to resist the urge (and incentives) to measure their success by how much they cover; and districts and states will need to fight the desire to control teachers and schools and focus instead on supporting them as learners. None of these changes will be easy to enact and, given the inertial pull of history, if one had to make a wager it would be for the status quo.

And yet, there are reasons to think that adaptive learning can and will come to pass. Foremost among them are the economic imperatives—for most of American history, graduating from high school would secure you a middle-class living, regardless of how much you had learned. This is no longer the case, which radically changes the incentives for both parents and students in how they approach schooling.

Then there are technological changes. We currently have what Richard Elmore has described as a "portal" view of schooling: states, then districts, then schools make decisions about how to divide the skein of knowledge, and the result is what a student receives in biology at 10 a.m. on Thursday. But everything ever known about biology is sitting on the student's phone. At some point, you have to think, we will shift to an educational model that is more responsive to students' interests—where teachers scaffold student learning, yes, but students also profit by directly engaging with their peers and with the limitless information and resources available on almost any topic.

Finally, there is the fact that deeper learning is captivating. Hard to achieve, yes, but once you have experienced it, shallower learning looks like black and white compared to full-spectrum color. Change will be slow, and it may take several generations, but deeper learning can spread gradually, as each one teaches one until we live in a world in which all students experience an education of power and consequence.

2

The Power of
Work-Based Learning

Nancy Hoffman

*The pitcher cries for water to carry
and a person for work that is real.*
—Marge Piercy, "To be of use"

BETWEEN THE AGES of twenty and sixty-five, the average U.S. adult works roughly ninety thousand hours—that's forty-seven hours per week over four and a half decades.[1]

Why forty-seven hours, rather than the stereotypical forty-hour week? At either end of the earning spectrum, Americans are spending more time at work than ever before. For many low-wage workers, it now takes two or more jobs just to get by and, for many professionals, work—whether it involves doing deals or doing good—provides the central organizing structure in their lives, keeping them busy from early in the morning until late at night.

Americans now spend a larger portion of their lives working than they do sleeping, studying, or spending time with family and friends. It may be a source of satisfaction or distress, engagement or alienation, excitement or tedium, or, most likely, a mix of all these things. Whatever its quality, though, work tends to have a major impact on identity and character, on self-esteem, on one's belief in the future, and ultimately on one's feeling of entitlement to participate as a citizen and social being in the world beyond the family.

For young people in the United States, whatever their backgrounds, an essential purpose of schooling should be to help develop the knowledge, skills, and competence needed to search for and obtain work that they find at least reasonably satisfying. And yet, our educational system does precious little to introduce young people to the working world or to prepare them for just how large a role work is likely to play in the rest of their lives.

While the phrase "college and career readiness" appears seemingly everywhere in the current discourse about the goals of high school, the "career readiness" part often seems like an afterthought, tacked on as if to suggest that if students pursue an academic, college-prep course of study—the real priority of most recent school reforms—they will also, as a side benefit, have better job prospects.[2] This lack of attention to career preparation only serves to intensify the class divide, leaving the most privileged students to anticipate and prepare for professional careers like those of their parents, while students from low-income families continue to think of work mainly as a way to survive.

What it means to be "ready" for a career is complicated and deserves real attention on its own. If one asks teenagers what the point of going to high school is—and many researchers have—they don't describe career readiness as a mere by-product of academic studies. To the contrary, they tend to say things like: What's the point of sitting there if you don't know what jobs or adult life school leads to? School is mainly about academics, and it's pretty boring.[3]

Today, few students experience a visceral connection between classroom learning and what they call "the real world." For stronger and/or relatively affluent students, work is something far off, expected to begin after a four-year college degree. And even among students who take some career and technical education courses in the formative middle and high school years, it is widely understood that the main point is to keep them motivated to stay through high school graduation, not to give them genuine preparation for and an initial experience of the workforce.[4]

But, some might argue, the Internet provides more free advice than any one job seeker can absorb. Plus, high schools have guidance counselors, and many offer service-learning programs, work-study jobs, co-ops, and assemblies featuring speeches by local business leaders. Moreover, teachers are forever admonishing students to study hard, or else they won't be able to go to college and get a good job.

But something's missing from this logic, something that would provide young people with a much more powerful, explicit introduction to careers.[5] In strong vocational education systems abroad, that something is called "preparation for working life," a phrase that signals that the two—work and the rest of life—are intrinsically connected. In Switzerland, Germany, Austria, the Netherlands, Singapore, and some of the Nordic countries, for example, it means that starting around age fifteen, young people actually learn about, prepare for, and begin to experience the workplace. And the way in which they do so responds to the developmental needs of adolescents, to the needs of the economy for a pipeline of young professionals who will take over from aging baby boomers, and, more grandly, to a basic human need to make meaning in the world by acting in the public sphere and producing goods and services used by others.

In the United States, by contrast, we tend to assume that young people are supposed to become educated first and then go to work. This assumption blinds us in important ways. In fact, work provides powerful opportunities to learn, and the workplace is where many young people are most receptive to applying academic skills and content as well as using critical interpersonal and intrapersonal capacities.

At times, work may seem like the enemy of life and leisure, but it can also be—and often is—an important source of meaning. Moreover, experiencing the workplace tends to be a prime force in helping young people grow up.[6] Indeed, a first job is a crucial rite of passage. As economist Andrew Sum (arguably the nation's leading expert on the youth labor market) puts it in a 2014 report titled, alarmingly, *The Plummeting Labor Market Fortunes of Teens and Young Adults*: "Finding and keeping a job is a key step in a young person's transition to adulthood and economic self-sufficiency."[7]

This chapter argues that the current discussion about deeper learning in the nation's high schools should be reframed to acknowledge that career readiness isn't just an outcome of deeper learning. Rather, career readiness is better defined as a process through which young people learn deeply and become prepared for the American version of working life.

The workplace can be a particularly good setting for deeper learning. It immerses and engages young people in developmentally appropriate, real-world tasks that challenge them—not only to learn advanced subject matter, but also to regulate their behavior; complete difficult assignments; work in teams; solve the unexpected, everyday problems that occur in workplaces; and communicate effectively with colleagues of differing ages and backgrounds. In short, the deeper learning movement can and should be aligned with current efforts to create better transitions from school to the workforce.

My argument is grounded in both economics and psychology (with a touch of philosophy mixed in). The economic case is purely pragmatic, based on the recognition that young people are being treated roughly in today's job market, and that young job seekers will likely continue to struggle in the coming years. The psychological case draws from research findings suggesting that most people, especially the young, learn best and most deeply through a combination of theory and practice (sometimes called "praxis"). Practical experience—particularly job-related experience—plays a central role in the formation of personal and group identity.

I begin by reviewing where the United States now stands with regard to youth experience in the labor market; it's a troubling story. I then turn to a more hopeful subject, discussing the psychological benefits of learning through a combination of school- and work-based activities. I continue with a description of an existing education system that relies on partnerships between employers, unions, a central government, and educators to make work a source of deeper learning that meets both the developmental needs of young people and the economic need for a steady supply of well-trained talent. Finally, I review some promising initiatives that aim to promote high-quality, work-based learning for a wide range of U.S. students.

PUTTING THE CAREER IN "COLLEGE AND CAREER READINESS"

As recently as a generation ago, the nation's young people grew up knowing that if they worked hard and stayed out of trouble, they could expect to find jobs with decent salaries when they left high school, and those jobs would allow them to become independent and self-sustaining adults. Today, though, millions of young Americans step into the labor market after high school only to discover that the best they can do is piece together a series of part-time, low-wage jobs that barely allow them to support themselves, much less build a satisfying life. And the same is true even among young people with some college credits or a poorly chosen two- or four-year degree.

The Great Recession of 2008 (which lasted, technically, until 2009 in the United States and even longer overseas) had a major impact on the well-being of many Americans, especially those who lack the technical expertise now required in almost every occupation. But it has had an inordinately heavy impact on the young, especially young people of color, youth from low-income backgrounds, and those who either dropped out of high school or who completed it but had no postsecondary plan.

Andrew Sum and colleagues review the dire situation in their 2014 Brookings Institution report: "Employment prospects for teens and young adults in the nation's hundred largest metropolitan areas plummeted between 2000 and 2011. On a number of measures—employment rates, labor force underutilization, unemployment, and year-round joblessness—teens and young adults fared poorly, and sometimes disastrously."

In 2000, 44 percent of teens were in the labor market; by 2011, the figure had dropped to 24 percent (see figure 2.1). For urban, low-income teens of color, the odds of having any job at all stood at roughly 10 percent. In fact, the teens with the highest employment rates came from families earning $120,000 or more. The rates were lowest among teens with family incomes below $40,000, the young people most in need of earning power.[8]

And lest readers suspect that disadvantaged teens are choosing not to work, Sum and his colleagues provide another data point: labor market underutilization, which includes those who desire work but who have stopped looking, and those who are working part-time but want full-time employment. In 2011, they note, black teens had the highest rate of underutilization (60 percent), followed by Latinos (52 percent), Asians (48 percent), and whites (35 percent). In other words, teenagers' desire to work is as high as ever—perhaps higher. If they are not working, it is mainly because they can't find jobs.

FIGURE 2.1   Youth experience in the labor market

Employment rates of teens aged 16–19 in the nation's 100 largest metropolitan areas by educational attainment/school enrollment, 2000 and 2011

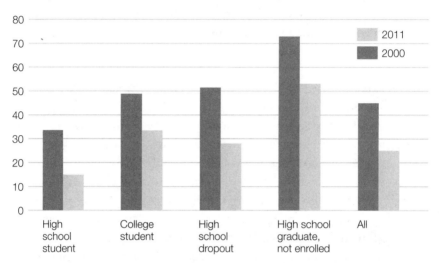

Source: Adapted from A. Sum et al., *The Plummeting Labor Market Fortunes of Teens and Young Adults* (Washington, DC: Metropolitan Policy Program and the Brookings Institution, 2014), http://www.brookings. edu/research/interactives/2014/labor-market-metro-areas-teens-young-adults, using data from the Current Population Survey, Bureau of Labor Statistics, http://www.brookings.edu/~/media/Research/Files/ Reports/2014/03/14%20youth%20workforce/BMPP_Youth_March10EMBARGO.pdf.

Youth Experience in the Labor Market

What do we know about the kinds of work experiences that are available to sixteen- to nineteen-year-olds today? First, if they work at all, high school students do so only part time and often sporadically. Second, for those teens lucky enough to find paid employment, first jobs are limited to a narrower range of options than ever before. Increasingly, teens must start in the low-wage service economy, where they compete with other low-wage, unskilled workers, many of them immigrants who have major family responsibilities.

The data are grim: according to a 2013 report from Georgetown University's Center on Education and the Workforce, the percentage of young people working in low-wage jobs in the food and personal service categories (e.g., cooks, cashiers, waiters, hair and beauty workers, home-care aides) rose from 15 percent in 1980 to 27 percent in 2013.[9] It has become much more difficult not only for teens to find work but also for them to find work that pays a decent wage. Further, young adults change jobs 6.3 times, on average, between the ages of eighteen and twenty-five.

In this environment, all young people, not just those from low-income families or with weak academic preparation, need more information about careers, more structure in their school to postsecondary pathways, and much more experience of the workplace than ever before. And that includes those who will become overeducated baristas or discouraged temps moving from office to office until their late twenties, despite having college degrees.

To be clear: There is nothing inherently wrong with these starter jobs for teenagers, especially if responsible adults help young people make sense of where such jobs fit in the economy and what kinds of skills they can teach.[10] It can be motivating to find out what one hates doing as well as what one finds enjoyable and rewarding. But the recent decline in even low-wage, service-sector opportunities means that a majority of young people from low-income backgrounds are unable to land the starter jobs that would allow them to gain initial work experience, earn some money, and feel the pride that comes with a paycheck.

More affluent young adults, especially those with social capital and family incomes in the top 5 to 10 percent, often struggle to find paying jobs too. However, those young people are far more likely to use personal connections to find internships in places such as child care centers, nonprofits, scientific research labs, and the businesses of family and friends. They may also get to go abroad over the summer, participate in wilderness training, or serve as unpaid junior camp counselors—experiences that contribute to identity development, to maturation, and to inequality.

No matter their background, though, young people who start looking for work after they finish school—whether high school or a two- or four-year degree program—tend to face the same conundrum: if you don't have experience, you can't get a job, but if you don't have a job, you can't get experience.

Employers tend to list "experience" in job postings not because they are biased against young people per se but because they are wary of the high costs and long timelines for training new workers. The real bias in U.S. business culture is in favor of short-term gains rather than long-term planning.

Indeed, employers are correct to assume that a high school or college graduate who has never worked will be unlikely, if hired, to quickly translate school knowledge productively to the workplace. It takes time for new workers to figure out not only how to apply what they have learned in school, but also how to behave at work—not to mention how one should deal with the knotty, unexpected, and complicated problems that arise every day in every workplace. In fact, young people and employers in countries with strong apprenticeship systems tend to cite this latter challenge—how to handle what social scientists call "messy" or "ill-formed" problems—as precisely the sort of thing that can be learned only on the job, not in a high school or college classroom.[11]

In an effort to help more youth and young adults gain a foothold in the labor market, many policy makers, philanthropists, and nonprofit leaders have begun to focus on helping our most vulnerable young people reconnect with education and workforce training. For example, *opportunity youth*—seventeen- to twenty-four-year-olds who neither work nor attend school—are poised to benefit from initiatives like the Opportunity Youth Incentive Fund (managed by the Aspen Institute's Forum for Community Solutions) and the work of President Obama's My Brother's Keeper coalition, among others.

These investments are timely, welcome, and high priority. Yet they focus entirely on getting young people back on track, while too little is done to prevent them from falling off the rails in the first place. What is needed today, more urgently than ever, is a more comprehensive and determined effort to help every young person make a smooth transition into the workforce.

Until high school educators, supported by policy makers, begin to take the career readiness part of their mission as seriously as they do college readiness, teens will continue to experience leaving school as a sudden shock, like being tossed into cold, turbulent waters knowing only the theory of how to swim.

Many middle-class and affluent young people can at least rely on family and friends to help them stay afloat while they attend college or graduate school, do an unpaid internship, or piece together temp work. For teens with fewer resources, though, the prospects tend to be bleak. And as long as schools and employers fail to address the youth employment crisis, those young people will struggle just to keep their heads above water, much less establish themselves in the adult world.[12]

Work and the Maturation of Adolescents

Perhaps the most eloquent and persuasive scholar writing about this topic is Robert Halpern, a professor at the Erikson Institute for Graduate Study of Child Development in Chicago. I draw liberally from his 2013 book *Youth, Education, and the Role of Society: Rethinking Learning in the High School Years*, which presents a powerful argument that schools are failing to engage adolescents in ways that align with their developmental needs.[13]

As Halpern points out, many young people find school to be terribly boring, and it is not because boredom comes naturally to teenagers. A wealth of evidence suggests that many apparently disengaged students are, in fact, lively and engaged thinkers outside of school. Often, students who seem listless and uninterested in math or social studies turn out to be self-taught experts in computer programming, civil war history, music, or some other field of their choosing, which they pursue with passion and commitment. School may fail to grab them, but they certainly are looking for things to grab onto that can help them define themselves as they grow up.

Unfortunately, notes Halpern:

> The very types of experiences that young people most need are the hardest to come by in American culture. . . . There's a kind of catch-22 here. Like every culture, ours needs young people to grow up. But because they are not yet grown up, because we cannot readily see their desire to participate and contribute, and perhaps because we are not fully comfortable with who they are, we deny young people access to what would be most helpful to them.[14]

What kind of experiences do young people need to support them in growing up? Most helpful, Halpern argues, are activities that take them out of their comfort zones, challenge them, place them among adult workers in authentic settings, and ask them to perform. We need to change the balance, he asserts, between in-school and out-of-school learning. School as it is currently organized has an "outsized role . . . in addressing developmental needs."

In an influential 1991 article, "Cognitive Apprenticeship: Making Thinking Visible," Allan Collins, John Seely Brown, and Ann Holum argue that the traditional apprenticeship model provides the right sort of support, relying on a process of "modeling, scaffolding, fading, and coaching. . . . The expert shows the apprentice how to do a task, watches as the apprentice practices portions of the task, and then turns over more and more responsibility until the apprentice is proficient enough to accomplish the task independently."[15]

The authors were interested in the ways in which the apprenticeship model could be translated to schools where, they argue, knowledge tends to be presented in abstract ways, denying students the opportunity to do and reflect on concrete tasks. But much has changed since 1991. At that point, they could still take it for granted that, while young people were not getting anything like an apprenticeship experience in the classroom, many of them were at least getting a taste of it while working at their first jobs in the evenings, over the weekends, and during the summer. Given the abysmally low rate of youth participation in today's labor market, however, that can no longer be assumed. It remains an urgent priority to give students more opportunities for concrete, hands-on learning at school. But it has become just as urgent a priority to give young people chances to learn about the sorts of thinking and doing that go on in the workplace, too.

If Collins, Brown, and Holum's goal was to translate this apprenticeship model to the school setting, Halpern would connect it back to the workplace. Using language quite similar to theirs, Halpern argues that students need many opportunities for "observing, emulating, practicing, applying, and revising," both in and out of the classroom. Schools could support the transition to working life by mixing in-school learning with out-of-school, work-based experiences that gradually lengthen as students advance toward the completion of high school and then into postsecondary education and/or the workforce.

How Some Other Countries Initiate Young People into Working Life

Until recent years, the U.S. educational policy community showed little interest in the world beyond our borders. That changed dramatically in 1995 with the release of findings from the Third International Math and

Science Study, followed in 2000 by the results of the Program for International Student Assessment (PISA), sponsored by the Organization for Economic Cooperation and Development (OECD).

Together, these assessments provided clear evidence that U.S. students were outperformed in math, science, and literacy. In comparison with peers from twenty or thirty countries, U.S. students scored at average and below-average levels. This has been confirmed by subsequent rounds of assessments, repeated as recently as 2012, while additional studies have shown that other countries have also overtaken the United States in the production of high school and college graduates. Though for many decades it was the world leader in high school and college completion, according to the most recent data, the United States now ranks twenty-second in high school graduation among the twenty-eight OECD member nations that have data available and tenth in tertiary degree attainment by twenty-five- to thirty-four-year-olds among all thirty-four OECD member nations.[16]

Today, U.S. policy makers regard such findings with alarm, seeing them as an indicator of declining economic competitiveness. At the same time, they are becoming more inclined to look overseas for insights into how we might address three critical problems. First is a growing skills gap (a mismatch between the skills workers have and the jobs that are available), suggesting that the country is not producing the highly trained "middle-skill" technicians needed to fuel the recovery. Second, the crisis in college costs is making families more attentive to the economic return of a degree. Third, new evidence from the fields of brain science, achievement, motivation, and adolescent development confirm that adolescents tend to learn best when their learning environment provides, as Halpern puts it, "a window to the adult world by blending academic and applied learning through introduction of apprenticeships, project-based learning, and other real-world applications."[17]

Today, many U.S. educators are looking specifically to Germany, Switzerland, the Netherlands, the Nordic countries, and Singapore for insights into effective vocational education. (Nobody would argue that the United States can or should adopt any of those models whole cloth, only that an understanding of those systems can inform our own policy discussions and provide fresh ideas.) These countries have low rates of youth unemployment (single digits in the Netherlands and Switzerland), flourishing economies, and, not unrelated, strong vocational education systems that serve at least half of the sixteen- to nineteen-year-old population. (Further, the Netherlands and Switzerland were the only two European countries to rank in the top ten on the 2013 PISA mathematics results—a test indicating strong preparation for both advanced vocational education and college-level academic work.)

Various studies suggest that the existence of a strong vocational system ranks among the top four or five most powerful reasons why some countries are more economically successful than others.[18] Switzerland is a prime example: it holds the top spot on the well-known INSEAD *Global Innovation Index* (an annual report on world economies and their growth potential); it has a highly competitive export economy, sending 80 percent of what it produces abroad; at more than $80,000 per year, its per capita income is the third highest in Europe and the fourth highest in the world; and it is the best example of an innovation economy that relies on a highly skilled technical and specialized workforce educated in a vocational system.[19]

For the purposes of this book, however, the most important lesson to be learned from Switzerland has to do not with its economic success— impressive as it is—but with the thoughtfulness it has given to matters of teaching, learning, and equity, making it a particularly interesting model for U.S. policy makers to study.

Readers may wonder, why not feature, say, Germany—the better-known exemplar of a school system that prioritizes both academic and vocational education?

While there is much to admire about the German model, the fact is that in spite of major investments over many years, the country has had little success in engaging the least affluent quartile of its student population, composed heavily of immigrants and the children of guest workers. By contrast, the Swiss system seems to work well for 95 percent of its young people, including the majority of students from poor and/or immigrant families.

And unlike the German system, the Swiss system is highly flexible. Young people are not tracked into vocational studies. If they prefer applied rather than theoretical learning, they choose apprenticeship, and 75 percent of fifteen-year-olds make this choice. Nor do they or their families see it as a second-class option—most young apprentices say with no embarrassment that they are tired of sitting in classrooms and want to do something that feels more grown up. Often, parents comment on how quickly their teenager went from sleeping late in a messy room to being out the door in a suit with no prodding at all.[20]

After their apprenticeship, students have a wide range of options to consider: continuing in the labor force, entering a university of applied sciences, or—if they change their minds at any point—moving onto the academic track. About 40 percent of fifteen-year-olds who score a 4 or 5 on PISA (i.e., the top end of the range) choose vocational education, signaling that apprenticeship is a high-status way to learn. In fact, some calls for apprentices in the financial industry and in information technology (IT) attract nearly ten times as many applicants as job openings.[21]

No, the United States is not Switzerland, and the differences between the two countries are immense. But it is entirely conceivable that state school systems in the U.S. could adapt some of Switzerland's practices or, at the very least, be inspired by the Swiss example to rethink our assumptions about the ways in which young people come of age and the ways that work experiences can promote deeper learning.

The View from the Alps

Some facts to begin with: Switzerland is a small, rich country of roughly eight million inhabitants. It has limited natural resources and relies heavily on human talent for economic success. It is diverse not just linguistically but also ethnically, with nearly a quarter of its current population born outside of the country. It is the world's oldest direct democracy. And, most important for our purposes, over the past twenty years, it has modernized its vocational education system. Rather than expand its university sector, it has added to the list of occupations that can be studied through the vocational education and training (VET) system, which now includes fields such as dance, music, child care, IT, elder care, and engineering. (Fields such as the traditional trades, banking, insurance, and advanced manufacturing have long been included).[22]

In Switzerland, small and large companies, state-of-the-art factories, insurance agencies, banks, hospitals, retail stores, and child care centers host sixteen- to nineteen-year-old apprentices who serve customers, work on complex machines, carry out basic medical procedures, and advise investors. In short, they do everything an entry-level employee would do, albeit under the wing of credentialed trainers within the company, taking responsibility for implementing one strand of the carefully designed VET curriculum.

Roughly 30 percent of Swiss companies host this sort of "educational" employee. Young people rotate among three learning sites—the workplace, a training organization that focuses on the given sector, and school—in different proportions over the three- or four-year period of their apprenticeship. Students have electronic schedules that tell them whether it is a day to wear a suit, take their protective glasses and hairnet, or put on jeans and a T shirt and head to school for language, math, or history. Students' learning is highly personalized: their own interests and talents are at the core of their studies, and they are encouraged to consider their options for further education and/or a change of field. Further, they get paid an average monthly starting wage of around $700, rising to around $1,200 by the time they are in their third or fourth year, a rate substantially below the Swiss minimum but attractive for a teenager living at home.[23] They do productive work that returns the cost of training and a bit more to their employer.[24] And, as a result, the Swiss economy can rely on a talent pipeline of young professionals.

Further, with more than 90 percent of young people moving successfully through the apprenticeship system or university, Swiss educators can afford to focus intensively on the small percentage who struggle, providing counseling, an extra "bridge year" after ninth grade, and, when needed, individual case management.

To what extent does this model provide young people with a well-rounded education—teaching them high-level academic skills and content as well as critical interpersonal and intrapersonal capacities? Or does it provide a narrow sort of occupational training? And if students are expected to contribute to the bottom line of their companies, then how can we be sure that vocational programs are truly organized for their benefit, and not just to provide employers with cheap labor?

The superficial answer is that the Swiss schools are explicitly charged with helping each young person to "flower" as a person and to take responsibility for their private, social, and professional lives.[25] More concretely, the VET curriculum gives priority to the teaching of metacognition, providing students with regular opportunities to discuss what they are learning and why they are learning it. Thus, when foreign visitors ask VET students about their experiences, more or less all of them are able to describe the three pillars of vocational education, *wissen, konnen,* and *machen* (or know, know how to, and apply), and to explain why it is important to learn content, methodology, and social and behavioral skills (the what, how to, and how to behave).

Students seem particularly aware of why interpersonal skills are so important. After all, coming from the peer-centered life of ninth grade, the first days at work must be an eye-opener, revealing just how different professional norms of interaction are from social life in school. For example, on a recent study tour to Switzerland, a U.S. delegation was introduced to a young apprentice who recounted her first experience at age sixteen as a teller (the starting point in the banking curriculum) and her second six-month rotation working in a back office, where she carried out all her transactions by phone: "Of course, you can't see people on the phone," she said, "so you have to imagine much more about them. You have to listen in a special way. You have to tell by their tone of voice whether they want to chat or want the answer quick and goodbye. And they might yell at you or be mad, and they'll be more likely to do it if you can't see them, so you have to figure out how to calm them down and get them what they need."[26]

Further, Swiss curriculum documents are laid out with very clear goals, outcomes, and activities for each VET setting—school, training company, and workplace—and across all three. In addition to the usual academic subjects, schools teach the language, history, and basic concepts and theories related to the student's chosen occupation. Training companies are more applied and hands-on but still devoted to helping students learn and practice, not to produce. For example, students gain applied foundational knowledge (e.g., the rudiments of the banking system, the basics of welding) and are expected to learn essential workplace behaviors (e.g., contributing to teams, asking for help, making independent decisions). And in the workplace, students begin with structured learning tasks. Only gradually are they expected to contribute enough goods and services to allow the company to recoup, by the third or fourth year, the costs of training and, in most cases, to reap a small profit.

In sum, the experience adds up to much more than what, in this country, might be called "learning by doing"—which, though useful, rarely encourages this sort of deliberate, ongoing, and reflective practice. The Swiss model doesn't just give students hands-on opportunities but guides them through a process of learning, being taught to apply, and then independently applying skills and knowledge. The cycle is repeated and reinforced at each of the three learning sites, over the three or four years of apprenticeship.

Consider the presentations made recently by young people completing the highly technical first two years of the polymechanic program at LIBS, an intercompany training institution for the manufacturing and engineering professions. For a group of foreign visitors, these presentations offered a window into just how much these students had learned about mathematics, information technology, and physics, as well as more specialized skills in machining, drawing, and mechanics, while also having numerous opportunities to develop and practice the interpersonal and intrapersonal skills associated with deeper learning. For example, two young men provided a close look at a series of inventive assignments leading to their final year's project. They explained that they had designed and produced a hydraulic machine to lift heavy kitchen cabinets and hold them in place for an installer. However, their goal was not only to construct the machine but also to turn the design process into a demonstration problem for a group of fifteen-year-old students who were spending several days on-site to see whether they might want to pursue an apprenticeship.

Thus, the assignment required the second-year students not only to know the given mechanical principles but also to take a step back and think about what they had learned, so that they could translate those principles into a task that would be suitable for less-knowledgeable young people. Further, the project was totally self-directed and included self-assessments in workflow management, problem solving, explanation of the method, and the ability to seek help when needed.

Such activities and assignments are, to put it mildly, very different from and much more powerful than what typically occurs in high school classrooms, in the United States or elsewhere. In short, they amount to a truly deep learning experience, one that engages young people in advanced academic content, teamwork, metacognition, persistence, problem solving, critical thinking, effective communication, and more—all of it in the context of developmentally appropriate real-world challenges.

Note also that this form of work-based learning includes daily contact with and coaching from various adults representing various occupations. As Halpern argues, such multigenerational working communities tend to be much healthier environments for adolescents than schools filled solely with teens. While peer groups have their benefits, exposure to peers alone can work against the maturing process, too. As Halpern puts it, "The more powerful and complete the peer world, the more it is detached from pathways toward adulthood. . . . It makes little sense," he goes on, "to take large numbers of inexperienced individuals who are the same age and relative maturity, place them in an isolated setting, and ask them to use that particular setting to grow, mature, [and] gain knowledge and experience."[27]

WORK-BASED DEEPER LEARNING IN THE UNITED STATES: PROBLEMS AND PROMISES

Not surprisingly, there are no education systems in the United States that feature the length, depth, and specificity of the work-based learning system in Switzerland. Nor have any U.S. school systems turned the school/work equation on its head, with high schools supplementing what is learned at work rather than employers supplementing what is learned at school.

Few U.S. educators today would likely endorse the notion that a prime goal of high school should be for young people to learn to work and begin a first career. Age fifteen or sixteen is too early, they might argue, adding that internships, job shadows, and the like should be defined as career exploration activities meant to give students a taste of the work world and to encourage them to go on to higher education, where more specific career preparation takes place.

Yet this country does have excellent models of high schools that seamlessly integrate academics with career preparation and that treat the workplace as an important site for deeper learning. In fact, high-quality, work-related education is provided in many states by national initiatives and networks, by impressive "one-off" schools and programs, and through the long-standing tradition of vocational or CTE schools and centers. The problem is that they currently serve only a relatively small number of students. The question is: Can these excellent models be further scaled up and their approaches refined and adapted in our many comprehensive high schools?

Exemplary Models

Among the most impressive networks incorporating learning for specific careers are up-to-date vocational high schools and centers, career academies, High Tech High schools, Project Lead the Way, Big Picture Learning schools, Cristo Rey Network schools, and early colleges. Each provides some form of applied learning related to the labor market—from programs linked to industries (e.g., finance, veterinary technology, information technology, and health care), to individualized multiyear mentorships, to an engineering curriculum that starts students on design thinking in the elementary grades.[28] And each provides opportunities for students to become truly engaged in problem solving, teamwork, communicating with diverse colleagues, and other aspects of deeper learning.

For example, Cristo Rey students share a single full-time job (in a law firm, bank, hospital, or other setting), with each working one day a week to pay tuition for schooling. Big Picture students make personalized learning plans that have them work several days a week with mentors of their choice with the goal of defining their passions and finding work that is satisfying. In the Massachusetts system of vocational schools, ninth graders circulate among career areas for four months to a year before making a career choice. These schools typically host companies on-site as well as provide clinical training required for industry certifications.

A particularly interesting school is CART, the Center for Advanced Research and Technology, a career center located in Clovis, California. CART provides half-day programs for 1,300 eleventh and twelfth graders from fifteen high schools. The 75,000-square-foot building, designed to replicate a high-performance business, is organized around four career clusters—professional sciences, engineering, advanced communications, and global economics. Teachers, business partners, and invited experts work in large open spaces, similar to a science lab or high-tech start-up, that are filled with equipment, work stations, and student work. Within each cluster are career-specific laboratories in which students complete industry-based projects and receive academic credit for advanced English, science, math, and technology. Boundaries between disciplines don't exist; students solve problems and learn as one would in the "real world." Students do everything from testing water in the High Sierra to making industry-standard films to trying out aviation careers by actually flying planes. Teaching teams include business and science partners, and many teachers have extensive professional experience.

Another promising approach has taken root among some of the three hundred or so early college high schools across the country. Roughly one-third have a thematic focus on the science, technology, engineering, and math (STEM) fields, with health sciences being particularly popular. Since hospitals are accustomed to supervising people at the beginning of their careers, a number of them have agreed to partner with early colleges, providing students with work-based learning opportunities in various health care fields. For example, at Wake Early College High School in Raleigh, North Carolina, students spend a significant portion of their time on Wake Tech's health sciences campus and in Wake Medical's main hospital, where they participate in job shadowing, internships, and other activities that connect them with practicing medical professionals.

An adaptation of the early college model, New York City's Pathways in Technology Early College High School (P-TECH), was developed by IBM in partnership with the New York City Department of Education and the Early College Initiative at CUNY. Graduates of this six-year program emerge with an associate of applied science degree in computer systems technology or electromechanical engineering technology. This model has affinities with European approaches in that students are promised paid internships in their final year, at either IBM or a partner IT company. Since 2011, New York State has funded more than twenty-five additional P-TECH programs, and Chicago and several other cities have adapted the model.

Similarly, SAP, the German business solutions company, is sponsoring early college programs in the United States: B-TECH, which opened in New York City in 2014, and C-Town Tech, an IT pathway that opened in Boston in 2015 in partnership with the mayor's office, Charlestown High School, and Bunker Hill Community College. In addition, a major agricultural firm, the Wonderful Company, is designing and supporting five early colleges in the California Central Valley focused on careers in agribusiness, plant science, and agriculture mechanics. Their students will be able to earn at least a year of college credit, will be supported to complete an associate's degree, and will have paid internships in Central Valley companies.

Among statewide investments, the newest of the modernized integrated career/academic approaches is Linked Learning. An ambitious California initiative, it aspires over the next decade to have every high school student in the state—about 1.8 million young people—enrolled in a career/academic interdisciplinary curriculum with pathways into postsecondary education. Linked Learning combines the broad academic foundation needed for further education with depth of study in a career area and is implemented across entire school districts and regions.[29] Developed with major philanthropic investment, Linked Learning—along with National Academies Foundation schools and California Partnership Academies—helped to secure a California public investment of $500 million to create career pathways aligned with labor market needs, starting in ninth grade and moving through community college degrees or certificates. The first set of grantees started implementation in 2014; a second group began in 2015.

Finally, the Pathways to Prosperity Network—directed by Jobs for the Future in collaboration with the Harvard Graduate School of Education—is attempting to capitalize on the sporadic models that now exist to build a stronger career education system, one that is more responsive to the needs of the labor market and that engages students in deeper learning through work experiences. In 2016, Pathways was four years old, with eleven state members—Arizona, California, Delaware, Georgia, Illinois, Massachusetts, Missouri, New York, Ohio, Tennessee, and Wisconsin—doing significant work in creating career pathways in grades 9 through 14.

The network seeks to ensure that many more youth complete high school, attain a postsecondary credential with currency in the labor market, and launch a career while leaving open the prospect of further education. Key sectors of the economy identified for building career pathways across the states include information technology, health care, and advanced manufacturing. Along with the network states, the federal government, some philanthropies, corporate foundations, nonprofit organizations, and other states are also engaged in this work.[30]

Note that all of these models understand their mission to be more than just "vocational," as the term is typically defined in this country. Collectively, they represent a growing movement to rethink the role of career preparation in the high school curriculum. Furthermore, they are addressing the either/or curriculum dichotomy—either career-focused or college-prep—by creating integrated educational models meant to engage adolescents in learning advanced academic content through a combination of classroom activities and developmentally appropriate, work-based experiences. Moreover, all of these models understand the workplace to be a powerful site—and for some students, perhaps the most powerful site—for deeper learning.

FINAL THOUGHTS

As I write these concluding words, news keeps coming that makes preparing young people for the better jobs in the labor market more and more urgent. Although the economy is recovering, wages are relatively stagnant, especially at the low end; current employees are losing benefits; companies are outsourcing high percentages of their work to staffing agencies that hire on short-term contracts; and employers of fast-food workers appear prone to resist the growing pressure to raise wages.

My goal in this chapter is to use this exploration of the role of work in adolescent lives to argue that every young person should have the opportunity to gain the knowledge, skills, and competence needed to search for and obtain meaningful work—and that to provide such powers of self-determination to young people requires a substantial rethinking of what schooling should be like for teenagers.

As I hope readers recognize by now, the argument I'm making is not that kids need jobs—though that is certainly true—but a far more radical proposition both in its intellectual demands of educators and in the organization of learning for late adolescents. That is, I argue that learning to work, learning about work, and experiencing a productive workplace should be integral to secondary-level education, since these are particularly powerful ways to teach high-level content, collaboration, problem solving, and other dimensions of deeper learning.

3

Preparing for
Civic Life

Peter Levine and
Kei Kawashima-Ginsberg

A NATION AT RISK, the 1983 report of President Reagan's National Commission on Excellence in Education, tends to be remembered for its martial rhetoric ("If an unfriendly foreign power had attempted to impose on America the mediocre educational performance that exists today, we might well have viewed it as an act of war"), its emphasis on the country's ability to compete in a global marketplace, and its role in inspiring subsequent waves of education reform. Rarely, though, is it remembered for its stirring appeal to the civic purposes of American education. For that, one has to revisit the actual text of the report:

> Our concern . . . goes well beyond matters such as industry and commerce. It also includes the intellectual, moral, and spiritual strengths of our people which knit together the very fabric of our society. . . . For our country to function, citizens must be able to reach some common understandings on complex issues, often on short notice and on the basis of conflicting or incomplete evidence. Education helps form these common understandings, a point Thomas Jefferson made long ago in his justly famous dictum: "I know no safe depository of the ultimate powers of the society but the

people themselves; and if we think them not enlightened enough to exercise their control with a wholesome discretion, the remedy is not to take it from them but to inform their discretion."[1]

Since those words were published more than three decades ago, such aims have been all but forgotten by most educational policy makers and advocates. Instead, certain other priorities have risen to the fore:

First, basic reading and mathematics—and, to a lesser degree, science—have been the focus of most reform efforts. Subjects such as history and civics (as well as the arts and foreign languages) have been marginalized.

Second, skepticism about teachers' and schools' abilities to assess their own students' performance has encouraged a growing dependence on standardized tests, which measure an individual's knowledge rather than the ability to discuss, collaborate, or influence the world.

Third, the overwhelming emphasis of recent reforms has been on preparing students for a competitive job market in which they must try to sell their own human capital (i.e., their individual skills and knowledge).

However, the most recent wave of school reforms appears to have passed its crest. Today, many Americans seem to be tiring of narrow curricula and simplistic assessments, and growing numbers are calling for deeper and more ambitious approaches to teaching and learning.

In this chapter, we argue that civic education has a crucial role to play in this movement to pursue deeper approaches to secondary schooling. If education reformers are now ready to rethink the priorities that have held them in thrall for the past thirty years—the teaching of basic reading and math, testing, and accountability—then they should also be prepared to address the civic imperatives that were described so passionately in *A Nation at Risk*, and which have been waiting on the shelf ever since.

Specifically, we advance two theses: (1) Deeper learning has great potential to promote civic outcomes and, hence, to strengthen our democracy; and (2) strengthening civic education is an important way to promote deeper learning.

Indeed, we argue that civic education, when implemented effectively, *exemplifies* deeper learning, requiring students to work together with peers and adults to diagnose and define problems, to deliberate and choose solutions, to implement strategies, and to reflect on the results.

Such learning experiences not only build the skills and attributes young people will need as citizens, but also contribute a great deal to preparing them for college, for careers, and, ultimately, for the chance to attain the kind of economic security that will allow them to participate fully in civic life.

The skills required for effective civic action (e.g., deliberating and collaborating in diverse groups to address complex problems) have great value in the twenty-first-century workplace. So, too, do the skills learned in high-quality civic education programs, such as the ability to set realistic goals, develop concrete plans, and direct oneself to follow a plan toward its ultimate goal—skills that are often grouped together under the term *agency*.[2]

As we describe later in this chapter, research finds that teenagers who participate in community service have better academic outcomes than their peers, and at-risk youth enrolled in certain programs that involve civic action also see substantial improvements in academic and economic outcomes.[3]

For all these reasons, deeper civic education will prepare students for success in work and life as well as for active citizenship. And developing better curricula, pedagogies, tools, and assessments for civics will benefit education generally because civics is intrinsically interdisciplinary and demands excellence in English/language arts, mathematics, and other subjects, going well beyond social studies.

DEEPER LEARNING CAN REVITALIZE CIVIC EDUCATION

In 2011, following the release of the 2010 assessment of civic learning by the National Assessment of Education Progress (NAEP), the *New York Times* published a story under the headline "Failing Grades on Civics Exam Called a 'Crisis.'" The article quoted Charles N. Quigley, the executive director of the Center for Civic Education, who said, "The results confirm an alarming and continuing trend that civics in America is in decline. . . . During the past decade or so, educational policy and practice appear to have focused more and more upon developing the worker at the expense of developing the citizen."[4]

We share the premise that civic education is essential and is not receiving sufficient attention at a time of alarm about the job market. But we argue that the familiar way of framing the problem, as in this *Times* story, is somewhat misleading. The NAEP civics assessment does not reveal "failing grades." In fact, the national sample achieved the scores that were expected when the assessment was designed.[5] There has been no notable decline in NAEP civics results over time.

The rhetoric that this article exemplifies can also promote mistaken policy proposals, such as mandating a civics class or requiring that every student pass the test that is now required for naturalization as a U.S. citizen.[6] In fact, almost every state already requires a civics class. Almost every student already faces tests in civics that, whether created by the teacher or an outside vendor, are more demanding than the naturalization exam. And neither of these approaches—required civics classes or tests—has an impressive track record.

Our own careful assessment of existing state standardized tests found that they have a negligible impact on what students know about government and civics or how to behave as citizens.[7] To be fair, there is some evidence that requiring high-stakes civics tests can result in some improvement in students' knowledge of current politics, with the greatest benefits for students of color.[8] Overall, though, the evidence that testing improves pedagogy or student outcomes is equivocal, at best. Requiring courses and standardized tests is not the path we recommend.

We start with a different diagnosis, leading to different prescriptions: where civic learning has been weak, it is because the instructional model and the assessments have been wanting. To be more effective, we argue, civic education should exemplify deeper learning. It should enable students to take on problems that are meaningful to them through collaborative and iterative processes. It should begin with discussion and analysis, strategizing and planning, taking concrete actions, and reflecting on the results. By working with peers and adults collaboratively, and bridging differences of demographics and values when possible, students build relationships that enable further constructive civic action. Deliberation, collaboration, and civic relationships are the core aspects of effective adult citizenship, and they are also deeply educational experiences.[9]

Currently, some students do receive civic education that meets these criteria. For example, an excellent service-learning project will involve a whole arc of activity, from an initial brainstorming of topics to a final reflection on the service and its outcomes. Ideally, it will be informed by disciplined empirical inquiry, guided by demanding values, and effective in addressing a real problem. Of course, service learning is just one of many possible forms of deeper civic education. We also see promise in collaborative research projects, in student-produced news stories and media, in debates and deliberations, and in simulations of adult civic experiences that may take the form of mock trials or model legislatures.

However, such opportunities are rare and unevenly distributed. All states have civics standards, and a vast majority of high school seniors take at least one course that discusses American government. But the reality is that relatively few American students experience deep inquiry or opportunities to apply their knowledge of civics. These same students also tend to attend schools in wealthy and white communities where most students are college bound.[10] Low-income students and students of color tend to have fewer experiential civic learning opportunities than their wealthier, white counterparts, and they performed at a much lower level on the 2010 NAEP civics assessment.[11]

A particular weakness is education for any form of political engagement and media literacy. Only one in ten Americans aged eighteen to twenty-four met criteria for "informed voting" in the 2012 election, which included news consumption, issue awareness, voter registration, voting, general political knowledge, and consistency between the individual's political opinions and choice of candidates.[12] Many educators, it seems, regard it as safer to ask students to participate in apolitical community service projects and to study formal governmental systems (e.g., learning how a bill becomes a law) than to ask them to discuss contemporary, politically divisive issues and how we might address them as citizens.[13] But if teachers were to provide more chances to confront such issues, the likely result would be greater civic engagement. Indeed, studies have found such opportunities to have positive effects on civic participation.[14]

Background: The Decline in Concern with Civic Learning

The current status of students' political knowledge is especially troubling when one considers that the original rationale for creating public education in America was explicitly civic: to make citizens capable of fulfilling their responsibilities as voters and jurors.

By the Progressive Era of the early 1900s, the classic modes of civic education were already in place. In 1915, the U.S. Bureau of Education formally endorsed a movement for "community civics." Its aim was "to help the child know his community—not merely a lot about it, but the meaning of community life, what it does for him and how it does it, what the community has a right to expect from him, and how he may fulfill his obligations, meanwhile cultivating in him the essential qualities and habits of good citizenship."[15]

One method was to provide extracurricular groups and clubs where students could learn civic skills and habits from experience. Groups such as student governments and school newspapers were already well established during the lifetime of John Dewey, for example.

Another essential method was to teach citizenship in courses. By 1929, more than half of all American ninth graders took a class called "civics." Another course, "problems of democracy" was also popular in the first half of the twentieth century, reaching 41.5 percent of American high school students by 1949. A third popular course was called "American government."[16]

Although it is unclear whether the total amount of classroom time on civics has declined since then, it is entirely clear that the balance of content has shifted.[17] Overall, today's curriculum is more academic and more derivative of college-level social science than it was fifty years ago, while less time is spent discussing or addressing contemporary problems.

For example, the "civics" course of the early twentieth century was mostly about a citizen's role in the community, and "problems of democracy" courses typically required reading and discussing a daily newspaper. Those could be described as forms of "deeper learning," since they required critical thinking, communication, and application of academic knowledge. But these courses are mostly gone from American high schools. "American government," which remains, is modeled on an introductory college-level political science course and emphasizes the academic study of politics and government. That course has remained common for the past hundred years and has been joined by popular college-type social science courses, especially economics and sociology.[18] Generally speaking, then, the current emphasis of civic education is the acquisition of knowledge about systems. Less emphasis is placed on the development of skills and dispositions.

Further, even as the high school curriculum becomes increasingly derivative of college-level studies, colleges themselves have lessened their emphasis on preparing students for citizenship.[19] Liberal education, including various aspects of civic learning, has gradually come to be overshadowed by a focus on career readiness.

The original civic case for public schooling can still be detected in state laws and policies. All states have standards for civics, and forty states have a standardized social studies test, although not always in civics.[20] However, civic education is not usually regarded as a high priority in the current educational system. The U.S. Department of Education acknowledges this: "Unfortunately, civic learning and democratic engagement are add-ons rather than essential parts of the core academic mission in too many schools and on too many college campuses today."[21] But the department had no authorized funds or programming for civics at all between 2011 and 2016, and even before that, it merely administered a single earmark for the Center for Civic Education, a provider of curricula and textbooks. On a positive note, the Every Student Succeeds Act includes new targeted programs of support for teachers of civics, as well as research grants and grants for local civic education programs. The funding for these programs, however, is fairly modest, capped at less than $7 million per year.

At the state level, virtually all social studies and civics tests now use multiple-choice formats, following a gradual decline in the use of essay and short-answer testing formats. Service learning is incorporated in the social studies standards of thirty-five states, but only one state (Maryland) requires service for graduation.[22] And only ten states have a preservice certification requirement for high school civics or government teachers.[23]

At the school level, very few teachers routinely use pedagogical techniques that are designed to build civic participation skills. For example, Kei Kawashima-Ginsberg found that less than half of fourth-, eighth-, and twelfth-grade students ever experience a simulation in civics, such as a mock trial, mock election, or model legislature.[24] Also, the amount of time devoted to instruction in reading, math, and science has increased in recent years, further shrinking the time available for civics. And Martin

West found that, in states with stronger requirements for history, students spent more time learning about history as a discipline, but they did not spend more time engaging in civics-related activities.[25]

Evolving Contexts for Civic Learning

We have already noted some important changes in the context of civic education: an increasingly academic curriculum, a strong emphasis on testing, and a focus on job skills. Two other trends are also important to note.

Civic Life Is Moving Online

At a time when politics and education are becoming increasingly mediated by digital technology, it would be unwise to replicate the "civics" or "problems of democracy" courses as they were taught in the mid-1900s, when news sources, political campaigns, and social movements relied mainly on print media and face-to-face communication. Perhaps citizens should still be able to read a newspaper article and give a speech, but now they must also be able to search the Internet for reliable political information and enlist support via social media.[26]

In 2012, 41 percent of Americans between the ages of fifteen and twenty-five reported engaging in at least one act of "participatory politics," which was defined to include activities such as forwarding a political video or starting an online group focused on an issue of public import.[27] Recent social movements, such as the efforts to permit gay marriage and to create a pathway to citizenship for undocumented immigrants, have been driven largely by young people who use social media.

Online civic engagement can take the form of superficial actions, such as clicking to "like" a comment. However, online platforms can also diminish existing gaps in civic engagement by social class, and online engagement is correlated with offline participation in politics and community groups.[28]

According to our own analysis of the Pew Research Center's Digital Civic Engagement data, young people who actively and frequently discuss political and current affairs online are far more likely to participate in other forms of civic engagement as well.[29] For example, 31.8 percent of young people who said that they discuss political affairs online every day reported that they worked or volunteered for a political party or candidate in 2012, compared to just 2.5 percent of those who never discussed politics online. (The average rate for the age group was 7.1 percent.) More than half (52.2 percent) of youth who discussed political and public affairs online said that they worked with fellow citizens to solve a problem in their community, compared to 23.8 percent of those who never engaged in online discussions. Further, the strong relationship between online and offline civic engagement held true regardless of young people's educational attainment, ethnicity, gender, income, or reliance on welfare benefits. Altogether, after controlling for other factors, online engagement accounted for 20.5 percent of the variance in offline civic engagement.

But if many young people already use social media for civic and political purposes—and if online and offline engagement are positively correlated—then one might ask whether it is really necessary for schools to teach young people to be digital citizens. We would say yes, for four reasons.

First, there remains a social class divide in using social media for civic purposes (albeit not as serious as the gaps in voting and volunteering rates), suggesting that the least advantaged young people need help to take full advantage of the new media.[30] Second, much false and misleading information circulates on the Internet, especially among networks of like-minded individuals. Classroom teachers have an important role to play in encouraging young people to seek out new ideas, and in teaching them how to distinguish reliable from unreliable information online. Third, actually changing the world remains difficult. It requires a mix of skills and strategies, not just online organizing but also the ability to understand and influence formal political institutions. Finally, digital tools may offer other kinds of opportunities for deeper civic learning, both in and out of school. For example, iCivics, a nonprofit founded by retired Supreme Court justice Sandra Day O'Connor, offers a whole suite of free video games focusing on civic themes. And while most existing games for civic education involve single players interacting with the computer, digital games can also enable groups of students to collaborate on civics-related activities in a simulated environment.[31]

Politics Is Polarized

A second major change in the environment involves political polarization.[32] Today, Americans are angry about the political system and especially angry with those who represent a different part of the ideological spectrum than their own. Mistrust goes beyond political leaders and extends to fellow citizens. The Pew Research Center found that "a dwindling majority (57 percent) [of Americans] say they have a good deal of confidence in the wisdom of the American people when it comes to making political decisions."[33]

Teaching about politics and civic engagement will always be somewhat controversial because it can influence students' values and actions in ways that affect the long-term direction of the country. We would argue that civic education can be ideologically fair and open-ended and need not turn into propaganda, but we acknowledge that civic learning will always be subject to suspicion, and when that suspicion is intense and widespread, civics can easily be cut from the curriculum—or at least rendered anodyne. Today, the situation seems particularly delicate, as public schools and teachers are quickly accused of political bias, and youth have come to be viewed as a partisan constituency.

Moreover, many Americans resist engaging in any sort of controversy at all, including classroom debates.[34] That has long been true, but it is especially significant at a time when political controversy seems particularly bitter and unproductive—adults worry about what could happen if students are encouraged to discuss and argue about serious topics, and teachers fear the repercussions if parents and the media find out that such things are happening in their schools. According to our national survey of high school civics or government teachers, roughly one in four believe that the parents of their students or other adults in their community would object if they brought discussion of politics into the classroom.[35]

Thus, any effort to strengthen and deepen civic education must take into account the fact that many topics once viewed as good prompts for classroom debate are now seen as partisan and ideologically loaded. Yet, under such conditions of polarization and bitter debate, it is arguably more important than ever to teach civil, cross-partisan deliberation in schools.

We acknowledge that even if we invest in efforts to teach teachers how to moderate debates, restrain their own partisan views, and choose balanced materials, problematic examples will arise. However, we would urge educators not to throw the baby out with the bathwater. Discussing controversial issues boosts students' knowledge and interest and is especially valuable for children who come from homes where there is not much political discussion.[36] Parents and educators should tolerate flare-ups of public controversy in order to preserve the principle that it is important to talk about difficult issues in school.

Toward a Shared Agenda for Deeper Civic Learning

At a high level of abstraction, it is possible to achieve a broad consensus about civic education. For example, *The 2003 Civic Mission of Schools* report, which became the charter for the Campaign for the Civic Mission of Schools, had fifty authors whose affiliations ranged from the conservative Heritage Foundation to the two national teachers' unions.[37] In spite of their many political differences, the participants were able to agree on a diagnosis of what ails civic education and on a set of proposed reforms.

However, that's not to minimize the real disagreements that can arise when advocates debate their competing priorities, especially when they know that instructional time and other resources are scarce.

Some leading experts in the field are concerned primarily with ensuring that young people understand the basic structure of the U.S. government as it is enshrined in the Constitution and its amendments. They tend to emphasize the value of instruction that focuses on the founding era and the national level of government, and that fosters an appreciative attitude toward the political system and a sense of unity around our shared history and principles.[38]

For instance, consider "We the People," a curriculum that was funded by the U.S. Department of Education through the Center for Civic Education for many years. The program, which likely has reached more than 26 million students, was found to have "a strong positive impact on high school students' knowledge of the history and principles of the U.S. Constitution" and to further the goal of "promoting civic competence and responsibility," as defined by students' positive attitudes toward American political institutions, knowledge of these institutions, and political participation (e.g., working for a political party or candidate, or participating in a peaceful protest).[39]

In contrast, other advocates are concerned primarily with empowering young people to participate in civic life, with an emphasis on civic action that takes place at the local level (as most civic action does). From this perspective, it is important for students to gain some understanding of the U.S. Constitution (for instance, they should know that speech enjoys constitutional protection), but it may be just as important for them to investigate local social conditions or who exercises real power in the community.

Further, those who favor such "action civics"—a new term for an old idea, which likely was more prevalent in 1915 or 1945 than it is today—tend to value a critical stance toward the existing political system, and they often call for instruction that emphasizes the value of diversity, localism, criticism, and action, rather than instruction that aims to foster a sense of patriotism and unity and an understanding of core political documents and principles.[40] Thus, action civics programs tend to engage students in activities such as local elections, interactions with elected officials, debates, community organizing, and other forms of experiential and authentic engagement.

Divergent philosophical views of civics tend to suggest quite different pedagogies and subject matter, and they reflect divergent views of the current U.S. political system and society, mapping roughly onto left/right ideological debates. Such controversies can easily intimidate teachers and students. But controversies can also motivate students to learn and help them make sense of complex material. As Gerald Graff, the distinguished literary critic and former president of the Modern Language Association, wrote more than two decades ago:

> One does not have to be a tenured radical to see that what has taken over the educational world today is not barbarism and unreason but, simply, conflict. The first step in dealing productively with today's conflicts is to recognize their legitimacy. [We should] rethink the premise that the eruption of fundamental conflict in education has to mean educational and cultural paralysis. My argument is that conflict has to mean paralysis only as long as we fail to take advantage of it.[41]

Graff might recommend that debates about the purposes of civic education be brought into the classroom, that multiple ideological perspectives be treated as legitimate, and that students learn to integrate material into meaningful arguments by participating in these debates. "Organizing high school and college courses around compelling debates could make information and books more meaningful—and worth looking up—than they now often are to many students."[42]

Certainly, civic education should be ideologically open ended rather than propagandistic. Students should form their own views after appropriate reflection, academic study, and deliberation with others. Civics can thus be neutral even as it is a field of controversy.

Furthermore, the modalities of civic education are not as controversial as the goals. Despite ongoing debates about the proper purposes of civics instruction, participants in the Campaign for the Civic Mission of Schools managed to reach consensus on six "promising" or "proven" practices, which are well-supported by expert opinion and existing research:[43]

1. Instruction in government, history, law, and democracy
2. Discussion of current local, national, and international issues and events
3. Service learning that is linked to the formal curriculum and classroom instruction
4. Extracurricular activities that provide opportunities for young people to get involved in their schools or communities
5. Student participation in school governance
6. Simulations of democratic processes and procedures[44]

Note that such practices are not inherently partisan, and they can and should address the concerns of both conservative and progressive educators. Moreover, they are entirely consistent with the goals of deeper learning.

Teaching civics in this way means helping young people develop a sophisticated understanding of social studies and civics content, while also helping them develop into competent civic actors who possess the range of skills highlighted by advocates for deeper learning. For example, the capacity to collaborate and communicate effectively is required in order to have a respectful, articulate debate with those who hold different political views. The ability to reflect on one's own thinking is key to making sense of those other views and to questioning one's own assumptions. And the ability to persist in the face of complicated real-world problems is critical to the task of confronting important civic dilemmas.

In fact, deeper learning is the only kind of learning that seriously addresses the "civic readiness" part of the common slogan "college, career, and civic life." To date, the argument for deeper learning has tended to be made in reference to the cultivation of knowledge and skills that matter in college and the workforce. But deeper learning is truly preparation for civic life.

CIVIC EDUCATION CAN SUPPORT DEEPER LEARNING

The effects of civic education have not yet been assessed as comprehensively as we and others in the field would like. However, available studies tend to support the premise that civic education can be an effective means of teaching not just civics-related content and skills but also the various kinds of academic content and inter- and intrapersonal skills that are grouped together under the banner of deeper learning.

What's Known About the Effects of Civic Education in General?

The Campaign for the Civic Mission of Schools refers to the six practices described above as "proven" on the basis of favorable program evaluations and survey data that show positive correlations between these practices and civic knowledge or civic engagement.[45]

In 2012, we surveyed a large sample of young adults and asked, among many other questions, whether they recalled the following experiences in high school: discussion of current events, discussion of controversial issues in any classes, conducting research on social or political issues, projects on community issues or in the community, and keeping up with news media. Participation in more of these practices, we found, was associated with greater engagement with the 2012 election. Service learning also had positive effects when the young adults recalled that they had addressed the root causes of social problems; otherwise, its effects were negative.[46]

A large study of Chicago public school students found that having good "civic learning opportunities" increased adolescents' commitment to civic engagement—these opportunities were defined as a combination of "learning about problems in society, learning about current events, studying issues about which one cares, experiencing an open climate for classroom discussions of social and political topics, hearing from civic role models, learning about ways to improve the community, and working on service learning projects."[47]

Additionally, a number of studies have found benefits from discussion of controversial issues in classrooms, participation in extracurricular groups, and community service, whether required or not.[48] Service learning has also been found to enhance students' interest in voting and increase their academic success in social studies classes, but much variation was observed in the quality and impact of service-learning programs.[49]

We acknowledge that more rigorous methodologies (especially random assignment) might complicate the story by suggesting that other factors, beyond the civics class itself, are primarily responsible for the results. Further, we do not yet have answers to some important questions, such as whether civic education in adolescence has effects that persist decades later, whether subtle differences in content and ideology matter, and what it will take to narrow severe gaps in civic learning. (While many studies find that all students benefit from recommended practices, the most advantaged students tend to benefit most.[50]) However, the available evidence creates a fairly strong basis for the belief that recommended approaches to civic education have positive results, at least when well implemented.

Civics and the Whole Curriculum

Of course, students do not learn democratic and civic knowledge and skills in their social studies classes alone. For example, students in an English class may raise important questions about justice while discussing a novel. A biology curriculum may offer challenging and valuable opportunities to explore environmental issues. In mathematics, statistical problems can involve social issues and teach important civic skills.

When designed and implemented thoughtfully, civic learning is a way to make any subject more authentic, helping students to become more engaged in the given content by allowing them to apply concepts from textbooks to real problems of public significance. In short, civic learning can provide a vehicle for deeper learning.

Particularly when students have a chance to apply what they learn in the classroom to a real-world setting—for example, through service learning or a community project—they are required to think critically, strategically, and collaboratively. Inevitably, they will be confronted by unexpected circumstances and complex problems that need solving, often in partnership with other students and adults, and often demanding that they communicate effectively with people who hold different values, perspectives, and backgrounds.[51] Confronting opposing views and dilemmas is also a critical part of service learning that helps students reflect deeply on their learning and define their values.[52]

Further, students who become involved in experiential civic learning opportunities often have a chance to see tangible results from their efforts to confront meaningful challenges, helping them develop an academic mind-set by teaching them the value of hard work and collaboration. As one study found, civic and leadership programs in afterschool settings provide particularly useful contexts in which to develop persistence, a sense of agency, and a sophisticated understanding of complicated real-world issues.[53]

Exciting Trends in Civic Learning

The federal government has allocated some funds for civics over the past decade through the Corporation for National and Community Service. However, very little federal funding has gone toward the creation of novel teaching models or materials, and recent investments in research and development for civic education have been paltry overall. For their part, when it comes to civics, the states have commissioned the cheapest and most traditional exams possible—that is, multiple-choice written tests—and only a small number of foundations have supported K–12 civics in any form. And while it should be possible to design reliable and valid measures of students' ability to work together to address common concerns, we know of no serious efforts to do so. With the exception of a recent draft framework from the Program for International Student Assessment, there has not even been much discussion of the value of measuring students' ability to work together on social or community problems.

Nevertheless, there have been several important recent developments in civic education, with promising implications for high school education writ large.

First, Advanced Placement American Government is currently the fastest-growing AP course, and—insofar as it emulates college-level political science—it often serves as a model for other high school civics courses. Because it requires relatively rapid coverage of a large body of information, some argue that the course gives too little attention to helping students learn how to address contemporary problems. However, University of Washington professor Walter Parker has been developing an alternative method of teaching AP American Government that involves group projects, and he explicitly describes it as a "deeper learning" approach. In a randomized experiment, Parker and his design team (which includes teachers) have been able to match the AP scores achieved with the traditional approach while considerably boosting students' civic skills and interests.[54]

Second, in 2013, the National Council for the Social Studies released a new framework to help inform states' efforts to revise their social studies standards. It is shorter, more coherent, and more demanding than typical state standards (which tend to be long lists of miscellaneous topics), but it makes new room for civic participation with the addition of "taking informed action" as a major learning outcome.[55]

Third, three states have recently enacted new policies to strengthen civic education on a large scale. Florida has imposed a new high-stakes civics test along with a set of other requirements, such as mandating the inclusion of nonfiction texts in elementary reading curricula. Tennessee also added a required assessment, but in lieu of mandating a high-stakes standardized test, it requires students to compile a civics portfolio for graduation. And Hawaii created—and then protected from a planned cut—a new mandatory high school course that focuses on applying academic content and skills to solving important real-world problems.[56] While it is too early to know whether these reforms will work, they are all bold and, at the same time, intriguingly different in their approaches.

Fourth, action civics is gaining recognition as an engaging pedagogy that enables students from diverse backgrounds to address relevant and serious community issues through action-oriented pedagogy. Harvard professor Meira Levinson gave the movement a strong theoretical basis in a recent book (although she prefers the phrase "guided experiential education"),[57] and many organizations, including our own, have joined a National Action Civics Collaborative to strengthen and expand the action civics model.[58] There is some evidence of its impact on students, but empirical research so far is limited.

Fifth, there is an emerging field of game-based and technology-assisted civic learning. Based on the concept of "gamification" (the use of games to engage users/students in solving problems and learning), these tools aim to support the active learning of key civics concepts (such as the branches of power and function of the Supreme Court) integrated with the development of deeper learning skills such as collaboration, effective communication, and persistence in the face of complicated problems.[59] The Center for Information and Research on Civic Learning and Engagement's evaluation of one iCivics game, Drafting Board, indicated that students who played it achieved the desired learning outcomes while reporting greater engagement with the class than did a control group of students who did not play the game.[60]

Sixth, civic learning can be incorporated into settings outside of traditional social studies curricula, and some prominent national organizations have successfully done so. For example, YouthBuild USA defines civic engagement and leadership as important pillars of its work, and it actively engages its participants in leadership development activities, mentoring, and civic activities. As a result, many graduates of YouthBuild serve in key leadership roles in their home communities.[61]

Finally, there are ample opportunities for engaged civic learning in extracurricular activities. For example, Junior State of America provides forums for students to join peers in exploring their interests in politics and foreign affairs, and it encourages them to take leadership roles in all aspects of the organization. Similarly, studies find that students who participate in the National Association for Urban Debate Leagues increase their chances of academic success dramatically compared to similar students who do not participate. The latest evaluation finds that the program not only teaches debating skills, leading to better overall academic performance, but it results in young people becoming more engaged in civic life and more optimistic in their views of the future.[62] Such out-of-classroom opportunities are critically important, we argue, because they offer pathways for students who are not well served by traditional educational settings. And by giving young people a chance to engage on their own terms with civic content and to participate in deliberations about civic matters, they allow diverse students to discover their love of learning.

CONCLUSION

Even though *A Nation at Risk* was explicit and eloquent about the critical importance of civic learning, the waves of education reform following that report have generally ignored civics. Since 1993, education for effective citizenship has been an afterthought in most federal and state policies and has received minimal investment from government and philanthropy. As a result, current programs and assessments in civics tend to look old fashioned and small scale, even as the political and technological contexts that confront young citizens have changed rapidly.

The few bold recent efforts to strengthen civics have taken the form of state-level tests or course mandates. Although we do not oppose those reforms (which may help if very well implemented), we think they miss the main point. Civics needs new approaches that involve deeper and more collaborative learning, that take better advantage of advanced technologies, that are assessed in more authentic ways (without sacrificing rigor), and that pervade the curriculum—including social studies but also reaching into other subject areas.

If states choose to require civics courses and exams, they should design the tests to measure students' ability to think critically about current issues and to interact with institutions and with other citizens (at least in hypothetical scenarios). Teachers will also need strong professional development to prepare their students for these tests without sacrificing opportunities for deeper learning. It is possible that professional development, mandatory courses, and thoughtful standards and tests could generate excellent pedagogy and outcomes. But tests are not particularly promising on their own and may not be necessary for improving civics.

Nor would we recommend requiring particular experiences, such as service learning, at the district or state level. The positive effect observed from some small-scale projects probably depends, at least in part, on the teachers' enthusiasm for undertaking these efforts; making them mandatory might well reduce their benefits. If any pedagogy has a strong case for being made mandatory, it is the engagement of students in moderated discussions of current, controversial issues. However, to support such discussions, districts and states should also adopt policies that explicitly protect teachers who address controversies in the classroom, while giving them guidance about how to moderate such discussions fairly and effectively.

Above all, we recommend the application of deeper learning to civics and the integration of civics in deeper learning. Deeper learning's emphasis on inter- and intrapersonal development seems very much in line with civic educators' long-term interest in cultivating the development of active and engaged citizens. Both movements seek to develop youth as people who not only understand how our political and legal systems work, but who are equipped to join their fellow citizens in responsible and respectful debate, to reflect on and revise their own positions, to negotiate and work through thorny conflicts, and ultimately to address local and national problems.

PART TWO

Access and Opportunity

4

Equal Opportunity for Deeper Learning

Pedro Noguera, Linda Darling-Hammond, and Diane Friedlaender

TO HELP ALL STUDENTS learn deeply, the nation's schools will need to provide them with regular opportunities to practice high-level skills such as solving complex problems, conducting research, communicating in multiple forms, and using new technologies to find, analyze, and evaluate information. However, when it comes to creating such a rich learning environment, schools serving low-income students and students of color tend to have the farthest distance to travel.

Since 2001 and throughout the No Child Left Behind (NCLB) era, schools serving relatively affluent students have continued to offer rigorous instruction (particularly in their honors, Advanced Placement, and college prep courses) and a wide course selection, including world languages, science, history, music, and the arts. In contrast, schools serving underprivileged students, already underresourced, have struggled to maintain a broad curriculum. Faced with repeated budget cuts and looming consequences if they fail to make Adequate Yearly Progress, many have shifted significant amounts of classroom time to test preparation in an effort to boost student performance on high-stakes exams.[1]

Complicating matters further, the segregation of students on the basis of race and socioeconomic status has intensified over the last thirty years.[2] While dropout rates in the United States have declined overall recently, they remain extremely high in some parts of the country, particularly in urban areas. As of 2011, 25 percent of the nation's African American high school students and 17 percent of Latino high school students were enrolled in what some call "dropout factories"—schools that see their enrollment decline by 40 percent or more between ninth and twelfth grade; only 5 percent of white students attend such high schools.[3] In short, inequities in funding, learning opportunities, and learning conditions continue to divide the American educational system, contributing to the persistence of the so-called "achievement gap."

In a recent report to the U.S. Secretary of Education entitled *For Each and Every Child: A Strategy for Education, Equity and Excellence,* the Equity and Excellence Commission documented these widespread disparities and defined an equity agenda to address the following needs:[4]

- a restructuring of the school finance system to ensure equitable distribution of resources
- access to high-quality teachers
- access to high-quality early childhood education
- external supports to address the social needs of children
- a new accountability system to hold policy makers responsible for conditions within schools

This chapter builds on that agenda, focusing on the specific kinds of instruction and support that all children deserve. We argue that to ensure equity in access to deeper learning, practices and policies must address the context for education both outside and inside of schools. To enable students from low-income backgrounds to learn deeply and successfully, schools that serve them must offer a high-quality, student-centered instructional experience and the wraparound services that can help ameliorate the stressful conditions they experience in their communities.

To inform efforts to prepare greater numbers of students for college, careers, and civic life, we first describe the obstacles that currently prevent schools from delivering high-quality instruction, and we then examine educational models, structures, and practices that facilitate deeper learning. Finally, we take a wider systemic perspective to consider how policy, practice, and research can be aligned to support the development of pedagogy for deeper learning in schools serving students who have been deemed at risk of school failure.

OBSTACLES TO OVERCOME

In this chapter, we define equity as the policies and practices that ensure that every student has access to an education focused on meaningful learning (i.e., that teaches the deeper learning skills contemporary society requires), taught by competent and caring educators who are able to attend to the student's social and academic needs, and supported by adequate resources that provide the materials and conditions for effective teaching and learning.[5] Equity-based reforms are central to the effort.

For many years, critics of the accountability movement have argued that its emphasis on narrowly framed academic goals has made it more difficult to pursue deeper learning with students. Even before the adoption of NCLB, advocates such as Ted Sizer, author of *Horace's Compromise* and the founder of the Coalition of Essential Schools, argued that the high school curriculum had become little more than an amalgamation of scattered facts and skills, lacking coherence and more likely to elicit boredom than serious engagement. As an alternative, Sizer and others called for educators to choose "depth over breadth" by emphasizing instruction in critical thinking, problem solving, and other "habits of mind" that would foster lifelong learning as well as the ability to acquire and use knowledge to tackle new problems and develop new ideas, products, and possibilities.[6]

However, advocates for such teaching and learning have struggled to gain much traction in schools serving children of color, particularly in areas where poverty is concentrated. As Harvard Graduate School of Education associate professor Jal Mehta recently noted, it tends to be the case that "students in more affluent schools and top tracks are given the kind of problem-solving education that befits the future managerial class, whereas students in lower tracks and higher-poverty schools are given the kind of rule-following tasks that mirror much of factory and other working class work."[7] Moreover, he adds, today's advocates of deeper learning appear to have a "race problem," in that the movement "is much more white than the nation as a whole," and African American civil rights leaders often have been skeptical of calls for deeper learning.

But while this divide may exist, there is also a long tradition of support for deeper learning in the black community. Since the days when W. E. B. DuBois and his colleagues in the NAACP argued for a liberal arts curriculum for African American students, civil rights groups have fought against the lower-level, skills-based curriculum that society has typically reserved for students of color. Only in the last ten to fifteen years have accountability hawks cloaked arguments for test-focused reforms in civil rights language, even as the effects of those reforms have deepened the gulf between the curricula offered to the haves and the have-nots.

Although NCLB brought a needed measure of attention to the achievement of often-neglected groups of students, high-stakes testing has inadvertently reinforced long-standing tracking systems based on assumptions about differential ability and the future life roles of students. This has occurred because (1) in many schools, especially those serving low-income students, the curriculum has been narrowed to mirror the content of low-level, multiple-choice tests in reading and math, reducing access to writing, research, science, history, and the arts; and (2) test scores have been used to allocate differential access to the curriculum, with the result that students of color and low-income students have often been denied access to a curriculum that teaches higher-order thinking skills, and instead relegated to remedial, rote-oriented, and often scripted courses of study.[8]

In short, recent policies have created a vicious cycle that exacerbates existing inequities. Evidence suggests that even when these policies do lead to a momentary bump in scores on low-level tests of basic skills, the lack of access to a broad liberal arts curriculum and to opportunities to engage in complex problem solving and inquiry ultimately contributes to poor performance on gateway tests for college (i.e., the ACT and the SAT) and in college courses that require deeper comprehension skills, the ability to write and communicate well, and analytic thinking.[9]

Where deeper learning remains unavailable to students of color and children of low-income families, the United States will never be able to solve its equity dilemma. The evidence is clear: students will acquire the skills to be truly college and career ready only if they have access to a higher-level curriculum.

The Effects of Poverty and the Environment

Educators have long understood that environmental factors—related to family background, peer groups, neighborhood conditions, and more—influence the health, nutrition, safety, and overall psychological and emotional well-being of young people, which in turn affect their development and learning.[10]

As numerous studies have shown, family income and parental education are two of the strongest predictors of student achievement and educational attainment.[11] Children in schools where poverty is concentrated underperform their counterparts in more economically mixed settings. Indeed, students who are not low-income but attend high-poverty schools have lower achievement than low-income students attending more affluent schools.[12]

Poverty also limits the amount and quality of academic and social support students receive outside of school. Whereas middle-class parents can generally provide their children with a broad range of opportunities—such as quality preschool, summer camp, homework assistance, music lessons, and the like—that support healthy development and enhance the likelihood of academic success, lower-income parents typically lack the education and resources needed to do so.[13]

Further, as poverty rates have risen in recent years, a growing number of researchers have drawn attention to the ways in which food insecurity, poor prenatal care, poor heath, lack of safety, housing instability, violence, and pervasive and persistent stress negatively influence children's welfare and well-being.[14] Many have argued that the rise in childhood poverty rates since the 1980s has been a major reason for the lack of progress in improving American schools, as federal and state education policies have done little to redress what has become an increasingly tattered safety net.[15] By 2013, according to a large-scale study on child health and well-being conducted by the United Nations Children's Fund, the United States ranked twenty-sixth out of the twenty-nine wealthiest nations.[16]

The educational consequences of poverty appear early. Studies have found, for example, that the working vocabulary of four-year-old children from low-income families is approximately one-third that of children from middle-income families, which makes it more difficult for them to read with comprehension and engage in academic learning when they enter school.[17] By first grade, only half as many students from low-income families are as proficient as students from more affluent families at understanding words in context and engaging in basic mathematics.[18]

These differences in early-year experiences among young children often lead schools serving low-income students to organize a remedial curriculum focused on rote skill development. Rather than creating an enriched environment that would provide robust linguistic and hands-on learning experiences that could develop higher-order thinking and performance, students are often subjected to a series of drills and learning experiences designed to develop low-level skills. The problem is often exacerbated by the prevalence of inexperienced teachers who frequently depart within the first few years of teaching. To compensate for high teacher turnover and a lack of highly skilled teachers, many districts have adopted highly scripted "teacher-proof" curricula. Such approaches cannot reach deeper learning goals as they generally fail to develop the capacity of teachers to teach the more sophisticated curriculum needed to develop higher-order thinking skills in students.

Moreover, research suggests that poverty and the social issues that frequently accompany it (e.g., housing instability, substance abuse, crime, and unemployment) have a negative impact not only on individual students but on the culture of their schools, undermining the collegiality and trust that organizations need in order to improve.[19]

None of this should be taken to suggest that demography is destiny or that children from low-income communities cannot be expected to achieve. However, it does mean that we must pay attention to the ways in which poverty negatively influences academic outcomes, and we must ensure that our schools provide the academic and social supports that enable students to thrive. Otherwise, we will be unlikely to reduce the race- and class-based disparities in achievement that characterize American education today.

Unequal Funding

Inequality in public spending on education further exacerbates the effects of high poverty rates and income inequality. In the United States, funding for schools in affluent communities is typically higher than in poor ones.[20] The differences are dramatic in many states, with wealthy suburban schools spending twice as much as urban and rural schools that serve higher-need students.

Contrary to the oft-repeated claim that increases in school spending levels have little impact on educational outcomes, funding affects the ability of schools to provide both high-quality instruction and the wraparound services (before- and afterschool care, health supports, and social services) that students need in order to be ready to learn.

A recent longitudinal study powerfully demonstrated the importance of providing adequate resources to schools in order to transform academic outcomes. It found that in districts that substantially increased their spending as a result of court-ordered changes in school finance, low-income children were significantly more likely to graduate from high school, earn livable wages, and avoid poverty in adulthood.[21] For low-income students who spent all twelve years of school in districts that increased spending by at least 20 percent, graduation rates rose by 23 percentage points and educational attainment levels rose by a full year. Between the ages of twenty-five and forty-five, these same children were 20 percent less likely to fall into poverty during any given year. Their individual wages were 25 percent higher than they would have been, and their family incomes were 52 percent higher. The effects were large enough in some cases to eliminate the entire gap in adult outcomes between those raised in low-income and high-income families.

In short, school funding formulas must enable all children to receive the fundamental supports and services they need, along with access to an engaging, relevant curriculum that promotes the acquisition of deeper learning skills.

WHAT SCHOOLS MUST DO FOR ALL STUDENTS

A number of studies have examined schools that are disrupting the status quo and engaging low-income and minority students in deeper learning.[22] These schools build on what we know about how children learn and develop, and research indicates they have stronger academic performance, better attendance and student behavior, lower dropout rates, higher graduation rates, and higher rates of college attendance and perseverance than comparison schools serving similar students.

In one of these studies, for example, the American Institutes for Research compared a set of thirteen schools in California and New York that belonged to school networks focused on deeper learning strategies with matched comparison schools serving similar students.[23] The study found that, on average, students who attended the network schools achieved higher scores on the OECD PISA-based Test for Schools, which assesses core content knowledge and complex problem-solving skills, as well as on state English language arts and mathematics tests. They were also more likely to graduate from high school on time and to enroll in four-year colleges and more selective colleges, and the benefits were similar whether students entered high school with low or high levels of prior achievement.

In this section, we examine the practices utilized by the schools in these studies to understand how they operationalize their simultaneous commitments to equity and deeper learning. Key elements include:

- authentic instruction and assessment, especially
  - inquiry-based and group learning
  - a focus on mastery
  - performance-based assessments
  - a relevant curriculum connected to the world beyond school
- personalized supports for student learning, especially
  - differentiated instruction
  - advisory programs
  - support for social-emotional learning
- supports for educator learning, especially opportunities for
  - reflection
  - collaboration
  - leadership
  - professional development

Schools that incorporate these key features are more likely to develop students who have transferable academic skills, feel a sense of purpose and connection to school, graduate and go on to college, and are prepared for a fast-changing job market. In short, they look at the student as a whole person.

At the heart of instruction that provides equitable access to deeper learning lie pedagogical approaches that emphasize the development of the analytic and communication skills needed to navigate and excel in a dynamic, information-rich environment.

INQUIRY-BASED PEDAGOGY AND GROUP LEARNING

Inquiry-based pedagogy and group learning prepare students for college, career, and life by promoting transferable skills such as critical thinking, problem solving, collaboration, and communication.[24] To help students develop these skills, teachers must create opportunities for them to engage actively with course content, grapple with real-world problems, explore core questions, develop and test hypotheses, make generalizations, and communicate with audiences beyond the classroom. For inquiry-based instruction to succeed, students need a base level of background content knowledge, a solid understanding of the process of inquiry, and the skills to design and manage a complex set of activities.[25] This requires teachers to provide access to background knowledge, along with substantial scaffolding for the analytic and inquiry processes, until students have had sufficient practice with these skills.

Schools use various strategies to structure inquiry-based learning. For example, in the San Francisco Bay Area Envision Schools, teachers design all class activities to give students the opportunity to build knowledge, apply their knowledge, and reflect on what they have learned and how they can improve. They tie this framework to their core competencies, which include inquiry, analysis, research, and creative expression.

At other schools, such as Oakland's Life Academy, teachers frame the curriculum around inquiry topics related to essential questions, such as, "How do people survive the horrors of war?" and "Was capitalism or socialism better for America in the twentieth century?" This type of instruction encourages higher-order thinking and requires more complex project-based and collaborative classroom activities, such as interactive class projects, role playing, mock trials, art projects, and presentations.

While students can engage in inquiry-based learning on their own, research has found that participation in group projects tends to be particularly effective, with hundreds of studies finding significant learning benefits—for young people of all ages and from all backgrounds—when students are asked to work together on well-structured inquiry activities.[26] Experimental studies have also shown that groups tend to outperform individuals on learning tasks and, further, that individuals who work in groups perform at a higher level on individual assessments.[27]

The largest positive effects appear when students receive explicit instruction on how to work productively in a group and when the work involves "group-worthy" tasks that require the talents of all participants and call for a significant amount of analysis and discussion. Structured student roles, interdependent group rewards, accountability for both individual and group efforts, and opportunities for groups to reflect regularly on their own process also make group learning more effective. Further, many studies have found that low-income students, students of color, and urban students tend to see even greater benefits from group work than do other students, making it a crucial strategy, in both elementary and secondary schools, for an equity agenda for deeper learning.[28]

A FOCUS ON MASTERY

For most schools, a turn toward deeper learning implies a seismic shift in the purpose of assessment—away from accountability measures designed to rank and sort students and toward performance assessments that diagnose individual student learning needs, promote skill acquisition, and enable students to gauge their progress.

Key to this approach is a focus on mastery—that is, a schoolwide commitment to ensuring that students truly grasp important academic material before they are moved along in the curriculum. For example, at Dozier-Libbey Medical High School in Antioch, California, teachers use a range of formative assessments to gauge students' progress in meeting academic standards, with an eye toward reaching a mastery level. A school staff member explains: "We look for opportunities for students to relearn and redo. Are the students learning and mastering the concepts that we want them to? If not, how can we give them the opportunities to learn? It is about meeting the standards or trying again. Not everyone learns at the same pace."

This perspective is diametrically opposed to the assumption, implicit in most schools, that effective instruction depends on sticking faithfully to a pacing guide, as though it were more important for teachers to cover the given material than for students to learn it. For young people who start with less prior knowledge—as do many students from high-poverty backgrounds—or who learn at a slower pace, such an approach makes failure almost inevitable. If they never get a solid footing in a subject's introductory material, they will stand little chance of keeping up with the more advanced concepts and skills to be encountered later.

PERFORMANCE-BASED ASSESSMENTS

Schools that teach for deeper learning gauge mastery through assessments that reflect the kinds of literacy, mathematics, and analytical tasks found in higher education and the workplace. Assessments such as exhibitions and projects result in tangible products and encourage learners to draw on multiple kinds of knowledge to demonstrate higher-order and integrated learning. (See the sidebar, "Performance Assessment: A Definition.") Often these schools require students to assemble portfolios designed to display their best work in a cumulative fashion and illustrate the range of skills they have mastered.

Many schools—including some that enroll mainly low-income students of color—use exhibitions as a way for students to demonstrate their learning, often across disciplines, and practice their communication skills. For example, at City Arts and Technology High School in San Francisco (one of three charter schools run by Envision Education), students do at least one exhibition every year. Tenth-grade students prepare an exhibition on *Animal Farm*, in which they conduct a literary analysis in English class, study the Russian Revolution in history class, and create a poster of the novel's symbols in art class. They present this work to an audience that includes parents and community members, who vote on the best citizen and leader in the novel. Exhibitions enable students to see the connections between their courses and understand how the knowledge acquired in one domain (history) can be relevant to what they learn in another (literature and art).

Reflection is a fundamental part of this assessment process, from the requirement that students fill out "exit slips" (quick descriptions of what they have learned) at the end of class periods to the expectation that their portfolio defenses or exhibitions include a discussion of their academic progress over time. For example, at Impact Academy (another of the Envision Schools, located in Hayward, California), students, advisers, and parents reflect on the student's academic and behavioral accomplishments and set goals for improvement during family conferences that occur twice per year.

PERFORMANCE ASSESSMENT: A DEFINITION

Linda Darling-Hammond and Frank Adamson define "performance assessment" in *Beyond Basic Skills: The Role of Performance Assessment in Achieving 21st Century Standards of Learning*:

For many people, performance assessment is most easily defined by what it is not: specifically, it is not multiple-choice testing. In a performance assessment, rather than choosing among pre-determined options, students must construct an answer, produce a product, or perform an activity. From this perspective, performance assessment encompasses a very wide range of activities, from completing a sentence with a few words (short-answer), to writing a thorough analysis (essay), to conducting and analyzing a laboratory investigation (hands-on).

Because they allow students to construct or perform an original response rather than just recognizing a potentially right answer out of a list provided, performance assessments can measure students' cognitive thinking and reasoning skills and their ability to apply knowledge to solve realistic, meaningful problems.

. . . [Performance assessments] allow teachers to gather information about what students can actually do with what they are learning—science experiments that students design, carry out, analyze, and write up; computer programs that students create and test out; research inquiries that they pursue, assembling evidence about a question that they present in written and oral form. Whether the skill or standard being measured is writing, speaking, scientific or mathematical literacy, or knowledge of

> history and social science research, students actually perform
> tasks involving these skills and the teacher or other rater scores
> the performance based upon a set of pre-determined criteria.[29]

RELEVANT CURRICULUM CONNECTED TO THE WORLD BEYOND SCHOOL

To successfully build the skills required for college and careers, students must be exposed to content and materials that are relevant to what they know, who they are, and who they want to be. However, this is not meant to imply that students should be limited to information within their experience; it simply means that, like adults, young people thrive in environments where their work has intrinsic value, meaning, and applicability beyond the classroom. An intellectually engaging curriculum that is challenging and connected to real-world issues supports in-depth reflection and engagement while providing better support for postsecondary education and the work world. And this is just as true for students from low-income backgrounds as it is for everyone else.

For example, Dozier-Libbey Medical High School and Life Academy of Health and Bioscience—both career-focused schools in the Oakland, California, area that serve large numbers of economically disadvantaged students—create relevance through interdisciplinary coursework, collaborative projects, and internships in the health and life sciences. They integrate their health careers focus not only through internships and projects in settings ranging from hospitals to scientific laboratories, but also through their coursework. At Life Academy, for instance, tenth-grade students investigate issues of mental health in an interdisciplinary project in humanities and biology, in which they read *Slaughterhouse-Five* while studying five mental illnesses through a biological lens. The project concludes with a written assessment in which students take the role of a psychiatrist and use textual evidence from the book to diagnose the main character. This type of interdisciplinary work incorporates the health care focus, brings relevance to the curriculum, and shows students how their academic subjects have value in the real world.

Similarly, the Envision Schools create relevance through a focus on art and technology, which encourages students to think critically about themselves and their environment. Here, too, internships engage students in learning outside of school, and the curriculum makes topics relevant through connections to current events and universal social themes. For example, the art rooms, hallways, and student exhibitions at San Francisco's City Arts and Technology High School display provocative art that speaks to both personal issues of identity and larger social issues. Teachers incorporate social justice themes as a strategy to empower youth and encourage them to think critically. While exploring key events in world history, students discuss overarching themes and questions related to culture and subjectivity, the power of perspective, and resistance and complicity that resonate from the era of Nazi power in Germany to American society and the world today.

PERSONALIZED LEARNING PRACTICES

Supporting high academic achievement for all students begins with a shared belief among all school stakeholders, including students, parents, teachers, and administrators, that all students can achieve challenging learning goals. However, for all students to attain high levels of success, schools must accompany high expectations with the academic supports students need to span any gaps between those expectations and their own preparation levels.[30]

Students from low-income backgrounds often enter high school underprepared for a college preparatory curriculum and lacking confidence in their own abilities. The numerous academic and personal challenges they face provide multiple points for potential failure. To overcome these barriers, schools need to clearly communicate their support for every student, use multiple and redundant support strategies, provide teachers with strategies to differentiate instruction and assessment, and offer external supports to address the needs of special populations. Teachers need to balance high expectations for all students with a sensitivity to individual real-life challenges, so they can provide strong support based on their relationships with and knowledge of each student, and within the context of the school's personalization structures. Schoolwide practices should support high expectations by providing extra help to students who need it and empowering teachers and students to do their best.

The use of personalized learning plans is common in the field of special education (and described in chapter 5 by Sharon Vaughn and her coauthors), including in well-researched approaches such as Response to Intervention and Multi-Tiered System of Support, which are designed to help struggling students in general education classrooms. Developing a personalized learning plan requires teachers to assess individual students' learning needs carefully in order to provide appropriate and effective instruction.

Many educators would argue that the only way to ensure that every student has the opportunity to engage in deeper learning is to provide *everyone*—not just students with disabilities—with a personalized learning plan and to train all teachers to modify and adapt their instructional strategies in response to students' particular learning needs.[31] This is complicated work, as anyone who has ever attempted to differentiate instruction in a classroom composed of students with a broad range of abilities and background knowledge can attest. However, a growing number of schools are showing that it can be done.

Formative assessment plays an especially important role in such schools. For example, to accommodate heterogeneous classes, Envision Schools has come to rely heavily on the use of ungraded assignments, exit slips, and other assessments to determine what sorts of scaffolding individual students need and what supports to provide them. Common scaffolding approaches and supports include peer learning strategies, extended time, and adapted work (tasks that vary by length and difficulty depending on the student, but which require all students to access the same curriculum concepts). As a history teacher at Impact Academy in Hayward, California, explains:

> [For] some students it's executive functioning stuff, for others it's skill deficits, or it's reading—changing how much they are being asked to read, or eliminating elements of a project, creating an alternative assignment, or doing lots of scaffolds for writing . . . I do a lot of literacy stuff with all the students, but basically I try to figure out what is their capacity, if they're working super hard, and just modify and scaffold as appropriate.

Educators committed to equity and to providing all children with the opportunity to engage in deeper learning often think creatively about how to design and implement responsive educational strategies to meet student needs. Such teacher creativity made it possible for a school in Sunset Park, Brooklyn, to arrange its classrooms so that monolingual English speakers (who were mostly African American) and Spanish speakers could work on projects together, thus forming relationships and helping each other in developing literacy skills. (Further, the arrangement has had the added benefit of reducing racial segregation in classrooms, the cafeteria, and the playground.) Similarly, when educators in Rockville Center, Long Island, realized that their practice of tracking students into different levels of algebra and geometry had produced racially segregated classrooms, they untracked the classes and lengthened math lessons so that teachers would have more time to differentiate instruction and provide students with individualized support.

In both of these examples, rather than lowering standards or expectations, teachers worked creatively to develop a learning context that made it possible for most students to engage in deeper learning and meet the demands of a rigorous curriculum. Similarly, programs like Reading Recovery, which extends time and provides differentiated supports in the early grades, can help educators address the learning needs of students in the critical area of literacy development before children internalize the notion that they can't—or don't like to—read.

ADVISORY PROGRAMS

Advisory programs, which provide a structure to facilitate deep and lasting relationships between teachers and students, have the power to become the touchstone for the school day, a central component of each student's high school trajectory, and the heart of the conjoined academic and wraparound support system that enables all students to succeed.

Effective advisory programs meet daily for at least thirty to sixty minutes with a consistent, small cohort of students (typically fifteen to twenty) who stay with the same teacher for several years. Within advisory programs, teachers focus much of their attention on building a safe and caring community that provides crucial peer support. However, the advisers themselves—who come to know their advisees well—also play a critical role in advocating for students and ensuring that they do not slip through the cracks.

Advisers are charged with making sure that students succeed academically, too. When students struggle, the adviser reaches out to their teachers to develop strategies to turn things around. Conversely, when problems arise in class, teachers often look to the adviser for insight and assistance.

Advisers act as liaisons to and partners with students' families as well. To parents and guardians, particularly those who did not have positive experiences in high school, it can be critically important to have access to a friendly school contact, someone who knows their child and is invested in his or her success. Typically, advisers contact parents to check in or schedule formal conferences and meetings, and in some schools they are expected to conduct home visits, serving as the bridge between the student, the family, and needed social services and emotional supports. Overall, advisers enable schools and families to work together to provide students with the support they need to navigate the intricacies of school in a productive and positive manner.

Further, strong advisory programs also teach a developmental curriculum that evolves as students progress. For example, advisory classes may focus on the transition to middle or high school; career exploration and organizational strategies; college preparation; and by the end of high school, college applications and senior exhibitions. The through line of this curricular development is the guidance and support students need to graduate from high school and enroll in postsecondary education or enter productive careers. Toward this end, advisers help students set and meet short- and long-term goals, monitor schoolwork and grades, review transcripts to ensure that students are meeting college admissions requirements, and collaborate with other teachers and support staff to provide the academic and social-emotional support students need to meet their goals.

SUPPORT FOR STUDENTS' SOCIAL-EMOTIONAL DEVELOPMENT

Some of the major obstacles to the success of low-income students of color are social and psychological in nature, rather than purely academic. Not only are these young people more likely than their peers to be exposed to violence in their neighborhoods, lack quality physical and mental health care, have limited access to transportation, and go without adequate food and housing—all of which can make it difficult just to get to school in the morning—but they face countless other everyday injustices related to poverty and racism. By the time they are fourteen, according to Preston Thomas, formerly the principal of Life Academy, the cumulative effect of these stressors means that students "see barriers in why they can't, why they don't belong, why it's not their right to succeed at things." Overcoming these barriers requires explicit teaching that addresses students' social, emotional, and psychological needs.

Thus, in addition to providing advisers and personalized supports, schools that aim for deeper learning tend to make proactive efforts to help students learn to manage their emotions, develop an academic mind-set, interact with others productively, and persist through obstacles. Advisers take on a pivotal role, addressing both social-emotional and academic learning, sometimes even weaving together traditional lessons and group counseling.[32]

Supports for Educator Learning

In addition to a focus on authentic instruction and assessments and personalized supports for learning, creating and sustaining schools that are committed to equity and deeper learning requires substantial investments in building staff capacity. This includes efforts to create a shared schoolwide vision; support teacher collaboration in grade-level and subject-matter teams; build teacher expertise in pedagogy, content, curriculum, and assessment with job-embedded professional development; and provide opportunities for staff to reflect on and revise both individual and schoolwide practices, so that they become ever more effective.

Because these issues are addressed at length later in this volume by Magdalene Lampert (in chapter 7) and by Meredith Honig and Lydia Rainey (in chapter 8), we forgo further discussion of them here. However, we return to the need for policy supports for deeper teaching in our concluding section.

PRIORITIES FOR EQUITY AND DEEPER LEARNING

When educators and policy makers give priority to authentic instruction, performance assessment, and personalized learning practices, and when they adopt strategies to mitigate adverse conditions in impoverished communities, they can significantly enhance the ability of schools to promote equity and deeper learning. Despite the many obstacles faced by students from low-income backgrounds, some schools have managed to offer all students access to a rich and engaging curriculum. And the research we have reviewed suggests that three areas of policy support can help to bring such opportunities to scale:

* Ensuring that all schools are funded and organized for deeper learning
* Ensuring that highly effective educators are available to all schools
* Investing in high-quality instruction and assessment

Funding and Organizing Schools for Deeper Learning

Across the country, inadequate funding prevents schools serving low-income and minority students from fully realizing their goals and addressing student needs. Insufficient funds impact the ability of schools to hire and retain quality staff, provide services that meet student needs, and offer rich curricular and extracurricular offerings. To address these shortfalls, most states will need new funding formulas. As the National Commission on Equity and Excellence observed:

> The common situation in America is that schools in poor communities spend less per pupil—often many thousands of dollars less per pupil—than schools in nearby affluent communities. Underserved schools can't compete for the best teaching and principal talent in a local labor market and can't implement the high-end technology and rigorous academic and enrichment programs needed to enhance student performance. This is arguably the most important equity-related variable in American schooling today.[33]

As we noted earlier, addressing these disparities can have a profound influence on achievement, dramatically reducing gaps in educational and life outcomes.[34] In the 1990s, Massachusetts adopted a weighted student formula funding system that allocates more funding for the education of low-income students, English language learners, and students who require special education services. Along with the state's investments in early childhood education, extensive professional development, and new standards and assessments, this move is credited for large gains in student achievement and a reduction in achievement gaps.[35] Similarly, a 2013 OECD report on international education achievement found that the highest-performing and fastest-improving nations invest a greater share of their education resources in schools serving the most disadvantaged students.[36]

Policies must not only ensure adequate funding to schools serving low-income students but also encourage those schools to spend their resources productively. To that end, we recommend:

- *Policy incentives for equitable funding.* The federal government should make it a condition of federal funding that states make progress toward funding equity as well as educational achievement. States should adopt strategies, such as weighted student formula approaches, that fund schools on the basis of the costs of educating students who live in poverty and/or have other risk factors. They should allow schools to use these resources flexibly to implement successful, innovative school models.

- *Incentives to develop new school designs.* Many current funding policies for school operations and facilities, along with other state regulations, determine staffing, schedules, and credits according to a factory model design that was developed a century ago. Policies at the federal, state, and local levels need to be changed to encourage new school designs that support practices aimed at deeper learning—including competency-based or mastery-based approaches to organizing learning, new staffing models that personalize relationships, alternative uses of time, and physical spaces that take advantage of technology and teams.

- *Resources for wraparound services that support student success.* States and the federal government should provide funding for school models that ensure that students in high-need communities receive wraparound services, including adequate preschool education, physical and mental health care, social services, summer learning opportunities, and before- and afterschool care.

Preparing Educators for Deeper Teaching

States must commit themselves to increasing the supply of educators—including teachers, administrators, counselors, and others—who are prepared to offer high-quality instruction in high-poverty schools. This means producing educators who understand how students learn, can motivate that learning through engaging pedagogy and real-world connections, and know how to address students' academic, social, and emotional needs. In addition, states must ensure that such well-prepared educators have incentives to work and stay in schools and districts serving high-need students. In particular, we recommend that states give priority to both standards and supports:

- *Teacher standards.* States should set standards that require teacher education programs to prepare educators who understand how to support students' academic, social, and emotional development. These standards should be enforced through accreditation and state licensing processes that look carefully at whether candidates have the opportunity to learn these skills and can demonstrate them in practice (through teacher and administrator performance assessments).

- *Supports for preparation and induction.* The federal government should invest in the creation of high-quality training sites and subsidies for practitioners in high-need settings to receive excellent training, as it does in medicine. This would involve funding high-quality preparation and induction programs that enable teachers and administrators to develop the more sophisticated skills needed to implement practices that lead to deeper learning. These programs should provide strong clinical training in teacher residencies or professional development partnerships with schools that prioritize deeper learning. To make such training available and affordable, governments should invest in service scholarships for a diverse pool of talented recruits who teach or lead in high-need schools and fields for at least four years, and they should support release time for accomplished mentors to coach beginning teachers.

Of course, educators need ongoing support, especially in schools that have not previously been engaged in the sophisticated instructional practices that support deeper learning. As noted above, schools must develop professionally informed, collaborative cultures with a focus on sharing practices to improve supports and student outcomes. To support such professional learning, we recommend:

- *Time for collaboration and learning.* States and districts should fund collaborative teacher learning, curriculum planning, and problem solving, including peer observations and coaching in classrooms, and schools should redesign schedules to provide time for this important work.[37]
- *Meaningful professional development and evaluation.* States and the federal government can promote meaningful professional development by developing and supporting teacher and school networks, professional development institutes, and coaching that all focus on deeper learning practices within and across content areas. Agencies can use established principles for high-quality professional development to guide the funding of learning opportunities.[38] In addition, states and districts can design teacher evaluation so that it reinforces deeper learning practices and rewards collaboration while encouraging teachers to engage in goal setting and inquiry to support their growth.

Implementing Instruction and Assessments Aligned with Deeper Learning

Under the greatly expanded state testing requirements of the NCLB era, many schools focused on deeper learning found that the rich and relevant curriculum they sought to offer was at odds with the multiple-choice expectations of high-stakes standardized tests. As a consequence, they struggled to balance preparing students for these tests with teaching them to demonstrate analytical thinking and problem solving in more applied and authentic ways.

We are optimistic that the new assessments that are emerging under the Every Student Succeeds Act will be more supportive of deeper learning goals, particularly if they are used to inform instruction and improve learning, rather than to sort and label students, teachers, and schools. Such assessments (described by David Conley in chapter 9), along with the deeper learning experiences and insights provided by school-level performance assessments, must be part of a capacity-building strategy that supports the goals of equity and excellence.

As Michael Fullan and Maria Langworthy have shown in their analysis of reform policies in New York, Toronto, and London, successful change occurs when policy makers focus on capacity building as the primary driver of change, rather than high-stakes testing and top-down accountability.

This means that accountability is mutual, with clearly delineated responsibilities for each constituency in the system. When schools fail to produce the desired outcomes, as measured by assessments, graduation rates, and other indicators, state and/or district officials intervene to figure out why. They assess state and district policies, along with school conditions, to determine what needs to be changed; they engage in collaborative problem solving with practitioners to devise new approaches to problems; and, where necessary, they recommend changes in personnel. For example, the Ministry of Education in Ontario has taken this approach for several years now, with the result that more high-poverty schools have improved their performance in Toronto than in any other large city in North America.[39]

To encourage and expand successful instruction and assessment practices that support deeper learning, we recommend these changes:

- *More supports and fewer constraints for instruction.* Districts, states, and the federal government should limit directives to schools that constrain practice in ways that may not be productive for all students or contexts, and that prevent schools from adopting more successful practices. Curriculum standards should provide information for instructional planning without pacing guides or other straitjackets that prevent teachers from meeting students' needs. To develop a twenty-first-century curriculum that is relevant to a new economy and society, states will need to allow schools to rethink curriculum structures, courses, Carnegie Units, credits, grading, and assessments. If this work is to succeed, governments should support it with ideas, materials, training, networking, and evaluation, and not seek to standardize it within a regulatory context. Once states have adopted high-quality standards and provided adequate funding and curriculum resources for educators to draw upon, their role in guiding practice should be modest, while their role in supporting learning should be robust.
- *New systems of assessment and accountability.* As permitted under the Every Student Succeeds Act, states should create broader accountability systems that emphasize meaningful learning and use multiple measures—including assessments, graduation rates, and postsecondary success—to inform schools and the public about student progress. Assessments should include a limited set of state-level assessments that

support deeper learning and more robust locally developed perfor- mance assessments that allow students to inquire, investigate, collabo- rate, present, think critically, be creative, and defend their ideas.

- *Systemic learning.* As other successful countries have illustrated, fed- eral, state, and local policies can move practice forward by creating opportunities for educators, schools, and agencies to learn from one another. States and districts can facilitate this learning by documenting and disseminating successful practices, promoting schoolwide learning so that educators can adopt and adapt practices that succeed in their settings, and supporting school staff in learning from research and from each other through conferences, networks, site visits, and other approaches. Governments can also develop and explicitly support net- works of like-minded schools that are working on similar problems or strategies, so they can learn with and from each other and share what they learn with the system as a whole.

Schools can reach all students when districts, schools, and teachers marry powerful and proven instructional strategies, support for student learning and social-emotional needs, wraparound services, and support for teacher collaboration and learning. If federal, state, and local govern- ments join in this work as collaborative partners, we can create systems in which deeper learning is equitably accomplished.

5

Deeper Learning
for Students
with Disabilities

Sharon Vaughn, Louis Danielson,
Rebecca Zumeta Edmonds, and Lynn Holdheide

MORE THAN SIX MILLION students with disabilities (comprising 13 percent of the total student population) attend public schools across the United States.[1] The majority of them—close to four million—spend most of the school day in elementary and secondary school general education classes, and most are capable of meeting the goals described by advocates of deeper learning.[2] However, discussions about deeper learning have yet to focus serious attention on the kinds of support these students require to become truly prepared for college, careers, and civic life.

One complicating factor is that this population is enormously varied. For example, students with identified learning disabilities (more than two million) differ in important ways from those with speech and language impairments (nearly 1.5 million), autism (nearly 500,000), intellectual disabilities (over 400,000), emotional disturbances (nearly 400,000), or visual, hearing, and other impairments.[3]

How can general education teachers provide opportunities for deeper learning to such a wide range of students? While we are mindful of the many ways in which individuals and groups of students can differ from one another, we also find strong support in the research literature for several core instructional practices that are feasible to implement in every classroom and that facilitate learning for students with many kinds of needs. Further, we argue that the field of special education has important insights and expertise to share with the deeper learning movement in general.

As defined by the William and Flora Hewlett Foundation, *deeper learning* includes not just mastery of high-level academic content but also the development of capacities such as thinking critically, solving complex problems, working collaboratively, communicating effectively, and learning how to learn.[4] These are, it should be noted, learning goals that special education teachers and researchers have long prioritized. Indeed, a number of instructional strategies that are now considered mainstream were originally developed for students with disabilities. Supporters of deeper learning would no doubt endorse these strategies, such as the teaching of peer-mediated learning activities, self-regulation, and problem solving.[5] And among special education's recommended practices are several that would likely prove just as beneficial to the wider student population, such as modifications to pacing, direct and systematic instruction paired with explicit practice, strategies to support motivation and attention, and increased instructional time, among others.[6]

In this chapter, we review previous efforts to promote better educational outcomes for students with disabilities. We also describe research-based instructional strategies that can support these students and other struggling learners and the local resources needed to ensure that all young people have meaningful opportunities to learn deeply.

We hope that at the conclusion of this chapter, readers will understand that when schools make use of readily available teaching strategies and supports, even students who face quite serious challenges (related to severe dyslexia, for example, or autism or physical challenges) can develop the full range of knowledge and skills associated with deeper learning. Finally, we hope also that readers will have increased confidence that all students stand to benefit from instructional practices known to be effective for students with disabilities.

ACCESS, EQUITY, AND OUTCOMES

Enacted in 1975, Public Law 94-142, the Education for All Handicapped Children's Act—later known as the Individuals with Disabilities Education Act (IDEA)—was meant to ensure that all children with disabilities have access to a free and appropriate public education and that their rights, and those of their parents, are adequately protected. Before the act was passed, most public schools provided few, if any, services for students with disabilities, and many of these students dropped out of school (if they attended at all) as soon as they were legally permitted to do so.

P.L. 94-142's most important provisions are still in effect today. These include the requirements that students with disabilities be educated to the maximum extent possible with their nondisabled peers (often referred to as the "least restrictive environment") and that they be given an individualized education program (IEP). Also required are due process provisions designed to ensure that students and their parents are kept fully informed about their IEP status and services and are given ample opportunities to participate in and/or challenge relevant decisions by their schools.

In theory, these due process provisions add up to a guarantee that all students identified with disabilities are eligible for an IEP and will receive appropriate supports. Schools are required to assess each child's specific needs and spell out their individual learning goals in writing in order to provide clear guidance to their parents and teachers as to appropriate instruction and classroom accommodations (e.g., giving students more time to take a test, permitting them to use a computer to take notes in class, and so on).

In reality, though, the results have been mixed. Around 1990, findings began to emerge from a congressionally mandated study (the National Longitudinal Transition Study) that focused on the high school and post-school experiences of youth with disabilities. The data revealed a pattern of high dropout and course-failure rates and low rates of postschool employment and college enrollment.[7] In turn, many policy makers, researchers, and other stakeholders began to wonder whether the law might have erred by placing too much emphasis on monitoring schools' procedural compliance (e.g., documenting that students and parents were able to participate in the IEP conference) and doing too little to ensure that students were actually learning, passing their classes, and reaching other desired goals.

However, while the Transition Study was eye-opening, as of the early 1990s there existed no reliable, ongoing sources of data that would enable states or the U.S. Department of Education to know precisely how well students with disabilities were doing in any given school or district, or whether their results were improving over time.

That changed dramatically over the subsequent years. First, in the mid-1990s, the National Assessment of Educational Progress (NAEP) began to require that students with disabilities be included in its regular assessments. Second, the 1997 reauthorization of IDEA specified that students with disabilities must be included in state assessments and that the data must be reported publicly. And finally, the 2001 No Child Left Behind Act (NCLB) required that states, districts, and schools be held accountable for the performance of students with disabilities.

Together, these policy initiatives provided a forceful response to the earlier concern that IDEA had been too narrowly focused on procedural compliance. From this point on, the monitoring of schools' adherence to the law was to be combined with efforts to use both NAEP and state assessment data to monitor the actual performance of students with disabilities and to push schools to get better results. Among many in the field, these steps led to optimism that students with disabilities would begin to make real progress in their academic performance, both in K–12 education and beyond.

The Current Status of Students with Disabilities

According to the most recent NAEP, 38 to 45 percent of students without disabilities performed at the proficient level or above in reading and mathematics in fourth and eighth grade, while a mere 8 to 17 percent of students with disabilities did so (excluding those students whose IEPs indicated that they would be unable to access the NAEP materials and participate in the assessment).[8] In short, despite the policy reforms of the past two decades, and despite an improved knowledge base in the field of special education, achievement results for students with disabilities have remained virtually unchanged.[9]

Due to continuing concerns about poor outcomes for these students, the U.S. Department of Education's Office of Special Education Programs announced a new approach to state monitoring—results-driven accountability—requiring states to submit systemic improvement plans, beginning in 2015, that detail precise steps they will take to improve the results of students with disabilities.

This is meant to open the door for educators to implement proven practices for providing deeper learning opportunities for these students. As with NCLB, however, the challenge will be for states to show that they have the will, the resources, and especially the *capacity* to do so.

On that score, many advocates have pointed out that for all of the recent efforts to improve services for students with disabilities, perhaps the most important piece of the puzzle—educators' capacity to provide those services—has not been adequately addressed. Not only must schools comply with IDEA, they argue, and not only must states monitor student progress and create incentives for schools to provide better services, but serious investments must also be devoted to professional development and organizational change. Unless teachers actually know how to provide effective instruction to students with disabilities, and unless schools create the conditions under which such instruction can take place, it is unlikely that compliance, monitoring, or incentivizing will impact student outcomes.

Toward Better Outcomes: Problems and Priorities

What are some of the challenges that will have to be overcome to ensure that students with disabilities have real opportunities to learn deeply?

For one thing, some educators and policy makers might not accept the premise that deeper learning goals are feasible for all students. Indeed, they might point to the fact that NAEP scores have remained low, even after two decades of legislation and reform, as evidence that large numbers of students with disabilities are simply not capable of meeting core academic standards.

We would argue, however, that a lack of improvement on NAEP scores does not provide a compelling reason to doubt these students' innate potential. If anything, those scores should be taken as an indication that many, if not most, students with disabilities continue to be held to low expectations and denied access to high-quality instruction and interventions. As recent findings suggest, when they are taught using well-established, effective instructional practices, students with disabilities do tend to make significant gains in their academic performance, particularly with respect to problem solving and knowledge application in content areas (which are key aspects of deeper learning).[10]

Another challenge is that most schools are not, and never have been, organized to deliver the intensity of services that many of these students require. But here, too, lessons can be learned from schools that do achieve good results for students with disabilities. Perhaps most important, they tend to be relatively flexible in their daily schedules, allowing teachers to devote extra time to students when it seems important to do so. Further, such schools also tend to implement multitiered systems of support, meaning that they carefully monitor student performance to identify those who are struggling and might need more intensive intervention and instruction.[11]

A third challenge is that few educators receive the kinds of preparation, professional learning, and support needed to promote effective instruction to students with disabilities, much less to help them learn deeply. For example, observational studies in elementary and secondary settings reveal that students with disabilities are frequently taught using methods that have no basis in research, are often excluded from participating in classroom learning activities, and are often given assignments that are so far beyond their reach that they become discouraged.[12] By contrast, effective special educators provide instruction that is explicit and systematic, and it often features considerable scaffolding and modeling from the teacher, designed to ensure that students gain a strong foundation in the given content and skills before they are expected to proceed on their own, without scaffolding.

A complicating factor is that, while such explicit instruction is well supported by empirical evidence, existing teacher evaluation systems may not value it, resulting in poor performance reviews for teachers who are actually quite skilled. Imagine, for example, that a teacher modifies a class writing assignment for a few students who struggle to process and organize written text—say, by requiring them to use a specific paragraph structure. This could be a wise and effective instructional strategy. However, a classroom observer might conclude that the teacher has singled out those students unfairly and denied them the chance to express themselves freely.

Teacher evaluation practices are very much in flux, at present, but whatever direction they take, it should be a priority for school leaders to ensure that those charged with observing and rating teachers are able to recognize when instruction has been tailored, appropriately, to meet the needs that many students with disabilities have for relatively explicit guidance.

Another challenge is that current accountability requirements—also in flux, especially since the passage of the Every Student Succeeds Act—can easily run counter to best practices in special education. One of NCLB's goals was to increase the percentage of the students in each subgroup (including students with disabilities) who score at the proficient level or better on state assessments. Yet many students with disabilities attend schools where this subgroup is too small to count toward Adequate Yearly Progress, as it was defined under NCLB. Among the rest, many tend to score far below proficient on standardized tests, such that school leaders see it as futile to try to raise their scores to the given threshold.[13]

Finally, an additional problem with many state tests—particularly those created during the NCLB years—is that they are designed to show only whether students are functioning at or close to grade level, which means that they include few items meant to assess lower-level knowledge and skills. For many students with disabilities, then, the tests show only what they *cannot* do. As to precisely what they do know, or exactly which content gives them trouble, such assessments provide very little information, leaving educators unsure how to adjust their instruction.[14]

We believe that many of the challenges described in this section—lingering prejudices against students with disabilities, insufficient organizational flexibility, lack of attention to special needs when preparing and evaluating teachers, and poorly designed student assessment systems—can be resolved with research-based instruction. Quite a lot has been learned in recent years about effective teaching for students with disabilities and, perhaps just as important, the evidence strongly suggests that when teachers implement these practices, all students benefit—typical learners included.

EFFECTIVE INSTRUCTION FOR STUDENTS WITH DISABILITIES

To teachers, parents, or anybody else who interacts regularly with individuals identified as "students with disabilities," it is hard to ignore just how varied these students are in their skills, talents, interests, likes, dislikes, and countless other characteristics. The diversity that characterizes this population is truly extraordinary. How, then, can teachers provide instruction that meets everyone's learning needs?

A suggestion often given to both general and special educators is to "differentiate instruction for each learner." However, while that is an appealing slogan, trying to implement it in practice—actually providing differentiated support to dozens of students at a time—would be enough to physically and psychologically exhaust even the most capable and motivated of teachers. Further, some students enrolled in general education classes exhibit learning challenges that are serious and persistent enough to require additional time and attention, which they cannot receive if their teachers are stretched too thin already.

We argue, instead, for an approach that may be both more realistic and more effective: the professional repertoire of every classroom teacher can and should include a number of specific instructional approaches—designed for students with disabilities but often effective for students of all kinds—that will allow them to respond to most learning needs, while leaving them time to provide more intensive support as appropriate. We outline these approaches below, and they are described at length in guides and resources offered by the National Center on Intensive Intervention.[15]

Teaching Core Concepts in the Content Areas

Deeper learning was described by a panel of the National Research Council as "the process through which an individual becomes capable of taking what was learned in one situation and applying it to new situations (i.e., transfer)."[16]

In part, this suggests just how critical foundation skills in reading, writing, and mathematics are, since they transfer to every other part of the curriculum, allowing students to gain access to the more advanced content to be found in various academic domains. Thus for many students with disabilities, who may struggle with basic reading comprehension and arithmetic even into the secondary grades, the call for deeper learning implies a redoubling of efforts to teach those skills.

By no means, however, does this mean that students with disabilities should be limited to the study of foundation skills alone.[17] Like all other students, they should have every opportunity to engage cooperatively with others, to learn to persist at challenging tasks, to communicate effectively in many contexts, and to experience other aspects of deeper learning, including the study of advanced content and skills in the academic subject areas.

What must content-area teachers understand in order to ensure access to these kinds of deeper learning for all students? Most important, students with disabilities may need more time to learn and practice new skills, they may need to be given somewhat different tasks and assignments (e.g., the option to provide oral rather than written summaries, or to answer fewer problems on quizzes and tests), and they may need particular kinds of instruction.

For example, Sharon Vaughn and colleagues have developed a set of instructional practices that are specifically designed to help students with disabilities learn academic content in social studies and other secondary-level subject areas.[18] These include (1) guiding students in creating a *comprehension canopy* by identifying the field's big ideas and key concepts and, over time, explicitly connecting them to specific examples and cases; (2) *defining essential words*, which are meant to assist students in learning and using the academic vocabulary of the discipline; and (3) *team-based learning*, in which students work independently at first to demonstrate comprehension, and then with team members to build, correct, and extend learning about content-area issues.[19]

What does this look like in a classroom that enrolls a mix of "typical" students as well as students with disabilities? When introducing a unit on, say, the Revolutionary War, the teacher will begin by posing a concrete but high-level question meant to frame classroom discussions (creating a comprehension canopy). For example:

> The colonists almost lost the war. General George Washington put it best when he said that American victory was "little short of a miracle." The British had the most powerful army in the world; it was made of professional soldiers who were disciplined and well trained. The Colonial Army was mostly made up of farmers and part-time soldiers. They were poorly paid, and few had formal training. How, then, did the colonists win the Revolutionary War?

Over the course of the unit, the teacher will return to this overarching question many times, asking students to refine and elaborate on it in increasingly sophisticated ways, both on their own and through group discussions and projects. Further, the teacher will make it a priority to identify and define key words that are critical to understanding the given content and which will likely appear in future readings and discussions.

Such practices may not seem so remarkable—content-area teachers often ask framing questions, highlight new words, and assign group work. However, research evidence strongly suggests that, for many students with disabilities, it is critically important that the teacher provide such supports *deliberately, explicitly, and systematically.* According to randomized control group studies—so-called gold-standard research—when teachers make conscientious efforts to apply these practices, students with disabilities (and many without disabilities) see significant improvements in their content knowledge and academic vocabulary, outpacing the gains made by students in matched classes studying the same content.[20]

In short, subject-area instruction can be organized in ways that allow students to access meaningful content, grasp key concepts and vocabulary, and participate fully in high-level discussions and projects, even though they may struggle to read and comprehend the given material on their own. And while such scaffolding is especially helpful to students with disabilities, it tends to benefit all learners.

Further, it requires no extraordinary effort or extensive professional development for general education teachers to provide such support. Rather, as described below, in "Explicit, Systematic, and Responsive Instruction," the chief requirement is that they become aware of and are willing to make some accommodations for students who need more time, practice, and explicit guidance as they process new content and ideas.

Supporting Cognitive Processing

Recent research into cognitive processing has done much to tease out precisely what is meant by the goal of "learning how to learn," which has been described as a key part of deeper learning.[21] Specifically, studies have zeroed in on the roles that executive functioning and self-regulation—both of which can be successfully promoted by instruction—play in learning.

Many students with (and some without) disabilities struggle with one or more aspects of cognitive processing, including challenges with memory, attention, and the generation, selection, monitoring, and implementation of learning strategies. These executive functioning and self-regulatory mechanisms are, in effect, the "control processes" that manage goal direction for learning, and they overlap with other cognitive and be-havioral processes such as short-term memory, processing speed, and nonverbal reasoning.

For example, many students with short-term memory difficulties struggle with reading comprehension, particularly when asked by teach-ers to read and respond to texts immediately.[22] If it is hard to recall critical information from the sentences one has just read, as is often the case for such students, then it is doubly difficult to describe the main idea of the given paragraph, or multiple paragraphs.[23]

As recently as forty years ago, the prevailing view in the field was that such students had neurological damage that required treatment *before* they could begin to access and comprehend academic texts.[24] Thus, prob-lems related to visual, auditory, and motor processing were assessed and treated in isolation, without being integrated with other learning goals.

However, this approach had limited value for students, and newer evi-dence—drawing from far stronger theoretical frameworks and a robust empirical base—suggests that it is a mistake to provide isolated treatments for processing disorders (e.g., training children in auditory processing alone, divorced from any particular academic context).[25] Rather, current research on executive functions and self-regulation supports the use of systematic and explicit instructional routines that are integrated with the teaching of specific academic content and skills.

Consider, for example, language-processing difficulties that interfere with students' efforts to solve mathematical word problems. Rather than trying to teach those students how to process language more efficiently in general, it is far more effective to teach them concrete strategies *that help them solve specific math problems*—such as showing them how certain everyday words can be expressed in mathematical terms, how they can restate an algebraic problem in their own words, or how they can break a problem down into a functional sequence of steps—which they can then apply to new math problems.[26]

Another practice that has been shown to be particularly effective for students with cognitive processing difficulties is to teach them to define specific learning goals and monitor their own progress over time, such as by keeping track of the number of word problems they are able to answer correctly or the number of math assignments they have completed.

Similarly, researchers have found that students can be taught to monitor their own comprehension while reading academic texts, becoming aware of any "breakdowns" in their understanding as soon as they occur. For example, teachers can instruct them to use "self-talk" as they make their way through a history text or literary narrative (e.g., asking themselves, "What's happening in this chapter? How does this relate to what I know? What's confusing to me?"). Often, it is helpful for teachers to model this strategy for students, giving them an out-loud demonstration of how they would talk themselves through the given text. (See "Thinking Out Loud: Modeling 'Self-Talk.'") Likewise, teachers can assign students to underline important passages or to use tools such as mnemonic devices or graphic organizers, which have been found to be effective in helping students with disabilities to remember and understand what they are learning.[27] Overall, students who struggle with cognitive processing tend to trail behind their peers in measures of academic learning and motivation.[28] When taught to use such self-regulatory practices, however, they often see significant improvements in school performance and self-efficacy.[29]

Finally, researchers have found that students' capacity to self-regulate is also closely linked to their beliefs about the causes of their academic failures and successes ("attribution" is the term most often used in the field of special education, though it has been described as "academic mind-set" in discussions of deeper learning). Students who struggle with cognitive processing often attribute their lack of academic success to stable, internal causes that they cannot change, while they attribute success to unpredictable factors, such as luck. However, when provided with instruction designed to improve their self-regulation (e.g., when taught to use self-talk while reading academic texts, or to paraphrase complex ideas, or to use rereading as a way to "repair" their own misunderstandings), these students often come to recognize that their concrete actions can, in fact, have positive effects on their learning and performance.[30]

THINKING OUT LOUD: MODELING "SELF-TALK"

For students who struggle to process and comprehend complex texts, it is often helpful to practice "self-talk" while reading— pausing to ask themselves questions meant to check their own understanding and to remind themselves to use specific comprehension strategies. A simple but highly effective instructional practice (one that all teachers should have in their repertoires) is to model this sort of self-talk out loud, showing students exactly how they can use it to improve their comprehension. For example, while looking over a text with a student, the teacher might say things such as:

> With a difficult book like this, the first thing I do is to look for key words that the author uses. There are several here that confuse me—like *colonial* and *regiment*—so I am going to read the text around them to see if that gives me any clues as to what those words mean. And if that doesn't work, then I'll check the dictionary.
>
> Now that I know what these key words mean, I'm looking at the title, headings, and questions provided in the text to see if they tell me what this chapter is going to be about, and whether it relates to things I already know.
>
> After finishing this paragraph, I'm going to pause and make sure I understand everything. And if something seems confusing, then I'm going to go back and read it again, and then I'll try to restate it using my own words.
>
> And now that I've read this page, I'll stop and look over our questions for class discussion, to see if this part of the text can help me answer them.

In short, the teacher demonstrates a number of very specific things students can do to monitor and improve their comprehension while reading. Not every reader needs this kind of support—many students pick up these sorts of strategies on their own, without being coached. But for those who struggle to organize and process information, such explicit modeling can be extremely helpful.

Intensifying Instruction

Regular classroom teachers, in addition to using instructional practices that support cognitive processing and helping students with disabilities access core academic content, should be prepared to provide more intensive support to students who need it.

This is not to suggest that all teachers must become experts in special education, or that they should devote a large portion of their time to helping just a small number of their students. But it is to argue that, for some students, the strategies described above may not be enough, and they will require additional kinds of support.

Explicit, Systematic, and Responsive Instruction

As described above, in "Teaching Core Concepts in the Content Areas," a relatively low-cost way to intensify instruction is for educators to adopt a strongly teacher-driven approach at times, combining direct instruction with efforts to coach students in the use of research-based learning strategies. For many students with learning disabilities, significant gains have been associated with teaching that is explicit, systematic, and filled with ample opportunities to practice their skills and receive targeted feedback.[31]

Explicit instruction refers to the overt teaching of the steps or processes necessary to accomplish a task or learn a given skill, and it often involves teacher modeling and demonstrations that illustrate precisely what students are expected to do. While this sort of highly directive approach may not be effective—or even appropriate—for all learners, research strongly suggests that, for many students who struggle to plan, organize, and monitor their own learning, it often leads to improved mastery of both foundation skills and higher-level concepts.[32]

Systematic instruction refers to how effective teachers organize instruction into manageable pieces of learning and then integrate these pieces into an overall learning goal. (For example, a teacher might break down a complex math problem into a number of smaller steps or processes and then bring them back together to solve the whole.) Further, it refers to teachers' efforts to introduce progressively more challenging tasks over time, to give students the scaffolding they need to complete those tasks successfully, and then to pull away that support gradually, as students become more accomplished and independent.

Also, in addition to providing explicit and systematic instruction, teachers can intensify the support they provide by giving students frequent opportunities to practice new skills and receive feedback on what they can do to improve. (For example, this could mean asking some students to get started on a class project early and to schedule a few brief check-ins in advance of the official due date to go over their work and suggest revisions.) According to an exhaustive review and synthesis of research in this area, teachers' feedback tends to have a significant influence on student outcomes, particularly when it is timely, relates clearly to students' goals, provides specific information as to how they can complete tasks more effectively, and allows teachers to monitor their progress closely.[33]

Finally, teachers should keep in mind that these students may already be discouraged—given that they were not helped by earlier, less-intensive kinds of support—and a fresh dose of discouragement could make it even harder for them to benefit from a new approach. Thus, teachers should consider modifying their classroom tasks and assignments in ways that will allow these students to experience some success. For example, they can make it a priority to give extremely clear instructions for each assignment, provide examples of the kind of work that will count as high quality, and provide graphics or other concrete illustrations of the concept to be learned.

Time and Class Size
The teaching practices just described do not necessarily require major new outlays of time or money. However, it would be misleading to suggest that there are no costs associated with providing more intensive supports to students with disabilities. Time, in particular, tends to be a precious commodity in schools, and choosing to spend more of it with certain students often means spending less on others.

Whatever local educators decide, they should keep in mind that scheduling decisions tend to be especially important to students with disabilities. Increasing instructional time has been shown to be one of the most effective ways to help such students learn advanced content and skills, giving them a chance to master cognitively complex tasks—such as reading high-level material and connecting ideas across texts—that they simply could not process over the course of a forty-five-minute lesson.[34]

For example, intensifying instruction in this way could mean providing a given intervention every day, or even twice a day, say, morning and afternoon, rather than three times a week.[35] Or, depending on students' capacities for attention, it could mean providing instruction in longer stretches, or increasing the duration of the intervention (e.g., from fifteen weeks to thirty weeks). To be sure, that extra time does have to come from somewhere—never an easy decision—but for this student population, it tends to be time well spent.

More expensive but equally important to consider is the option of reducing teacher-student ratios. Small group size can be a powerful factor in improving outcomes for students with disabilities, since it gives teachers far more leeway to provide the kinds of responsive instruction—including frequent opportunities for practice and feedback—that research shows to be effective for students who require intensive support.[36]

Differentiating When Appropriate: Data-Based Individualization

As we noted above, it would be impractical for general education teachers to provide truly differentiated instruction to every student. However, at some times, and for some students with disabilities, such instruction is absolutely critical.

More than forty years of research suggests that if students have several and persistent learning needs, and if they show little or no improvement despite teachers' efforts to intensify instruction, they can probably benefit from what is referred to as clinical or experimental teaching, or "data-based individualization" (DBI), a term that highlights the role that systematic assessment plays in the process.[37]

DBI is typically implemented within a multitiered system of support (such as Response to Intervention), which is to say that schools tend to offer it only after they have tried to help the given student in other ways. If regular core instruction (known as Tier 1) was not successful, and if the student did not benefit from a secondary (Tier 2) intervention—assuming it was a proven approach, implemented with fidelity—then the DBI process kicks in.

First, the teacher tries increasing the intensity of the instruction (e.g., spending more time with the student). Next, the teacher monitors the student's progress to determine whether intensifying the instruction had an impact. Third, the school uses diagnostic assessments to identify the student's specific skill deficits and develop a hypothesis about effective ways to modify instruction. Fourth, the teacher implements an adapted program (which may include some of the teaching strategies described in the preceding sections). And finally, the teacher continues to monitor and collect data on the student's progress, to see whether the approach is working or should be modified further.

This careful integration of assessment and intervention can meet the needs of individual students who have not been helped by the kinds of supports described earlier. But how expensive is it to provide such services? Typically, schools train and rely on their regular classroom teachers to provide effective Tier 2 interventions, monitor student progress, and, when students continue to struggle, perform diagnostic assessments to pinpoint their needs. In turn, when the DBI process reveals a need for more intensive interventions, students usually are referred to special education teachers, reading specialists, and other specialized staff and/or instructional aides. In short, DBI can be quite labor intensive, and most schools would be hard-pressed to offer it to more than a very small percentage of their students at a time. As is true of other means of intensifying instruction, however, research suggests that when implemented well, it is associated with improved outcomes for students.

FINAL THOUGHTS

The practices described in this chapter have been shown to promote effective instruction for students with significant learning problems and disabilities in general education classrooms. When practiced thoughtfully and consistently, they can help these students to gain access to deeper learning. They can also be expensive—such as when schools choose to reduce class sizes or offer additional, specialized services—but in many cases they are not, requiring only that classroom teachers learn how and when to implement a number of specific, proven instructional practices.

With these considerations in mind, we urge educators and policy makers at the local and state levels to ensure that

- *all* students—including those with disabilities—have access to high-quality instruction in the core content areas
- general education teachers' professional standards, licensure requirements, and job descriptions assign them clear responsibility to provide effective instruction to students with disabilities
- teachers' pre- and in-service programs equip them to provide the kinds of intensive, evidence-based interventions that can help students with disabilities to access deeper learning
- state policies require schools to provide tiered levels of instructional and behavioral supports
- state policies create incentives for all teachers to share responsibility for providing effective instruction and supports to students with disabilities
- state and local educator evaluation systems reward—or at least do not penalize—teachers who use appropriate, evidence-based instructional strategies when working with students who have disabilities
- states implement college and career readiness assessments that address the full range of deeper learning competencies and include accommodations that enable students with disabilities to show what they know and can do

We are confident that if states and districts integrate these recommendations with the practices described above, all students will benefit as a result. Deeper learning can and should be the goal for *every* young person.

6

~~~~~

Deeper Learning for English Language Learners

Patricia Gándara

WHILE THERE IS no single, fixed definition of "deeper learning," the term tends to be used to describe a mix of academic, personal, and relational capacities, including elements such as collaborative learning, critical thinking, conceptual understanding, and learning how to learn. Typically, deeper learning is said to have an affective dimension as well, touching on characteristics such as persistence and self-motivation, and advocates often argue that students should be taught to take responsibility for their own learning through active engagement in their education.[1]

In this chapter, I argue that the nation's immigrant students and English language learners (ELLs) are likely to benefit from such focused, critical, and engaging classroom instruction. In fact, one could argue that these children tend to be better equipped for such teaching and learning than monolingual, nonimmigrant students. However, to the extent that ELLs are framed as deficient and in need of remediation, schools tend to overlook their affinity for deeper learning.

Our public schools have always enrolled significant numbers of immigrant students, though the numbers have varied over time. But in 1968,

Title VII of the Elementary and Secondary Education Act (ESEA) brought into being the official category of "English language learners" (or, as they are still sometimes called, "Limited English Proficient students"). Title VII, also known as the Bilingual Education Act (BEA), was the first federal acknowledgment that immigrant students and children who come to school speaking a language other than English need special accommodations to ensure their academic success. This naturally led to the need to identify and label these students, for the purpose of targeting resources to them.

It is important to note that ELLs and immigrant students are not one and the same. Most (though certainly not all) immigrant children spend a period of time as ELLs, but today most ELLs are not immigrants. According to current estimates, almost 90 percent of all ELLs were born in the United States. Overwhelmingly, then, the resources dedicated to educating ELL students support native-born U.S. citizens.

How to best utilize resources to support ELLs' learning has been an ongoing national debate. In 1967, U.S. Senator "Smilin' Ralph" Yarborough of Texas, the chief sponsor of the BEA, went on record in favor of "the creation of bilingual-bicultural programs, the teaching of Spanish as a native language ... designed to impart to Spanish-speaking students a knowledge and pride in their culture."[2] Many other education activists, heady with recent victories on civil rights, advocated similar positions. However, because Yarborough and his allies were unable to win the support of the Johnson Administration, they had no real hope of passing legislation that would privilege the language and culture of Spanish speakers.[3]

As Natalia Mehlman Petrzela recounts, passage of the bill depended on its ability to fit into the overall objectives of ESEA, which focused on remediating the disadvantages of poor children, and to not challenge the popular notion of the "melting pot," which demanded that immigrants relinquish their distinctive cultural characteristics.[4] Moreover, as Rachel Moran notes, "[Yarborough's] vague statement of purpose masked fundamental differences over whether the programs were designed to promote assimilation by overcoming a language 'deficiency' or were intended to foster pluralism by acknowledging a linguistic asset."[5] In the end, the former perspective—defining ELLs as having a deficiency that requires remediation—won out. Multiple reauthorizations of ESEA, up to and including the Every Student Succeeds Act (ESSA), have only furthered the emphasis on deficiency.

Like the No Child Left Behind Act (NCLB) that preceded it, ESSA omits mention of bilingual education. (Then again, nothing in the federal legislation explicitly prevents schools from using funds to hire more bilingual teachers or counselors, or to provide professional development to strengthen dual language instruction. Thus, while it does not promote bilingual education, neither does the law impede it. School personnel can choose to be proactive in assigning funds for these purposes.)

But while federal lawmakers have been relatively silent on this issue in recent years, that hardly means that the debate has ended. Since 1967, countless educators, researchers, state and local politicians, and others have continued to wrestle over how best to support immigrant students and ELLs. If anything, the debate has only intensified. We now have nearly fifty years of research on ELL students and classrooms from which to draw and almost fifty years of experience with deficit-based policies and practices upon which to reflect. Moreover, this is now a very different nation, demographically and politically, than it was fifty years ago.

In this chapter, then, I return to the vision that Yarborough outlined in 1967, asking once again whether our students might be better served if we understood their linguistic and cultural backgrounds as assets, not deficiencies.

I begin, in the following section, by describing the current educational status of the nation's ELLs and immigrant students. I then describe the ways in which their skills have been denigrated, and I consider a number of ways in which linguistic and cultural diversity and immigrant experiences might be reframed as valuable resources for deeper learning.

FRAMING AND REFRAMING ENGLISH LANGUAGE LEARNERS AND IMMIGRANTS

In 2015, nearly five million students across the United States, comprising almost 10 percent of the total school-age population, were designated as ELLs.[6] (If one considers all students who come from homes where English is not the primary language spoken, the figure doubles to more than 20 percent.[7]) Many students who today do not carry the label of ELL were once designated as ELLs and may still be on a continuum of learning academic English; most of these students go home every day to an environment in which English is rarely heard. Because there is no national test of English proficiency or even agreement as to what constitutes "proficiency" in English for academic purposes, any count of the number of ELLs is, in reality, a best estimate. And while these children are often referred to as "immigrant children," as noted above, the truth is that very few ELLs are born outside the country. As of 2013, 88 percent of children of immigrant parents were native-born citizens.[8]

In the United States today, more than seventeen million children under age eighteen live with at least one immigrant parent, constituting one in four children overall.[9] Contrary to popular perceptions, most of the forty-one million foreign-born residents of the United States are legal residents. Almost half are naturalized citizens, while only about one-fourth are unauthorized—which still means that millions of children live in a household in which at least one person is at risk of being deported.[10] This threat often places strains and restrictions on the entire family. Children can be distracted from learning due to fears that one or more of their family members will not be there when they return from school, or they may hesitate to become engaged in school, knowing they could be removed at any moment. This is not an exaggerated concern: according to recent estimates, roughly 450,000 U.S.-born children now live in Mexico, most having returned with family members forced to leave the United States.[11]

According to recent findings from the Migration Policy Institute, 71 percent of the nation's ELLs speak Spanish. The next largest language group is Chinese (both Mandarin and Cantonese dialects) at just 4 percent, followed by Vietnamese at 3 percent.[12] Only five states claim a language other than Spanish as the primary non-English language spoken. In nineteen states, more than three-fourths of ELLs speak Spanish.

Thus, while there is great linguistic diversity in the United States with respect to both numbers of students from different groups and their geographical concentrations, a few languages predominate, with Spanish being overwhelmingly the primary non-English language spoken. This could begin to change, though; in recent years, the largest share of immigrants to the United States has come from Asian countries, particularly China, outpacing the flow of immigrants from Latin America.[13]

The size and concentration of languages other than English has significant implications for how education systems can serve students. Trying to educate students from many different language backgrounds in a single school or classroom can be especially challenging and can restrict the programmatic options available to educators. However, where there are large concentrations of a single language, or just a few languages, and where there are teachers who speak those languages, there are more instructional options. For example, bilingual programs can be mounted in schools that have many children of the same language group and teachers prepared to teach in that language as well as in English. However, where many different languages are spoken and trained teachers from those language groups are not available, other program models must be considered.

The five traditional immigrant "gateway states"—California, Texas, New York, Florida, and Illinois—continue to be home to nearly two-thirds of all ELLs nationwide, but the greatest growth in English language learner students has been in "new destination" areas. In 2009, for example, South Carolina, Alabama, and Tennessee experienced the most rapid growth in immigration, mainly from non-English-speaking countries.[14] This development presents major challenges, since states with no history of such immigration often lack policies and infrastructure to support these students. Also, the sudden influx of new immigrants can stimulate a hostile reception in areas where people feel unprepared to receive newcomers, exacerbating the trauma many immigrant students experience.[15]

FRAMING STUDENTS WHO ARE SPEAKERS OF OTHER LANGUAGES

Whether they are immigrants or native-born U.S. citizens, students who arrive at school with a primary language other than English are usually defined by what they lack: English language skills. Thus they have been dubbed "limited English-speaking," "Limited English Proficient," or "English language learners," among other labels. This framing has resulted in these students being viewed as deficient, remedial, or lacking in fundamental skills that are critical for "normal" academic achievement. Thus, most programs that serve these young people are designed to fix a deficiency, and students are deemed ready to join the mainstream and have full access to a regular curriculum only once this is accomplished.[16]

A central goal of NCLB was to increase the numbers of students moved from ELL to "English Proficient" status. Further, its accountability provisions—which called for students to take their math and reading tests in English no more than a year after entering the U.S. school system—created an incentive not just to reclassify ELLs as proficient but to do so as quickly as possible. Unfortunately, this placed very little emphasis on students' content learning, which was to be dealt with separately under Title I, once students were English Proficient. (And since ESSA provides no guidance related to appropriate instruction for ELLs, the insistence on testing them in English is likely to continue.)

In effect, this encouraged states to reduce support for bilingual instruction (in which students continue their academic studies while shifting from the use of their primary language to speaking more and more English) in favor of Structured English Immersion (SEI) programs (which are designed to provide instruction in English only).

The result has been a surge in the rates at which ELLs have been reclassified as proficient in English, but it has come at the expense of academic learning. For example, Arizona created a statewide SEI program that consists of four hours of English language drills every day, to the exclusion of most other subject-matter instruction. And while the state aspires to have ELLs reach proficiency quickly, "normally in one year," the reality is that students tend to remain in such programs for far longer than that.[17]

In a 2006 study of California's program for ELLs, researchers found that the average student had less than a 40 percent chance of being reclassified to English Proficient within ten years.[18] Since that time, pressure by the state to speed up the process has resulted in increased rates of reclassification, but even so, students rarely achieve this goal within a year or even two.[19]

In any case, one might ask why educators and policy makers don't pay more attention to the *quality* of the programs offered to ELLs, rather than simply focusing on the speed at which students escape them. To date, very little research has been conducted on the quality and appropriateness of the instruction in such programs, or on the preparation and skills of the teachers (apart from small qualitative studies that look at only a handful of schools). Currently, all we know is that there is great variation in programs and teacher preparation across and within states—and that states with specific guidelines related to the quality of instruction for ELLs have better outcomes for these students than those without.[20]

Unfortunately, by the time ELLs are considered proficient in English, they have often lost so much content-learning time that it becomes all but impossible to catch up with their native English-speaking peers.[21] And this puts many of these students at a disadvantage that continues throughout their schooling.

Of course, all students in the United States need to develop strong English skills. However, as I will argue in this chapter, building on ELLs' native linguistic strengths as they acquire English makes better sense than holding them back from learning content on the (unsupported) assumption that they will "catch up" later. Finally, it should be noted that this insistence on a sequential approach—first learn English, then gain access to the regular curriculum—begs the intent of the 1974 Supreme Court ruling in *Lau v. Nichols*, which found that ELLs must be given access to the same curriculum as English-speaking students.[22]

Framed by the Tests

The poor performance of ELL students on standardized assessments only adds fuel to the belief that they are fundamentally deficient and in need of remediation above and beyond all else. On average, ELLs score lower on academic achievement tests than almost any other subgroup except special education students. This remains true throughout the grades. For example, the 2013 National Assessment of Educational Progress (NAEP) found that 69 percent of ELLs were below basic proficiency in eighth-grade mathematics, compared to just 25 percent of non-ELLs. Eighth-grade reading scores were similarly dismal, with 70 percent of ELLs scoring below basic, compared to 21 percent of non-ELLs.[23] Scores at the fourth-grade level were comparable.

However, it is important to note that since the highest-performing ELLs are constantly being moved out of the ELL category (reclassified as English Proficient), such reports include only lower-performing ELL students. Thus, "English language learners," by definition, will have low scores. This has prompted many researchers to argue that, for purposes of monitoring the performance of former ELLs, and for making appropriate comparisons between ELLs and non-ELLs, data should be collected and reported for a new category, "Ever ELL," including students who have been reclassified as well as those still considered English learners.[24]

Nonetheless, comparisons over time should reflect whether ELLs are gaining ground, losing ground, or maintaining the same level of performance relative to non-ELLs. On that score, it appears that the education reforms of the last couple of decades have not closed gaps. For example, nationally, since 1996 (the first year for which the NAEP shows gap trend lines for ELLs), the gap between ELLs and all others in eighth-grade math has not narrowed, and in fact has begun to widen. In 2003, the gap between ELLs and English speakers who scored at the proficient level in math was 20 points; in 2013 the gap had grown to 24 points. Eighth-grade reading proficiency showed a similar widening of the gap (3 points) over the same period. At least from the perspective of math and reading score gaps, educational achievement has not improved nationally for ELLs, who, across the grades, remain significantly behind their native English-speaking peers.

Barriers to Academic Achievement

Language difference is just one—and perhaps not even the most important—of many reasons for these achievement gaps, although the way schools treat language difference certainly plays an important role in sustaining them. For example, many schools insist on teaching academic classes in English from day one, even though students may not yet understand what their teachers are saying. Further, many schools neglect to assess what their ELLs know and can do in their primary language, and thus often assign perfectly capable, even high-achieving, students to remedial courses solely because their English is weak.

With a few exceptions (including New York, Texas, and Illinois), states require students to take achievement tests in English. In some cases, the state has the capacity to test students in their native language but chooses not to because it has adopted English-only instructional policies, which educators interpret as requiring English-only assessment, too. Other states, however, simply lack the capacity to offer tests in other languages and have not dedicated resources to developing them. Whatever the reasons, when schools test students in a language they do not fully comprehend and make educational decisions based on these invalid scores, they contribute to ELLs' low performance.

That said, many immigrant students and ELLs are significantly disadvantaged educationally, but not necessarily for reasons having to do with language. Rather, their struggles may result from a history of weak and interrupted instruction, or from the effects of poverty, frequent migration, or other challenges. Some educators or policy makers may be tempted to blame students for their poor performance or attribute it to their lack of English proficiency, when in fact other variables constrain their achievement.

Poverty is perhaps the greatest threat to all low-income students' academic achievement because it can directly affect cognitive development through inadequate nutrition, poor health care, mental health challenges, distractibility, and other factors.[25] Chronic health problems associated with poverty are also related to high absenteeism from school, putting students even further behind.[26]

More than 40 percent of children of Latino immigrants are born into poverty.[27] Further, this population is especially likely to fall into deep poverty. In 2014, more than one in eight of these children lived below 50 percent of the poverty line (less than $12,000 a year for a family of four), compared to about 6 percent of all other children.[28] Since Latino immigrants make up about half of the nation's immigrants, that means that a significant portion of the nation's immigrant children and ELLs are living in poverty, many of them below subsistence level.[29] To make matters worse, many social services are not available to immigrant families (even those who are legally authorized to be in the country) because of punitive federal and local laws.[30] Additionally, Latino children of immigrants are less likely to attend preschool than any other subgroup, so the ameliorating effects of early childhood education are not available to nearly half of these young ELLs.[31]

Barriers to effective learning continue into the secondary grades, where these young people are often lost in the shuffle, placed with teachers who may not know they have ELLs in their classes. Overall, middle and high school students identified as ELLs are roughly twice as likely to drop out as their peers.[32] Thus, it should come as no surprise that Latino youth, approximately half of whom begin school as ELLs, are the least likely to complete a college education compared to the other major racial/ethnic subgroups.[33]

For most immigrant students and for those classified as ELLs at the secondary level, two-year colleges are the only viable option because of weak preparation in high school and the costs of postsecondary education.[34] Unfortunately, most students who enter two-year colleges will never complete a degree, and end up simply incurring debt without seeing the increase in earning power that a college degree provides.[35]

THE TRAUMA OF THE MIGRATION EXPERIENCE

While most ELL students are U.S.-born, their parents are usually immigrants. Many of these families have experienced great trauma, having left their home countries to escape war, gang activity, deep poverty, natural disasters, and other crises. Often, this means leaving everything behind, including close friends and relatives, which can take an enormous psychological toll on family members.[36] This adds to the stress of the migration experience and weighs heavily on children as they try to adapt to a new country, new language, and new expectations—with few, if any, support services. Once they arrive in the United States, immigrant families are often isolated from the mainstream and segregated by ethnicity, language, and poverty.[37] Further, they tend to lack knowledge of how to navigate the educational system. Frequent residential moves (as parents seek employment) can mean frequent changes in school enrollment, putting these students at increased educational risk.[38]

Of course, there are enormous differences in socioeconomic status among the children of immigrants in the United States. For example, two-thirds of Taiwanese immigrant mothers hold at least a bachelor's degree, while only slightly more than 3 percent of Mexican mothers have a college degree. Similarly, less than 20 percent of Taiwanese immigrant families live at or near the poverty level, but more than two-thirds of Mexican immigrant families fall into this category.[39] Indeed, many Asian immigrants enter the country with higher levels of education, and often greater ability to navigate the educational system, than the native U.S. population.[40] Such examples notwithstanding, the great majority of children of immigrants come from low-income families with relatively low levels of formal education.

Further, the many undocumented young people known as "DREAMers"—those who were brought to the country at an early age and may have discovered only recently that they aren't U.S. citizens—live in constant fear of being apprehended.[41] Unable to apply legally to work or drive a car or (in most states) pay in-state college tuition, DREAMers often struggle to find the motivation to work hard in school and prepare for a career. The Deferred Action for Childhood Arrivals (DACA) program, launched in June 2012 by the Obama Administration, has provided some relief for more than half a million young people who meet its very strict criteria. However, it is estimated that at least another half million meet the criteria but have not come forward, perhaps because they fear identifying themselves to government officials, lack information about the program, worry that they cannot provide the necessary documentation, or are simply unable to pay the $465 application fee.[42] They may worry, also, that DACA protections could disappear overnight, as has been called for by some politicians. Thus, the specter of deportation still hangs over many of these young immigrants, casting a shadow over every part of their lives, including education.

REFRAMING ELLS AND IMMIGRANT STUDENTS: ASSETS AND OPPORTUNITIES

In spite of the many challenges they face (and perhaps because of them), these students can also be viewed as advantaged in certain ways—possessing some important skills and dispositions that monolingual and monocultural students may lack. Their most obvious asset is the ability to speak another language (in most cases, a major world language that is highly valued in the labor market), but there are others. Often, ELLs and immigrant students have complex, multinational perspectives on history, culture, and politics; belong to a culture that prizes collaboration (which is now seen as a critical twenty-first-century skill); display greater motivation to learn than many native-born peers; and have become strongly resilient and self-reliant.[43] What these characteristics all have in common, of course, is their association with key features of deeper learning.

Multilingualism

Multilingualism has been shown to be associated with a series of cognitive advantages, including a greater ability to invoke multiple perspectives in problem solving.[44] The multilingual student knows intuitively that there is more than one way to get to the right answer or define a concept because she does this routinely. Research also shows that multilingualism is related to less distractibility and greater ability to focus attention on a task, another prerequisite to engaging learning in a deeper way.[45] In fact, Guadalupe Valdés has argued that young immigrant children who function as interpreters for their family members exhibit a special kind of giftedness in moving back and forth across languages and cultures, as they extract and represent meaning for others.[46]

A recent analysis of data from the U.S. Department of Education's Education Longitudinal Study of 2002—which has followed the progress of more than fifteen thousand young people since they were in tenth grade— offers further evidence that bilingualism confers a strong advantage. Lucrecia Santibañez and Stela Zárate found that students from immigrant families (both Asian and Latino) who maintained their primary language at high levels, and thus became balanced bilingual speakers, were more likely to go to college than those who lost their primary language; among Latinos, they were more likely to go to four-year colleges.[47] The researchers hypothesized that the bilingual speakers' greater success in getting to college was probably due to having more extensive social networks. That is, they had greater social capital than the monolingual children of immigrants and therefore more support and access to knowledge about enrolling in higher education. Ruben Rumbaut has found similar advantages for balanced bilingual adolescents with respect to high school graduation, perhaps due to greater social networks or perhaps, as others have theorized, because adolescents who maintain the family language communicate more intensively with parents and extended family, and therefore are more likely to receive and heed advice about completing school and going on to postsecondary education.[48] Certainly, the development of sophisticated cognitive skills coupled with greater social assets paves the way for equally sophisticated learning.

Multiculturalism

Having an insider's knowledge of another country and having learned to navigate everyday life in more than one culture may also help students to be more cognitively flexible—that is, to understand that problems can be assessed and solved in more than one way.[49] Cognitive flexibility is also related to creativity, the ability to imagine alternative ways of representing ideas and experiences—also known, in psychological parlance, as divergent or novel thinking.[50]

The biological concept of "hybridization"—bringing together two or more varieties of an organism to create stronger, more resilient progeny—may be a useful analogy here: a hybrid cultural identity can be a powerful asset for individuals and groups. For example, Scott Page has shown through a variety of novel experiments that diverse groups tend to be more creative and better at problem solving than homogeneous groups.[51] Thus, by bringing greater diversity to classrooms, the inclusion of immigrants and ELLs can benefit all students, prompting them to think differently about concepts and problems presented in the curriculum.

Further, by virtue of having learned to live and study within a new cultural environment, immigrant students can be particularly welcoming of differences, skilled at intercultural communication, and comfortable working on diverse teams—characteristics that employers often describe as highly valuable.[52]

Immigrant Optimism

Research on adolescent ELLs has found that motivation is the key prerequisite to educational success.[53] Students from immigrant backgrounds can be especially motivated by their parents' strong belief in the "American dream" for their children. In examining the educational trajectories of immigrant students, Grace Kao and Marta Tienda famously observed that this contributes to what they called the "immigrant paradox."[54] They found (and this has been confirmed by several other studies) that the children of immigrants, as a group, often attained better educational outcomes than subsequent generations—that is, the opposite of the classic immigrant paradigm, in which each generation outperforms the one that came before it.

In a more recent study of four generations of Mexican immigrants in Texas, Edward Telles and Vilma Ortiz found that the children of immigrants completed more years of education than third- and fourth-generation members of the same families.[55] Telles and Ortiz offer structural explanations (e.g., weak schooling) for the failure of postimmigration generations to prosper, but other researchers suggest a psychological explanation: to a large extent, the success of first-generation immigrant students may be due to their belief that success is in fact possible, combined with a strong appreciation for their parents' sacrifices. According to researchers Carola and Marcelo Suárez-Orozco, the "immigrant optimism" of parents—the belief that opportunities are greater in the new land—often propels children to work harder to achieve the American dream, even in the face of daunting obstacles.[56] And in contrast to the limited options available in the old country, that dream may seem all the more tangible.

Further, confronting the challenges associated with the immigrant experience (learning a new language, adapting to a new culture, perhaps having to cope with the hazards of a difficult neighborhood or contending with peers who are disengaged from school) can also lead adolescents to develop certain dispositions that psychologists have found to be far more important than sheer intelligence.[57]

Disillusioned with the limited ability of measured intelligence alone to predict life outcomes, researchers have looked increasingly to affective variables to help explain young people's varying levels of success in school, work, and other settings. Especially important seem to be characteristics such as stress management, adaptability, interpersonal skills, and persistence, each of which is highly relevant to the experience of trying to make one's way in an unfamiliar country and new language, often with few resources. As Birgit Leyendecker and Michael Lamb attest, "Successful immigration demands enormous resourcefulness and flexible adaptation to new and changing circumstances."[58]

Collaborative Orientation

It is important to keep in mind that Latinos and Asians comprise the overwhelming majority of immigrant students in U.S. schools. Of course, not all members of an ethnic or racial group can be presumed to share the same values and beliefs. That said, however, some patterns of socialization do tend to be broadly shared within cultural groups, which can have important implications for teaching and learning. For example, consider Uri Triesman's work in mathematics education at the University of California, Berkeley, four decades ago, which served as the foundation for his well-known Emerging Scholars model of instruction.[59] Observing the study habits and academic outcomes of Chinese and African American students, Triesman noted that the Chinese students naturally formed study groups and helped each other to figure out problems, while the African American students tended to study alone, without the help or support of peers. Reasoning that this difference in study habits could help explain why the Chinese students were outperforming the African American students, Triesman incorporated their model of peer teaching and support into his math program for minority students at Berkeley, and he quickly saw a dramatic increase in their academic achievement. Although Triesman did not use the term "deeper learning," what the Chinese students were doing was entirely consistent with its tenets—they were figuring out collaboratively how to make sense of and solve complex mathematical problems.

Similarly, psychologists have long noted a preference for cooperative versus competitive peer interactions among Latino students, especially those raised in traditional Latino cultures.[60] This preference is believed to be linked to socialization in the home, particularly to Latina mothers' greater emphasis on cooperative and respectful family interactions, relative to Euro-American mothers' tendency to encourage more individualistic behavior and independence.[61] While an emphasis on individualistic behavior serves students well in settings where they are expected to study alone and compete with their peers for the right answer, preference for cooperative behavior would seem to lend itself to the kinds of shared inquiry and teamwork that are cornerstones of deeper learning.

Resilience

Psychologists have been keenly interested in the topic of resilience for more than fifty years, and a number of leading researchers have dedicated themselves to exploring its role in human development.[62] Defined as "a dynamic process encompassing positive adaptation within the context of significant adversity," its relevance to the lives of immigrant children is readily apparent.[63]

In spite of often traumatic uprootings from their homes, harrowing migration passages, and hostile receptions in the new land, immigrant children often arrive in the United States full of hope for the future, with a drive to succeed in school. There is no consensus as to what, exactly, leads so many young people to develop positive outlooks in the face of extreme adversity. However, such resilience does appear to be common. Indeed, some researchers have found that immigrants, in spite of their travails, actually demonstrate better mental and physical health than the native-born population.[64]

Bonnie Benard argues that four "personal strengths," or manifestations of resilience, can be observed in immigrant children: (1) social competence, (2) problem solving, (3) autonomy, and (4) sense of purpose. Virtually all research studies of resilience have associated it with characteristics that fit easily into these four categories (though the terminology may vary).[65] To survive and prosper in an alien environment, immigrant children must attend carefully to the behaviors that constitute social competence, must learn to solve problems in novel situations, and often must do these things with little peer or adult assistance because they do not speak the same language—literally or figuratively—as their classmates and teachers. A sense of purpose, the fourth strength, is often provided by parents, who embody the notion of sacrifice for the chance at a better life, a lesson their children learn daily.[66]

Having developed these forms of resilience, many immigrant students would seem to be well-suited to the kind of engaged, critical, challenging school experiences that advocates describe as deeper learning. However, to the extent that these students are framed as deficient and in need of remediation, these strengths tend to be overlooked.

This is not to say that the performance of immigrant students would greatly improve if only their teachers could recognize the assets they bring with them to school. As the researcher Gordon Allport hypothesized more than sixty years ago, to reduce the prejudice and negative stereotypes that affect the performance of minority students, conditions would also need to be created that allow those students to engage in equal status interactions with individuals from majority groups.[67]

Three decades later, Elizabeth Cohen demonstrated how this theory can be applied by creating instructional contexts in which students of minority and majority backgrounds have opportunities for equal status contact, allowing them to break down their negative stereotypes of each other.[68] In these classrooms, nonmainstream students are also viewed as purveyors of knowledge with commensurate, albeit sometimes different, skills as mainstream students. Such classrooms level the educational playing field for minority (in this case, ELL and immigrant) students. However, Cohen also has shown that this "complex instruction" requires considerable skill and diligence on the part of the teacher, and interactions must be carefully planned and choreographed. Students must be organized so that each can make an important contribution to the group, and groups must be mixed often so that students do not acquire fixed labels (e.g., "the smart kid," "the dumb kid"). Thus, teachers must be both amenable to extensive training and committed to the goals of equity in education. With those conditions in place, ELL and immigrant students could exploit their advantages to lead the way to deeper learning for the whole class.

WHAT WOULD TRULY EFFECTIVE SECONDARY SCHOOLING LOOK LIKE FOR ELLS AND IMMIGRANT STUDENTS?

Over the last several decades, policy makers frequently have engaged in debating the most effective way to educate ELL and immigrant students. But virtually all of those debates have centered on how best to achieve rapid transition to English and assimilation to the dominant culture, without real consideration for other goals.[69]

If the only goal were for students to achieve rapid transition to oral English in the early grades (and concomitant assimilation in the mainstream culture), then it might indeed be preferable to provide an English-only instructional program. As Fred Genesee and his colleagues found in a massive review of research on the education of ELLs, "Evaluations conducted in the early years of a program (grades K–3) typically reveal that students in bilingual education scored below grade level," and were outperformed by students in English immersion programs.[70]

But if one takes a longer view—defining the goal as helping students to achieve at high levels over the course of their schooling, as well as becoming reclassified as English Proficient—then bilingual and dual language instruction show the strongest outcomes.[71] Genesee and his colleagues go on to note that "almost all evaluations of students at the end of elementary school and in middle and high school show that the educational outcomes of bilingually educated students . . . were at least comparable to and usually higher than their comparison peers."[72]

For example, Ilana Umansky and Sean Reardon followed a large cohort of ELL students from kindergarten through high school.[73] The students had been in English-only, bilingual, or dual language programs in the same large district. Carefully controlling for all observable characteristics that could influence educational outcomes, the researchers found that by middle school the bilingually educated students outperformed the English-only students on all outcome measures: proficiency in English, reclassification as English Proficient, and achievement in English language arts.

Further, if the educational goals for ELLs include preparing for and going to college, then there is additional reason to support bilingual and dual language instruction. As noted earlier, an exhaustive analysis of federal data found a significant relationship between balanced bilingualism and going to college.[74] Using another U.S. Department of Education data set, Orhan Agirdag found that once students "with immigrant roots" who maintained their primary language entered the labor force, they earned several thousand dollars a year more than students who lost their primary language abilities.[75] A study of yet another merged data set, which focused on adolescence and early adulthood in Southern California, found a similar earnings advantage for balanced bilingual speakers, in addition to higher rates of high school graduation.[76] Finally, the host of personal and interpersonal benefits that accrue to people who speak more than one language provide yet another reason to choose a program of study for ELL students that includes development of the primary language. For example, evidence suggests that a strong identity plays an important role in school success for ethnic minority students, and families that maintain strong ties with a native culture are more likely to reinforce this identity and sustain the primary language in the home, thus providing critical support for bilingualism.[77]

It is commonly believed that most ELLs enter kindergarten or first grade not speaking English, and they can quickly become fluent English speakers because "they are little sponges." In truth, however, ELL students enter the education pipeline at all grade levels. Significant numbers of ELLs attend middle and high school, either because they have recently entered school in the United States or because their prior schooling has been so weak or interrupted that they have not acquired the academic English that allows them to advance. In California, for example, as many as 30 percent of ELLs are found in secondary schools, and immigrant students are scattered across the grade levels.

Regardless of the strength of the education they received before entering the United States, schools assess relatively few of these students in their primary language to determine what they know or are actually capable of doing, and provide few of them with a rigorous curriculum, including a full complement of college preparatory courses.[78]

Notable exceptions to this pattern include International Baccalaureate programs, offered at various schools across the country, that focus on developing the linguistic and academic skills of immigrant and secondary ELL students. Ursula Aldana and Anysia Mayer report that these programs often spring up in response to intense dissatisfaction with local schools serving ELL students, and they provide rigorous, college-preparatory courses in both English and a second language.[79] They require competence in at least two languages (one being English), but do not privilege any language, so students can learn in their strongest language while developing the other. These and other two-way dual language programs also have the benefit of increasing the prestige of the school and thus attracting more middle-class and high-performing students from surrounding communities, breaking down the cultural isolation that ELLs often experience, and increasing the benefits of diversity for all students in the program or school.

Project SOL (Secondary Online Learning) is another innovation designed to provide rigorous, college-preparatory mathematics, aligned with the Common Core State Standards, in an online and Spanish/English bilingual format. It can be accessed by secondary students who are not yet ready to read textbooks in English, and by teachers who lack the materials to teach those students in Spanish. In recent years, Project SOL has allowed hundreds of immigrant students in California to take and pass the courses they need to graduate from high school and prepare for college. Because the format is totally bilingual, students are able to use and build on both languages.[80]

ONGOING CHALLENGES AND
NEW OPPORTUNITIES

When discussion turns to legal and political matters, it is important to note some key differences between ELLs and immigrant students. While most immigrant students are ELLs at some point in their lives, relatively few ELLs are immigrants. As noted earlier, an estimated 88 percent of ELLs are native-born citizens of the United States.[81] Thus, they enjoy the same legal protections and should receive the same access to education provided to every other U.S. citizen.

Although unauthorized immigrant students do not enjoy the privileges of citizenship, the Supreme Court's 1982 decision in *Plyler v. Doe* did accord them free access to public education through high school. Inadvertently, this also created the predicament that now faces the "DREAMers," those students brought to the United States at a young age by their parents, without legal authorization; once they leave high school, they lack educational rights or even opportunities to work.

Ironically, as the research has converged on the many benefits of bilingualism, for both academic and other deeper learning outcomes, education policy appears to have moved in the opposite direction. The Bilingual Education Act was already being undermined at the law's first reauthorization in 1974, and for the most part continued to move, in subsequent reauthorizations, away from instruction in the primary language. In 2001, with the passage of the NCLB, the BEA disappeared altogether. The Office of Bilingual Education was renamed the Office of English Language Acquisition, Language Enhancement, and Academic Achievement. The term *bilingual* was nowhere to be found. (And as noted earlier, ESSA does not contain the term, either.)

During his time as U.S. secretary of education, from 2008 to late 2015, Arne Duncan touted the importance of bilingualism many times, asserting, for example, that "[it] is clearly an asset that these kids are coming to school with," which should be "maintained," and "The fact that our kids don't grow up [bilingual] puts them at a competitive disadvantage."[82] Similar assertions have been made by Duncan's successor, John King, who was recently quoted as saying that "bilingualism is an asset . . . to be leveraged on behalf of student success."[83] However, the federal government has no policy to foster bilingualism, maintains no office dedicated to bilingualism, and has made no effort to promote biculturalism. Rather, policy makers have focused on the rapid acquisition of English only. Moreover, ESSA's approach to accountability embodies this focus on English-only instruction: scores on tests given in English (often before students actually know the language) determine the academic progress of ELLs.

On the one hand, it is possible to see ESSA as an improvement over prior versions of the federal education law. It is less punitive and it does not rule out dual language instruction. On the other hand, it leaves most instructional (and accountability) issues to the states, and unfortunately many states do not have the expertise or teaching resources to meet these students' needs.

At the state and local levels, the original BEA served as a strong impetus for the creation of policies to guide the education of ELL students, to support the recruitment and training of bilingual teachers, and to support the creation and dissemination of resources for bilingual instruction. Prior to 1968, no state had a probilingual education policy on the books.[84] But by 1983, all fifty states permitted bilingual education and nine states had laws requiring some form of dual language instruction.[85]

However, attacks on primary language instruction continued to pick up steam over the 1970s and 1980s. By the mid-1990s, with immigration reaching exceptionally high levels, California led the way in anti-immigrant legislation, beginning in 1994 with an extremely punitive law that eventually was found unconstitutional. The state outlawed affirmative action in 1996 and culminated its attack with an antibilingual law—Proposition 227—in 1998.[86] Other states and regions followed California's lead, resulting in a steep national decline in primary language instruction. The most recent study commissioned by the federal government found that between 1992 and 2002, the number of ELLs receiving English-only instruction (allowing no use of primary language for any purpose) rose from 34 to 48 percent.[87] That figure is likely to be much higher today, given increasing restrictions at the state and local level.

A good way to begin writing a new chapter for ELL and immigrant students would be to return to Senator Yarborough's initial vision of a BEA that would incorporate not only the native language but also the culture of the children it serves. Many of the assets these students have are embedded in the traditions they bring with them from home, which are often the very same characteristics that can propel them to deeper learning.

Finally, it is also critical that the federal government develop an immigration policy that supports all students, rather than punishing some children for things that are beyond their control, and that respects immigrant families that have contributed to their communities and to the nation. States, too, can pass laws that protect students within their borders, such as policies that extend in-state college tuition rates to all residents, as well as providing all residents with access to driver's and professional licenses that allow them to be insured and to pursue meaningful occupations and professions.

With such fundamentals in place, ELLs and immigrant students could take full advantage of the assets they bring to school and could share these assets with their native English-speaking peers. These students could even be a leading force in the movement for deeper learning.

PART THREE

School Improvement
for Deeper Learning

7

$\sim\!\!\sim\!\!\sim$

Ambitious Teaching

A Deep Dive

Magdalene Lampert

"What sort of endeavor is teaching?" The answer seems simple:
One in which knowledge and skills are transmitted.
All true, but not all that is true. One might also say that
teachers try to improve their students' minds, souls, habits.
—DAVID K. COHEN, from *Teaching and Its Predicaments*[1]

AT PRESENT, most students in most secondary schools are accustomed to learning in two ways: by listening to the teacher and by reading textbooks and other materials.[2] And in a sense, these familiar, rote ways of "doing school" work well for them, because what they are expected to know and be able to do tends to be intellectually shallow.[3]

However, if students are going to be expected to learn deeply (i.e., to master core academic content, think critically and solve complex problems, work collaboratively, communicate effectively, learn how to learn, and develop academic mind-sets), then their everyday experiences in the classroom will have to involve a much more active and personal intellectual process—what Cohen refers to as "minds at work"—than the familiar scholastic exercise of memorizing terms, facts, dates, and formulas.[4]

The question is, what do such ambitious expectations imply for the everyday work of *teaching*? Precisely what does it look like to provide instruction that moves students' minds, souls, and habits toward deeper learning?

Mastering core academic content, for example, involves understanding "key principles and relationships within a content area" and seeing how they fit together within a larger conceptual framework.[5] But how, exactly, does one teach such a framework? What kind of instruction will help students to grasp a content area's organizing principles?

Further, if students are supposed to learn how to communicate and collaborate effectively, then teachers cannot just ask them to work quietly on their own. To get better at those skills, they actually have to try them out. Learning, here, is both the goal and the means of getting to that goal.[6] It requires not just a mind at work but a mind thinking critically and solving meaningful problems in concert with others.[7] And this too begs the question: What can a teacher do to make these things happen? What is involved in teaching students to reason, collaborate, and communicate with one another productively?

Finally, deeper learning is as much about *who* we want students to become—intellectually, at least—as it is about the knowledge and skills we want them to master. To "learn how to learn" requires "caring about the quality of one's work, enjoying and seeking out learning on your own and with others," which has more to do with commitment and interest than skills and knowledge per se.[8] Similarly, to "develop academic mind-sets" means that students

> develop positive attitudes and beliefs about themselves as learners that increase their academic perseverance and prompt them to engage in productive academic behaviors [so that they are] committed to seeing work through to completion, meeting their goals and doing quality work, and thus search for solutions to overcome obstacles.[9]

It goes without saying that such desires, attitudes, and beliefs are shaped, at least in part, by the kinds of interactions students have with peers and adults, both in and out of school.[10] Students learn how to learn and develop academic mind-sets by participating in many such exchanges over time.[11] But what, exactly, does teaching look like in these exchanges? And how can teachers persuade students to invest more of their time, and more of themselves, in their academic work?

Given what we know about U.S. adolescents, it seems reasonable to assume that, for most students, it will be impossible to build these competencies without simultaneously changing what they care about and, in a sense, who they are.[12] For example, in the 2009 High School Survey of Student Engagement, 77 percent of those surveyed said that they spent an hour or less per day on "written homework," and 87 percent spent an hour or less per day on reading and studying (between 40 and 50 percent said they spent less than an hour on these activities per *week*). By contrast, 56 percent said that they devoted at least six hours per week to video games, television, and surfing or chatting online, with significant numbers also describing these activities as "very important" or as their "top priority."[13] In short, teaching for deeper learning will need to support a kind of identity transformation. But, one might ask, what can teachers do to help students change their priorities and choose to dig into academic content? And how can they make the classroom a safe place for students to try out a scholarly identity?

The teaching that leads to these kinds of learning will not be teaching as we have known it over the past century or longer.[14] Perhaps all teaching changes students' minds, souls, and habits, as Cohen claims, but—as I describe in the rest of this chapter—teaching for deeper learning involves doing so deliberately, toward very specific and well-articulated ends.

A CONVENTIONAL WAY OF TEACHING: TEACHER A

To determine whether teaching or learning is "deep," we first must be sure that the given material is in fact worth learning. So I begin this section by introducing a bit of the "core content" that is widely understood to be central to the secondary school curriculum. I then describe—based on my own classroom observations—how two teachers taught that content and what students did to learn it.[15]

The first lesson typifies the most common sort of instruction in secondary schools across the United States.[16] The second features a teacher who is at the same point in the curriculum, teaching the same subject, but trying to practice what I call "deeper teaching," which pursues goals that are more intellectually and socially ambitious.[17] Over the next several pages, I put these two lessons under a microscope, focusing on moment-by-moment exchanges between the teachers and their students. My aim is to call close attention to what it means to teach deeply, how such teaching differs from the norm, and what sorts of knowledge and skills it requires.

I suspect that the interactions between teacher and students in the first lesson will seem entirely familiar to most readers. After all, these are the activities that many of us picture when we imagine a typical classroom: the teacher talks, usually to the whole class from the front of the room, and "explains" facts or procedures, while the class takes notes on what the teacher says or writes on the board.[18] If students speak at all, they provide answers to the teacher's questions, which the teacher judges to be correct or incorrect.[19] This form of teaching has persisted in the United States for more than a century.[20] Individual teachers don't invent it—it is a reenactment of the way they were taught, and it is what many students and parents expect.[21]

The second lesson presents a very different picture. Students frequently talk to one another, collaborating as they make sense of a complex problem. The teacher moves and talks in ways that engage students publicly as learners, listening to and representing their thinking for consideration by the whole class.

Although some teachers may find their own way to a form of deeper teaching—perhaps seeing themselves as mavericks, standing apart from their peers—the teacher in this example did not invent deeper teaching any more than the teacher in the first example invented her approach. Rather, her lesson was developed as a part of a purposeful effort to design instruction and professional learning that deliberately organizes interactions between teachers and learners to bring about the kinds of competencies that characterize deeper learning.

Both of the lessons are more or less consistent with the ways in which these two teachers taught throughout the school year, and they are representative of the regular patterns of interaction that characterized each classroom.[22] My purpose is not to compare two particular teachers, but to compare two different kinds of teaching.

An Example of "Core Content"

The core content I focus on here is algebra, which is usually taught as a distinct subject area sometime between eighth and tenth grade. Studying algebra can be merely an exercise in memorizing formulas and rules, as is the case in much of U.S. education. Or it can provide an introduction to a powerful mathematical language that people use to describe patterns and make predictions. It can be an opportunity to learn how to learn in new ways. And it can open up access to social and economic resources.[23]

For students to master algebra, they need to study functions—that is, mathematical relationships in which one quantity changes in relation to another. Here, I look at two lessons that have to do with the rate of change of a linear function. Mastering the concept of rate of change (sometimes referred to as *slope*) enables us to think productively about problems like how to finance an expensive purchase, determine the safest gradient for a road, or design an engine.[24] It can be a useful tool for making important decisions both in work and in civic life.[25] Students who understand functions and their rates of change can go on to study calculus, the mathematical gateway to engineering, medicine, economics, information technology, and many other fields.

When they study rate of change, students begin by working with linear functions, so named because, represented on a coordinate graph, they look something like figure 7.1.[26]

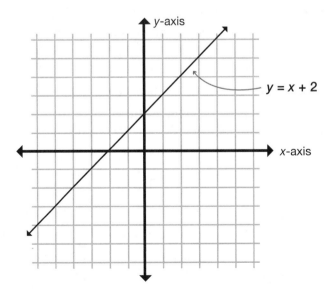

FIGURE 7.1

y-axis

$y = x + 2$

x-axis

The line on this graph tells us that no matter what quantity we start with (x)—whether it is expressed as a whole number or a fraction, whether it is greater or less than zero—the related quantity (y) is always two units larger. For this kind of function, it is possible to extrapolate important information about how y changes in relation to x from just two pieces of data: the slope of the line and the point where it crosses the vertical line that goes through the origin (called the "y-intercept"). We can predict what y will be for any x, no matter how great or tiny the quantity. The lines on the graph have arrows on their ends because they represent only a small part of infinite lines reaching in both directions.

Studying functions and their graphs can be an opportunity to learn how to learn and to learn how to think critically about mathematical problems and how to solve them. It can be a key to "belonging" to the community of learners who know they can succeed at math in high school. Or it can lead students to believe that math doesn't make sense and/or they are not smart enough to get it. Whether or not a student comes out of the study of functions having made progress toward the deeper learning competencies depends on how the content is taught.

Providing a Conventional Introduction to Slope

In the first math classroom, Ms. A stands at the board in front of her class, beginning a lesson on rate of change in linear functions. The goal of the lesson is projected on a screen at the front of the room:

Students will be able to: find the slope of a line given two ordered pairs.

Ms. A tells her class that this is their introduction to "slope," and they will connect finding slope to graphing lines. For a few days, they have been graphing lines using tables of ordered pairs like this one:

x	y
0	−1
2	3
3	5
4	7

They have not yet talked about what it means—or why it matters—if the line slants up or down or goes horizontally across the graph, or if it is "steep" or "gentle."

In a previous class, the students had copied this definition of a function from the board into their notebooks: "A function is a relation between a set of inputs and a set of outputs with the property that each input is related to exactly one output." On the same page, they have also written:

$$\text{input} = x$$
$$\text{output} = y$$

At the beginning of the lesson, Ms. A draws a horizontal line crossing a vertical line on the board. Standing next to the drawing, she gestures up and down, then left to right, saying, "The graph is divided into four quadrants by two axes: the horizontal x-axis, and the vertical y-axis." She then puts arrowheads at the ends of the lines, and writes an x to the right of the horizontal line and a y at the top of the vertical line. Pointing to their intersection, she says that they cross at a point called the "origin." (The words *quadrant, horizontal, vertical, axis,* and *origin* are projected on a screen next to what she refers to as the "graph.") Next, she ticks off equal segments on both lines and puts numbers next to them. She then draws a diagonal line from the top right to the bottom left of the graph, and she darkens and labels two points on that line, resulting in a picture that looks like figure 7.2.

She then reads from a projection on a screen next to the board: "Remember, every point on the graph can be labeled with two numbers, x and y, and indicated by the ordered pair (x, y)." This is review. Ms. A's students wrote this in their notebooks when they first learned to use tables like the one above to make the corresponding dots on a graph and connect them with a line. The only x and y on the board are the ones labeling the x- and y-axes; the letters are not visually associated with points on the graph. One of the students asks the boy next to him whether the y on top of the vertical line and the x next to the horizontal line have anything to do with the (x, y) on the screen. He does not ask the teacher his question, because he knows this is the part of the lesson where the teacher puts things up on the board or screen, and the students copy them into their notebooks. His seatmate writes something on a scrap of paper we cannot see.

FIGURE 7.2

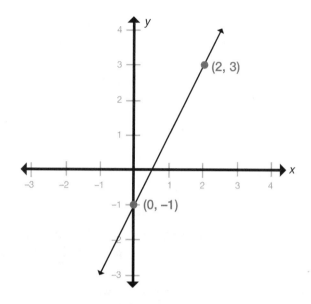

Ms. A next flashes what she calls the "definition of slope" on the screen:

$$\text{Slope} = \frac{\text{rise}}{\text{run}} = \frac{\text{change in } y}{\text{change in } x}$$

She tells students to copy this into their notebooks. Thus another x and another y appear in front of the class, but the teacher does not make connections among the three uses of the same two letters.

She then says, "The slope of a line is usually labeled by the letter m," and flashes another equation:

$$m = \frac{y_2 - y_1}{x_2 - x_1}$$

She tells students to copy this too, "because this is the rule for how to find slope."

She reminds the class that (x_1, y_1) is one point on a line and (x_2, y_2) is another. She further asserts that it is "really important to keep the x and y coordinates in the same order in both the numerator and the denominator; otherwise you will get the wrong slope." She then tells students that learning to find slope is important so that you can use a "table" to find a "line" and use a line to find an "equation." As the teacher passes out graph paper, she tells her students to use it to copy the graph she has drawn on the board. She explains that one finds the slope of this line "by calculating the change in y," being careful to "start with the dot on the top." She writes the equation on the board:

$$m = \frac{3 - (-1)}{2 - 0}$$

She asks the class what they get when they subtract $3 - (-1)$. Some students raise their hands, but she does not call on anyone to give the answer. Instead, she asks a student with his hand up to remind everyone of the rule for subtracting a negative. He says, "Two negatives make a positive." So, she says, the "change" or "difference" in y (the numerator of the fraction) is 4, and she writes a 4 next to $3 - (-1)$ and puts a line under it. She next asks, "What is the change in x?" Pointing to the board, she answers herself: "To find that, we subtract, $2 - 0$." She writes a 2 under the line below the 4. Then she puts an equals sign next to the 4, the line, and the 2, and another 2 next to the equals sign, and says: "So, the slope of this line is 2." She tells the students to copy what she has written on the board under the graph.

Next, she passes out a sheet with several line graphs similar to the one on the board, each with two points labeled, and tells the students to work independently "to find all of the slopes by following the formula we just learned." She goes around the room while they work, answering questions and putting check marks next to correct answers and Xs next to wrong answers, asking students to "do the wrong ones over and check in with me again." Before the bell rings, she says, "Remember, this is going to connect with tables and equations, which we will be working on soon."

Why This Teaching May Be Considered Satisfactory

Ms. A's lesson is well organized, and the facts and procedures she presents are mathematically accurate. She introduces two formulas and demonstrates how to plug values into one of them to find the slope of a line. She asks students to write those formulas in their notebooks and copy the work she has done on the board. She gives them a textbook definition of the new academic term *slope*. She builds her introduction on terms students have heard before—*quadrant, horizontal, vertical, axis,* and *origin*—and on their representations in graphical form, which students should have already learned to make. To some extent, she may be reteaching these terms and representations for the benefit of students who have never encountered them or have forgotten what they mean—and in this part of the lesson she is quite animated, speaking, drawing, and showing slides she has prepared, while students appear to be "on task," actively listening, watching, and copying material into notebooks.

Why This Teaching Does Not Support Deeper Learning

To be successful in this class, students need to demonstrate knowledge of the system the teacher presents. They are learning that "doing mathematics" means following the rules laid down by the teacher, and "knowing mathematics" means remembering and applying the correct terms and the correct rule when doing an assignment.

Although the teacher provides conventional terms, definitions, and formulas, she leaves out a number of key terms and concepts, including some that could be very helpful to her students. For example, she does not actually use the phrase "rate of change," even though the formula for finding slope describes the ratio between how much the value of y and the value of x change from one point to another. Although she tells the students that two points are used to find the slope, she does not mention the fact (a remarkable, even beautiful, bit of mathematics, some would say) that they can use any two points on the line, no matter how close together or far apart, and the slope will always be the same. What she has missed here, in other words, are opportunities to pique students' curiosity: *Why does it work? Does that always work?*

By the time they arrive at high school, most U.S. students have come to believe that they are not cut out for any math more complex than arithmetic.[27] They have learned that when their teachers put mathematical formulas up on the board, they are not expected to respond with curiosity and wonderment. Rather, they are expected to listen to the teacher, follow directions, and, perhaps, try to memorize what they write down in preparation for tests.[28] The students know that once the test is over, they will move on to a new topic and not be likely to see or hear these things again.

Further, in this lesson segment, the teacher communicates that mathematics is a fixed system, in which the student's role is to learn the rules for how to operate within that system. She does this by extending knowledge to students as facts and procedures in a compressed form, briefly unpacking that knowledge with an example and a drawing, but not opening it up to question or interpretation. Students do not practice communicating complex concepts or using mathematical vocabulary, nor do they have the opportunity to use graphs and equations to help them solve problems. They do not have chances to give or receive feedback in interaction with peers.

A DIFFERENT WAY OF TEACHING: TEACHER B

In the second classroom, we observe the exchanges Ms. B has with her students and the way she structures students' interactions with one another. I offer this lesson as an illustration of the everyday work of deeper teaching, which involves not only pushing students toward the deeper learning competencies, but convincing them to participate in a very different way of "doing school."

Like Ms. A in our previous example, Ms. B is standing in front of the room when we come in. She is introducing a new activity, which she tells students they will see multiple times, and which, she adds, is connected to "what we have been doing with functions." She begins by taping five pieces of chart paper to the whiteboard, covering the space across the front of the room (see figure 7.3). She says these are "three coordinate graphs" and "two verbal descriptions" that represent journeys of people traveling by car. She points to the place on graph A where the vertical and horizontal lines meet, and says that at this point the cars are in Boston and no time has yet passed.

As she puts up the papers, she explains how the class will proceed, namely by "looking for structure" and "connecting representations." She says, "We are going to look at a graph representation and a verbal description, or real-life scenario, in words. So, I'll set up all of these representations here."

From a deeper teaching perspective, it is as important to consider what the teacher is *not* doing when she puts up these charts as it is to understand what she *is* doing: she does not distract students from the task at hand—making sense of the concept of rate of change—by bringing in new symbols or terms, such as "positive slope" and "negative slope"; she does not mention that all of these lines are associated with equations; and she

FIGURE 7.3

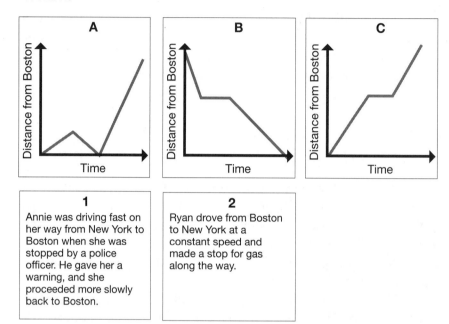

does not write those equations on the board. Rather, she sticks to the interpretation of graphs. In terms of the Common Core State Standards for Mathematical Practice, she focuses solely on Algebra Standard HSF.IF.B.4:

> For a function that models a relationship between two quantities, interpret key features of graphs and tables in terms of the quantities, and sketch graphs showing key features given a verbal description of the relationship. Key features include: intercepts; intervals where the function is increasing, decreasing, positive, or negative; relative maximums and minimums; symmetries; end behavior; and periodicity.

Her goal is to build a foundation for understanding the meanings of terms and formulas that students will learn in subsequent lessons. By linking the graphs with verbal descriptions, she enables students to think about what these abstract representations have to do with something familiar—a car trip. The familiar will provide an anchor as they move to manipulating abstract symbols, helping them judge whether what they are doing "makes sense."

In each of the graphs and scenarios, the distance from Boston is related to how much time has passed since the beginning of the trip. (Formally, we might say that the distance from Boston is a function of time. The rate at which the distance changes in relation to time determines the steepness of the lines.) The one thing she is asking students to investigate right now is why the lines are sometimes flat, sometimes steep, sometimes slanting upward, and sometimes slanting downward. She is, in short, giving her students an opportunity to engage with the visual representations and figure out what they mean in terms of real-life scenarios.[29]

Familiar scenarios like this often help to engage students in classroom activities. But evidence suggests that they are also key to the development of efficient mental structures that provide interpretive perspectives on problems and how they might be solved. In other words, scenarios are tools that can carry knowledge from one domain to another.[30] Students need to be able to do this to learn deeply in secondary school, and they need to know they can do it, so that they come to feel secure about their ability to move into unfamiliar academic and professional territory.

Ms. B teaches in a school whose students are 50 percent Hispanic and 45 percent African American. Some 85 percent are classified as "low income" and 96 percent as "high needs."[31] Students in these categories are less likely to finish high school, less likely to attend college, and even less likely to graduate if they get there.[32] They thus have the most to gain from acquiring the belief that they can make sense of mathematics and succeed at learning it.

Building on What Students Know, and Not Faulting Them for What They Don't

As she waves toward the pieces of chart paper, Ms. B asks if anyone remembers any of the different ways of showing a function that they have already studied.[33] The first student to answer says, "y-intercept." She is in the right ballpark, for the y-intercept is an important part of each graph, as it shows where the car started out in relation to Boston. But it does not "show" a function. To show a function, something would need to show a *relationship* between two quantities that vary in relation to one another.

By asking students to tap into their prior knowledge of functions, Ms. B opens herself up to the risk that students might not be able to answer correctly. The question is, how does she make them feel okay about volunteering ideas that may not be right? In this case, she has to respond to an answer that is "in the ballpark" in a way that lets the student know she is on the right track, while also taking her and the class further down that track toward mathematical precision.

Ms. B responds, "We've looked at the *y*-intercept. And we can see the *y*-intercept on all of them, in all these representations." She then gestures at the coordinate graphs. She chooses to recognize the relevance of the student's contribution in a way that will keep her engaged, while drawing her attention, and the attention of the class, to the different ways of showing functions and how to connect them with one another.

She also pulls the whole class in by repeatedly using the pronoun *we*— "We've looked at the *y*-intercept. And we can see . . ." Her language communicates that engaging with the content is a group effort, and that this content is not something "out there" and impersonal, but something "we," in this room, are working on. Ms. B's use of "we" is a deliberate choice, like many of the words she uses to indicate that the class is involved in a different kind of learning than what happens in Ms. A's classroom. It signifies that she and the students are co-constructing ideas, working collaboratively on building and maintaining a shared sense of the mathematical concepts under study.[34]

By making a habit of responding in this way to incorrect answers, Ms. B shows her students that she can be trusted not to belittle or embarrass them, and that learning is a process of connecting what you know to what you need to learn. This kind of teaching move encourages more student contributions, makes connections between the present and previous lessons, and builds students' intellectual courage to speak in front of the class, even if their thinking needs to be revised at some point. By taking the emphasis off right and wrong answers, she is constructing a classroom culture in which mistakes are an opportunity for learning, rather than a situation in which teachers judge students, and students judge themselves, to be "not good at math."

Ms. B is using what students know to help them grasp new material, a well-known and powerful strategy for building commitment to learning.[35] This move is one of many that make it possible for her students to try on an identity that includes being good at math.[36] By using a student contribution to call attention to something important in the lesson—even though the comment does not answer the question she had posed—she is positioning every student who answers a question as someone who belongs in a community of learners. Or, to phrase it in terms of deeper learning, she is building "academic mind-set" by challenging widely held beliefs that some people are just "good at math" and the rest can't learn it.[37] Every time she makes a move like this, she is attempting to connect students' sense of who they are and who they want to become with learning as a social and worthwhile activity. She is teaching the student who answered and all of her classmates to be learners.

Using Tools and Routines That Support Collaboration and Communication

After soliciting additional answers, such as "graphs" and "tables," to the question of how they have studied functions, Ms. B says that the goal of this activity is to "make connections between two things that look nothing alike but have the same underlying structure"—that is, to figure out which of the written scenarios correspond to which of the graphs. But, she adds, she expects them to do more than just figure out which graphs match up with which narratives; she wants them to practice skills they have worked on before, "like looking for structure in numbers and thinking like mathematicians."[38] She adds:

> It's going to be really important that you are justifying your representation and using language to connect both representations. So, for example, you could say, "The graph shows," and you name something that you see on the graph, and you say, "It's shown in the story by," and then you name something that you're seeing in the story.

She also explains that they will be using a classroom technique that they will repeat several times over the coming weeks: first, they will think about the problem alone; then they will share their thinking with a classmate; and finally they will share with the whole class.[39] This activity structure is designed to require every student to collaborate and communicate about a clearly defined task, working in pairs to hash out their answers and decide how to explain their reasoning to the rest of their peers.

This kind of talk—openly discussing their assumptions, making sure they all mean the same things by the words they're using, and being explicit about their thinking—is unfamiliar to Ms. B's students, almost to the point of learning a new language.[40] One learns to collaborate and communicate only by trying to do these things and being coached to improve.[41]

What Ms. B is prompting these students to do is radically different from what typical American students are used to. Many high school students simply do not talk in class because they don't want to call attention to themselves in an academic setting. They prefer the anonymity of worksheets and lectures and, for the most part, their teachers are willing to oblige.[42] But Ms. B is asking her students to justify their answers to their peers and challenge each other's justifications until they arrive at a solution that is mathematically legitimate.[43] Further, she tells them explicitly that this is her goal:

> I'm going to be pushing you to be connecting back and forth between the two [stories and graphs] and really using evidence to convince your partner, and then the whole class. By the end, you're going to have to create your own representation for a graph, and you're going to write your own real-world description.

This is Ms. B's equivalent of the "Students will be able to" statement that Ms. A wrote on the board in her classroom: she gives her students an end-of-class goal that will require them to invent something new, applying what they have learned from the earlier phases of the activity. While she provides many supports, she leaves the fundamental intellectual work of connecting the stories with the graphs to the students. They are to listen to how their partner matches the representations, ask clarifying questions when necessary, agree on a conclusion, and come up with a way to explain it to the class.[44]

Making It Safe for Students to Publicly Perform Their Academic Competency

When the allotted time for independent pair work ends, Ms. B calls the class together and asks for "one match." Tatiana raises her hand, and the teacher addresses her not as an individual but as "you and Floriana," the pair who worked together on the task.[45] By attributing the finding to a pair, she communicates that collaboration is the norm. She also lowers the personal risks Tatiana might face if she were asked to speak in front of the class only on her own behalf. Having thus put Tatiana at ease, Ms. B asks her to speak loudly, expecting that everyone is listening and anyone might have something to say about her answer:

> MS. B: First match? Tatiana, can you share what you and Floriana found? Nice and loud.
>
> T: We found that B and 1 go together because we said that she was going a certain speed. And then the police stopped her. And then if it was going to, from Boston to New York, it would have started there [points to the lower left-hand corner of the graph], but it didn't start there. So it started from the top. Which means that she started from New York.
>
> MS. B: Great, so can I have you two come up to the front? Okay, now Floriana, you're going to stand next to the representation, so make sure you can see both. And you are going to point to what Tatiana is saying. So Tatiana, can you turn and face your class? Nice and loud, and Floriana is going to help you by pointing to what you are saying, okay? Go ahead. Explain how you found your match.

Repeating what she said before she came up to the board, Tatiana addresses the class:

> T: We found that B and 1 go together because we said that she was going a certain speed and then the police stopped her, and then, if it was going from Boston to New York, it would have started there [pointing to the origin], but it didn't start there. So it started from the top, which means that . . .

As she speaks, her partner Floriana points to the section of the graph that represents the time before the police stop, then to the section that shows the stop itself, and then to the place where the line intersects the vertical axis, "at the top," showing that the car did not start in Boston (at the origin).

In this activity, the teacher has created a structure for public collaboration—giving each student in the pair a role—and explaining those roles publicly, so that everyone in the class can begin to learn them. She also provides a way to take ownership of their shared assertion that graph B connects to story 1.

She doesn't begin by asking which match they found (which might suggest that their job is simply to give an answer, right or wrong). Instead she presses for an explanation of "how you found your match." This puts the girls in a "think on your feet" mode that could be stressful for many students. Ms. B knows, however, from having listened to the pair's conversations, that these two girls have come to a clear, shared understanding of the material. Further, she asks them to face the class and speak loudly, communicating that their audience is everyone in the room, not just her. By asking them to explain their thinking in front of their peers, she gives them a relatively safe opportunity to show that they are capable of complex mathematical reasoning and, in a larger sense, to try on the identity of "serious math student."[46] This in turn shows their classmates that they too can likely do such work.

Tatiana begins the pair's justification that graph B goes with story 1 by focusing on the point that shows the speed of the car when it is stopped by the police, after which a horizontal line shows that the car's distance from New York and Boston did not change for a period of time. She clinches their argument with a logical move called a "counterfactual," raising the possibility that the car "was going from Boston to New York" and concluding that this would lead to a different graph. Focusing on the beginning of the journey, she explains that the car could not have started in Boston because the line that represents the journey does not start at the origin. Since this is the only one of the three graphs whose line does not start at the origin—it begins "at the top" and goes diagonally downward—it must be the one that goes with story B. That is, the girls focused on the y-axis, which measures "distance from Boston," and they noticed that the driver ended there.

Communicating in this way is not a natural activity for either teachers or students. Rather, it is a deliberately constructed instructional design intended to engage students in challenging but doable tasks that reinforce the idea that they are capable of deeper learning.

Structuring Students' Productive Struggle with Core Content

In the third part of the lesson, Ms. B deliberately takes students into new territory. She assigns pairs of students to write the story that goes with the graph shown in figure 7.4.

FIGURE 7.4

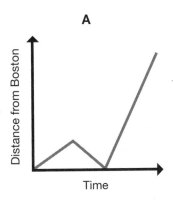

Coming up with a matching story for this graph entails a deliberate challenge. The two other graphs include a horizontal line between two upwardly sloping lines, signifying a stop in the journey. But in graph A, there is a downward-sloping diagonal between two upward-sloping diagonals. The questions are: What happens in a functional relationship when the graph suddenly switches from "going up" to "going down"? And what does it mean that the second line segment goes down to the x-axis and the next segment goes upward, more steeply than before?

This segment of the graph represents an important mathematical idea that is fundamental to linking graphs with stories. But it tends to be harder to grasp than the narrative interpretation of the upward-sloping and horizontal lines because it involves a visual contradiction that can only be resolved with mathematical reasoning. A downward-slanting line might seem to suggest that the car is slowing down, and when the graph turns upward again, it might seem to suggest that the car is speeding up. But this is a common misinterpretation of graphs that represent time, speed, and distance.[47] In fact, the second, downward segment shows that the car returns (at the same speed) to Boston, and the third segment shows that it sets out again to New York, moving at a faster speed (perhaps to make up time for having had to go back to Boston). In formal mathematical terms, we would say that the first segment has a positive slope, and the second has a negative slope, while the third has a greater slope than the first. For someone who does not regularly work with such graphs, though, the visual and verbal cues can easily overtake the conceptual.

In this beginning algebra class, then, Ms. B asks students to use what they know to confront a mathematically interesting inconsistency that leads them to need to come up with a new idea. Once they grasp one mathematical concept, she challenges them with a problem that requires them to figure out another, more sophisticated, concept.

This is a fundamentally different way to learn math—or, in a larger sense, to be a student—from what we saw in Ms. A's classroom, where the typical assignment required students to use a memorized formula provided by the teacher to figure out preestablished answers to the teacher's questions.[48] Constance Bowen, a New York City high school teacher, has described this sort of "deeper" instruction:

> These are rich questions that elicit reasoning and build understanding about how the variables being measured relate. If we had simply asked them, "What is the slope from point A to point B," then they would have applied the algorithm without any thought of its meaning. . . . Students typically grab onto the formula as the method and actually don't build understanding or the ability to describe what is happening in the relationship between the two variables at play.[49]

THE KEY DIFFERENCES BETWEEN CONVENTIONAL INSTRUCTION AND DEEPER TEACHING

In 1999, the National Research Council's Committee on Developments in the Science of Learning published *How People Learn: Brain, Mind, Experience, and School*, an exhaustive review of extant research. Briefly put, that work described three main principles for enabling students to learn in ways that we would now call "deeper":[50] (1) Teachers must build new understanding on the relevant knowledge and experience that students bring to the classroom; (2) they must help students to integrate factual knowledge into a network of concepts to support knowledge use in new situations; and (3) they must support students' capacity to become aware of and engaged in their own learning and to decide whether their answers make sense.[51]

Teaching according to the National Research Council learning principles is congruent with what I have called deeper teaching. To do this kind of teaching, teachers need to make appropriate decisions about what to teach, build on students' current understandings, use methods of instruction that link the two together, and respond to each student's contributions with feedback that is carefully formulated to communicate to all students that they are capable of becoming competent.

Consider the following contrast between the teaching of Ms. A and Ms. B. Midway through her lesson, Ms. A told her class, "The slope of a line is usually labeled by the letter *m*." On the overhead screen, she flashed this equation:

$$m = \frac{y_2 - y_1}{x_2 - x_1}$$

She told her students, "This is the rule for how to find slope." Referring to a graph she had drawn, she said that one finds the slope of the line "by calculating the change in *y*," being careful to "start with the dot on the top." She then wrote this equation:

$$m = \frac{3 - (-1)}{2 - 0}$$

If Ms. A had asked her students to make the equation for finding the slope of the line on the graph, rather than doing it herself, they might have had an opportunity to practice what the philosopher Alfred North Whitehead called "throwing inert ideas into fresh combinations," edging toward the deeper learning competencies of problem solving and critical thinking.[52]

But Ms. A did not even make it explicit that she arrived at this equation by inserting the numbers associated with the points on her graph. Nor did she go back to the graph to explicitly represent the link between these subtractions and the visual "rise" over "run" in what she called "the definition of slope," which would have entailed adding lines to the graph, as in figure 7.5.

Linking the equation to the rise and run lines would have given the students an anchor not only for understanding what the equation for slope represents, but also for seeing that 3 – (–1) is the length of the "rise," that is, the line from 3 to –1 on the *y* axis. Ms. A might have asked her students to use the graph to talk about why 3 – (–1) is 4, not 2, relating the quantity

FIGURE 7.5

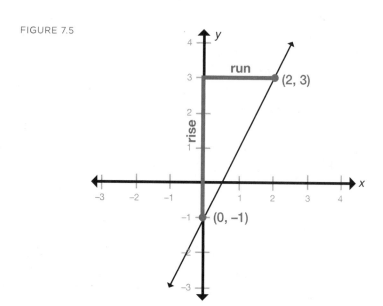

4 to the length of the "rise." She might even have linked what looks like a fraction to the idea that slope is a ratio between the change in x and the change in y, which would stay the same for any two points on the line. This might have at least given students an exposure to the conceptual framework that leads to core academic content or understanding "key principles and relationships within a content area and organiz[ing] information in a conceptual framework."[53]

Instead, when Ms. A asked the class what they got when they subtracted 3 − (−1), she did not wait for an answer but immediately asked a particular student, presumably one she knew she could rely on, to remind everyone of the rule for subtracting a negative. Repeating the rule he had memorized, he expressed an inert idea, as Whitehead calls it. Then Ms. A did the calculation herself, unwilling to risk that a student might call out the wrong answer. No student even had a chance to apply the rule. To the extent that what Ms. A did when she inserted the values from the points on the graph into the equation for slope might be called "intellectual work," she did that work, not her students.

The question Ms. B asked to elicit students' memories of the different ways of showing a function and the way she responded to their answers offers a signal contrast to Ms. A. Recall what Ms. B did when she asked a question about the different ways of showing a function that they had already studied. The first student to speak said "y-intercept," which is not a way of showing a function. But Ms. B did not judge this response right or wrong, which would have positioned her as the "owner" of the mathematics. Instead, she responded in a way that connected what the student said with what they would be working on. She also positioned students to try out being mathematical thinkers. By making a habit of not judging their answers immediately, but giving them a chance to make sense of things themselves, she let them know that the connections they make are valued, and that her classroom is a safe place to try on the "academic mind-set" one needs to do mathematics.

As Ms. B's work illustrates, deeper teaching requires setting up interactive structures for students that deliberately reposition them in relation to academic content and to one another, incorporating their agency, interests, and knowledge in ways that make accessible the meaning and relevance of academic material. Perhaps the most profound segment of Ms. B's lesson is the part where she moves to the graph that does not have a story, and asks the students to write the story. Putting too much emphasis on the familiar visual and not enough on the unfamiliar symbolic is a problem that comes up over and over again in algebra, geometry, and calculus, where graphs that model abstract mathematical relationships are often interpreted as pictures showing a concrete phenomenon.[54] Ms. B knew that if she gave her students two sets of graphs and stories to link together, and then a third anomalous graph, she would be building a foundation for one of the more important aspects of mathematical understanding.

CONCLUSION: TOWARD DEEPER TEACHING

I began this chapter by asking how teaching would have to be different if learning were to be deeper. Drawing on the learning principles derived by the National Research Council, and comparing the deeper teaching of Ms. B with the more common and familiar teaching of Ms. A, we might say that:

1. *Ms. B needed to be able to elicit students' current understandings and build from them toward the deeper learning competencies.* To do this,

she made student reasoning—rather than proffering known answers to teacher questions—the basis of teacher-student and student-student interactions.

2. *Ms. B needed to know her subject well enough to decide to teach and be able to teach core content, critical thinking, problem solving, collaboration, communication, a disposition to learn, and academic mind-set.* This involved choosing rich tasks, developing academic language for describing and communicating about ideas, and structuring interaction so that it was safe for students to express partially formed thinking in the classroom.

3. *Ms. B needed to choose and be able to use methods of instruction that link what the teacher is teaching with students' current understandings.* Students need structured, predictable routines for surfacing their interpretations and conceptions, and Ms. B needed to use strategies for linking individual work and small-group work with the learning agenda for the whole class.

This is a tall order.[55] For this reason, such teaching is sometimes referred to as "ambitious teaching."[56] While number 2 has to do with the skills and dispositions that teachers need to acquire ahead of a particular instance of teaching, much of the work entailed in numbers 1 and 3 requires the teacher to make quick judgments while working face-to-face with multiple students. The knowledge underlying those judgments includes the core ideas of a subject, how they relate to one another, and why they are important, as well as how students are likely to think about the content of a lesson, in order to prepare to connect their prior knowledge with the core ideas being taught.

The question is: How did Ms. B learn to teach in this way?

The way Ms. B interacted with students and mathematics did not just "come naturally" to her, although she entered teaching with a strong mathematics background. Nor did she invent it single-handedly. Although Ms. B is a beginning teacher, she could enact the lesson because she had learned a set of routines for carrying out the kinds of complicated interactions that support deeper learning. She did not learn these routines in a context-free, content-neutral way, for researchers have found that it is difficult for teachers to use teaching routines taught in the abstract in particular settings.[57] Rather, she learned them in repeated cycles of observing, planning, teaching, and analyzing an instructional activity called "Connecting Representations."

This instructional activity is one of a small number of protocols that can be used to teach mathematics ambitiously.[58] Instructional activities have been used for many years to organize balanced literacy instruction, and they are now being designed for use in mathematics, science, and social studies.[59] In effect, they are templates for organizing classroom instruction in a way that makes room for students to problem solve, communicate, and collaborate. They support students as they learn how to learn and develop academic mind-sets.

Making the structure of an instructional activity like Connecting Representations a regular part of lessons reduces the cognitive load of ambitious teaching, so that teachers can pay close attention to students and connect what they are doing to elements of the domain under study, thereby positioning them as agents of their own learning. Instructional activities are not one-off tasks that a teacher might find in a resource book or on the Internet; rather, they are protocols that are meant to be used repeatedly with varying content. They are deliberately designed to accomplish ambitious aims by specifying who (teacher and students) should be doing what, with whom, when, and for how long.

Instructional activities also provide very specific guidance as to how teachers can respond productively to students' contributions in class. Whenever teachers and students do an instructional activity, they are repeating patterns of social and intellectual interaction that students must learn in order to accomplish deeper learning goals. A system of instructional activities can organize teaching and learning to regularly include individual think time for students, students explaining their thinking to one another, making student thinking public by representing it for the class, and connecting student reasoning to core mathematical content.[60] Through repetition, both teachers and students acquire new ways of thinking about what it means to teach and learn, and what they are able to accomplish.[61]

In short, Ms. B is part of a coherent, albeit small, system of instructional improvement. She works in a group of teachers who use the same set of instructional activities, which are aligned with the Boston Public Schools' academic goals and targets and the Massachusetts Curriculum Frame-works. Ms. B and others in her group rehearse in front of one another, and coaches help them hone their skills in implementing the routine parts of the activities. Since instructional activities are designed to elicit students' mathematical input, this group of teachers prepares to teach with an instructional activity by deliberating together about appropriate ways to use student input to achieve learning goals, pooling their knowledge of students and mathematics. They also collectively plan adaptations to the instructional activities that suit their students and the mathematics they plan to teach. On occasion, they watch one another's lessons and give feedback on the practices they are learning together.

Such collectives can be built when teaching is supported by common instructional and assessment tools and opportunities to learn to use them. As individual teachers use common resources in instruction, they can make ambitious teaching happen across classrooms by scaffolding the risky and complex work of engaging each student in learning to perform authentic tasks. And because individual teachers use common resources, they have the shared language and artifacts that are pivotal for working together on common planning and on the shared evaluation of lessons and students. That is, they share a framework within which to figure out how to use what they know about mathematics and the students they teach.

Using common tools like instructional activities, teachers can learn to provide consistent instruction by preparing and planning together, teaching in a way that makes it possible for others to observe and coach them, and collecting and analyzing records of practice as a basis for refining their lessons and units.[62] Schools need to be structured to support collective teacher learning as a series of improvement cycles that quickly move in and out of practice.[63]

However, although common tools and well-organized schools are necessary, they are not sufficient. To come alive, they require a corps of teachers who have the knowledge of the content, the students, and the context in which they are teaching to make informed judgments about how to use an instructional design appropriately and how to respond productively to each particular student contribution—year by year, unit by unit, lesson by lesson, and moment by moment. Only in the particular interactions between a teacher and a class can an instructional design be implemented in a way that utilizes its power to achieve the learning goals its designers embrace.

Deeper teaching is a set of practices that support students in building a new scholarly identity, enabling them to become active agents in their own learning. Such teaching involves improving students' minds, souls, and habits, as well as their skills and knowledge.

8

~~~~~~

District Leadership
for Deeper Learning

Meredith I. Honig and Lydia R. Rainey

SCHOOL DISTRICT LEADERS nationwide aspire to help their schools become vibrant places for learning, where students have meaningful opportunities not only to study core academic content but also to develop critical thinking, communication, and other deeper learning skills that are essential to success in later life.

Historically though, school district central offices have been ill equipped to support truly ambitious goals for student learning. For example, a host of major school improvement initiatives have stumbled, or failed outright, at least in part because central offices did not help schools implement reforms successfully. Numerous studies of approaches, such as the "effective schools" movement, site-based management, and comprehensive school reform, conclude that productive participation by district-level leaders and staff is essential to bring high-quality teaching and learning to scale.

However, those studies generally do not elaborate on what productive participation entails, precisely, or how to help central offices engage effectively in districtwide teaching and learning improvement.[1]

175

As we describe in this chapter, a new wave of research has begun to fill this gap, identifying the very specific actions that central offices can take to support the goals of deeper learning. It suggests that ambitious instructional reforms can and often do succeed when district leaders and staff make a genuine commitment—not just on paper but in all aspects of everyday practice—to what we call "performance alignment," referring to an especially strategic and comprehensive approach to school system improvement. We base our claims on emerging evidence from the field, on our own intensive research in nine districts (which vary in size, demographics, and other characteristics), and on our experience as advisers to another seventeen central offices that have been implementing such reforms.

Performance alignment does not mean that central office staff simply adopt a new organizational vision, agree to make decisions with the best interests of children in mind, or pledge to do their current tasks more efficiently. Rather, it means that they continuously scrutinize everything they do to ensure they are spending their time and other resources on the right work: work that helps principals support teachers so that all students realize ambitious learning goals.

Central office staff working toward performance alignment recognize that they influence teaching and learning not directly but through their support for the many others who do have direct impacts on those outcomes. They coordinate their work so that the individual parts of the district system operate in concert, as opposed to working in separate silos or in competition for limited resources.

Why should central office leaders make performance alignment a key part of their efforts to help all students learn deeply? What, more specifically, does performance alignment entail, and how might district leaders move in that direction?

In this chapter, we identify several challenges that central offices often face when they try to support the improvement of teaching and learning districtwide. We then describe how pioneering districts are pursuing performance alignment. And we conclude by recommending specific strategies that can help school districts to realize deeper learning at scale.

The findings from our research point to the need for a fundamental redesign of most central office functions, as well as major departures from business as usual for most central office staff, especially those in human resources (HR), curriculum and instruction (C&I), and principal supervision. Such reforms can be challenging, but they are likely to be necessary for school systems to realize deeper learning outcomes in all schools and for all students.

WHAT DO CENTRAL OFFICES HAVE TO DO WITH DEEPER LEARNING?

For at least the past two decades, federal and state policy makers have called upon schools and districts to hold all students to high standards as part of a broader strategy to ensure that all students graduate from high school ready for college and careers.[2] The guiding assumption behind most reforms has been that if educators set high standards for all students, and if they truly believe that all students can meet them, they will likely create opportunities for all to learn at high levels.

Recent school improvement efforts such as the Common Core and curriculum standards created by individual states are grounded in this theory of action. They aim to define ambitious learning targets for all students, both in specific academic content areas and in essential skills such as critical thinking, problem solving, collaboration, communication, and the ability to direct one's own learning.[3]

At the same time, many researchers have found that, while high standards and expectations set the stage for student success, the *in-school* factors that tend to have the most powerful influences on student learning are teaching and principal leadership.[4] For example, students assigned to very high-quality teachers learn far more than peers assigned to very low-quality teachers, ending the school year up to a full grade level farther along.[5] And principals influence classroom instruction in a number of ways, such as by establishing a climate conducive to learning, ensuring quality professional development, and providing ongoing feedback to help teachers improve their practice.[6]

But what about district leaders and central office staff? How much and what kinds of influence do they have on teaching and learning? More specifically, what can central offices do to support the ambitious goal of deeper learning for all students?

Little Research or Policy Attention on Central Offices

Researchers have identified some broad roles that central offices play to ensure that teachers and principals have basic supports to succeed in their work.[7] For example, in districts of all sizes, schools tend to rely on their central office staff to provide professional learning opportunities and to identify and procure standards-based curriculum materials. Further, while school principals in many districts have the authority to select their own teachers, the pool of available candidates is often shaped by central office systems of teacher recruitment, hiring, and retention.[8]

In past decades, however, district central offices appeared mainly in the background of studies that focused on individual schools, and they were discussed mainly as impediments to school improvement.[9] The few researchers who focused on central offices did so indirectly—not by investigating what actually went on within central offices but, rather, by using available datasets to identify a handful of district-level characteristics that appeared to be statistically associated with positive school outcomes.

More recently, attention to districts has increased somewhat, with researchers using qualitative and mixed-methods approaches to study their effectiveness. However, most have described the influence of "the district" as a whole on school improvement efforts, and they have reported their findings in terms of broad categories of district action, such as "leadership," "vision," or "policy alignment," that, they argue, matter to school results.[10]

Because such methods leave the inner workings of central offices unexamined, researchers have been able to provide few insights into the specific and various ways that districts influence teaching and learning. For example, studies have made no distinctions among the myriad district-level staff members whose actions might have differing impacts on school outcomes.[11] Nor have they addressed why some districts that engage in particular actions, such as policy alignment, fail to see the positive results observed in other districts.[12]

Likewise, attention to school district central offices has been largely absent from recent policy debates about education reform. For example, the Education Commission of the States lists over seventy issues in its database of K–12 education policy topics, research, and resources, but not one of them relates to how the central office can better support school performance.[13] Similarly, many foundations and state and federal policy makers have chosen to bypass central offices altogether and work directly with schools, as was the case with both the small schools movement and school improvement grants.[14]

Limited Central Office Support for Teaching and Learning

The lack of attention to central offices' contribution to teaching and learning makes sense in light of their history. In the early 1900s, rural leaders formed central offices largely to help raise the local funds required as a precondition to receiving newly authorized federal support for schools.[15] Urban leaders created them mainly to manage burgeoning enrollments and handle business functions. Their participation in teaching and learning matters usually extended only to ensuring that teachers were properly licensed.

Earlier, in the late 1800s, superintendents had typically functioned as districts' head teachers, with authority over the curriculum. However, as the organizational ideal of "scientific management" gained prominence in the first decade of the 1900s, central offices came to focus mainly on ensuring the efficient use of resources and on monitoring compliance to regulations. The role of the superintendent followed suit.[16] And for the better part of the last century, central offices built up their capacity in those non-instructional areas, spurred in part by federal and state funding streams that treated local educational agencies as little more than fiscal pass-throughs.[17] In the 1960s and 1970s, superintendents found themselves under growing pressure from civil rights leaders, teachers unions, and federal and state governments to share decision making with local educators. This further eroded their influence on teaching and learning, even with regard to operational matters.

Considering these origins, it is no surprise that when, in the late 1980s and early 1990s, central offices were called upon to help implement standards-based reform and other efforts to improve the quality of classroom teaching at scale, their capacities turned out to be poorly aligned with this new role. For instance, in 1991, the National Council for the Teaching of Mathematics issued professional teaching standards that required a fundamental shift in pedagogy, from an emphasis on the memorization of mathematical procedures to efforts to deepen students' understanding of mathematical concepts and their applications. But central office staff tended to assume that the introduction of these new standards entailed only modest changes to their own work.[18] Even those staff members who were explicitly charged with supporting high-quality teaching—such as coordinators of professional development services—tended to lack the experience and resources required for realizing such outcomes.[19]

Why Central Offices Struggle to Support Improvements in Teaching and Learning

When district leaders do aim to shift their roles to support ambitious teaching and learning, the misalignment of central office resources, data, and other systems to those demands can frustrate their efforts. First, competition and lack of coordination *within* central office units can impede their support for teaching and learning improvement. For instance, one midsized urban district with which we partner provided teachers with state-of-the-art professional development in mathematics for many successive years. Experts agreed that the live and video-based coaching and the intensity of the supports likely contributed to significant improvements in students' performance in mathematics on standardized tests across virtually all grade levels for several years. However, to provide this support, central office staff used well over half of the days available for teacher professional development, as well as most of the allotment for substitute teachers, leaving few resources for other subject areas, such as English language arts and science. Student learning outcomes actually declined in those other areas during this period.

A second reason central office leaders struggle to support the improvement of teaching and learning at scale relates to limitations of available data about resources for improvement. For example, in one district that participated in our research, staff in the C&I department initiated a major effort to provide professional development for teachers in schools with the greatest need, as determined by a new system that placed schools into four "tiers" based on their students' performance on standardized achievement tests.[20] C&I staff targeted their most intensive supports to schools ranked at tier 1—those that did not adequately improve student performance for several years—and they offered fewer and fewer supports up to tier 4, which included schools whose test scores revealed strong performance and growth.

The district superintendent and school board praised the tiered system as an example of using data wisely to target limited resources to areas of greatest need, and other districts copied the approach. In our analysis, however, we found that many of the tier 1 schools already had a significant number of teachers performing at a high level, as well as on-site teacher leaders who were providing enhanced professional learning opportunities to their peers, thanks to a separate initiative that had directed strong teaching candidates to those schools. The principal of one tier 1 school reported that he now had more resources for professional development than he really needed. Meanwhile, his teachers told him that the district's required professional development sometimes took time away from learning opportunities that they found more meaningful. Other school leaders, too, reported that the professional development for tier 1 schools was too rudimentary to meet the needs of many teachers who were actually teaching at a higher level of quality than suggested by student test scores.

Central office staff acknowledged this problem. However, because they lacked reliable access to data that might better inform them about the actual quality of teaching in each school, they could not figure out how to provide services that aligned with teachers' true learning needs. We find such mismatches between teacher quality and professional development opportunities to be common. Further, we have observed that C&I staff sometimes engage teachers in professional development without first consulting principals to determine whether the support fits with the school's overall efforts to strengthen teaching practices.

Third, systems for the hiring and placement of personnel in many school districts do not function in ways that support improved teaching and learning. For example, in many of the midsized districts with which we work, it has long been standard practice for HR staff to screen teaching candidates' credentials very lightly before passing them along for principals to consider. As a result, for each vacancy, a principal might receive files for anywhere from fifty to a hundred candidates, forcing them to waste precious time looking through applications that the HR staff should have been able to exclude from the start. Further, a cursory screening process does little to identify candidates whose instructional strategies and experiences are most aligned with deeper learning. Principals report that they have lost promising candidates to other schools and districts due to these slow and cumbersome hiring practices. Districts with such systems also often spend significant professional development resources bringing new hires up to a basic level of performance—resources they could have used elsewhere, had they hired better-matched teachers at the outset.

Fourth, central office staff who supervise principals have rarely provided them with the kinds of intensive supports that can help them lead instructional improvement.[21] In many districts, principal supervisors devote much of their time to monitoring compliance with central office directives. Or they serve as all-purpose liaisons between the central office and schools, following up on requests from either party and filling in for nonresponsive central office staff. For instance, in one of the districts that we have studied, HR staff were so slow to assign teachers to schools that the principal supervisors stepped in and made the assignments.[22] Not only did this leave less time to do their own jobs—working directly with principals—but it also shielded the other staff from the consequences of their low-quality service, likely prolonging the office's dysfunction.

These problems with the resources, data, and systems within central offices have deep roots, and they will not be resolved by the kinds of actions that districts typically take in response to calls for ambitious teaching and learning standards. For example, in many districts, leaders assume that efforts to improve teaching and learning belong largely within the purview of the C&I department. Often they overlook the pivotal roles played by principal supervisors and the responsibilities of HR staff for personnel recruitment and selection.

In a potentially promising development, some district leaders have begun to assign cross-functional teams—including representatives from several central office units—to work together to support teaching and learning in a cluster of schools. Such teams may be able to build bridges among organizational silos, and we find that they sometimes lead to better working relationships between principals and individual central office staff members. However, like the traditional forms of principal supervision mentioned earlier, such teams can also have the unintended effect of *delaying* real reform, insofar as their work may distance other district leaders from direct interactions with local principals that might have made them more acutely aware of the urgent need for deeper changes.

Given the significant barriers to central offices' ability to support deeper learning, are advocates on a fool's errand when they call on central offices to do so? Or—as we argue in the next section—is it realistic to pursue meaningful improvements?

WHAT CAN CENTRAL OFFICE LEADERS DO TO SUPPORT SYSTEM-WIDE DEEPER LEARNING?

Some districts have succeeded in confronting the mismatch between the ambitious goals of deeper learning and the longstanding limitations of central office systems and staff capacity. In so doing, their leaders have demonstrated that this work requires not just tinkering with staff and systems but transforming them.[23]

We conducted one intensive study of three districts that tackled the problem of central office performance misalignment head on, as well as of another six districts that aimed to use findings about those districts and other research to inform their own transformation efforts.[24] We also currently partner with an additional seventeen districts and their support providers across the country to help them use the emerging knowledge base about central office performance improvement and to learn from the experience of pioneering districts.[25]

We find that central office staff can do much to ensure that their daily work meaningfully supports principals as they enable teachers to help all students realize ambitious learning goals. Further, they can strategically coordinate their work with that of others throughout the district so that the individual parts of the district system operate in concert with one another, again toward the goal of engaging all students in deeper learning.

Our research and district partnerships reveal that such performance alignment entails a fundamental redesign of many central office functions, with particular attention to C&I, HR, and principal supervision. In the sections that follow, we draw upon our own research in and other experience with districts to describe three strategies often pursued by high-performing central offices:[26]

- Define high-quality teaching and principal instructional leadership.

- Ensure that principal supervisors are truly focused on supporting principals' instructional leadership growth.
- Enable all district staff to focus their time and other resources on activities that support schools' pursuit of deeper learning.

Although the districts with which we work have not been pursuing deeper learning per se, they have been working toward similar goals, and their experiences provide important lessons for other central offices interested in supporting ambitious teaching and learning.

Define High-Quality Teaching and Principal Instructional Leadership

Districts that align to performance, like performance-oriented organizations in other arenas, clarify their performance target—in this case the kinds of teaching that have been linked, theoretically and empirically, to deeper learning. These districts also clarify the proximate supports for realizing that target—here, school principals as supports for teachers and high-quality teaching, or what some call "instructional leadership."

At the school level, clear and explicit definitions set the stage for teachers and principals to develop a shared understanding of (1) the kind of teaching they aim to develop and (2) what principals can do to support it. Such joint sense-making is fundamental to professional learning, providing educators with a common image, or mental model, of the kind and level of performance to which they aspire, and which they can use to guide improvements in their practice.[27] We have found that teachers and principals are likely to benefit from district improvement efforts when they have opportunities to participate in defining their professional standards and deciding which of them to prioritize.[28]

Definitions of high-quality teaching and principal instructional leadership can also function as important tools to support performance alignment in central offices. For example, school districts that have successfully improved the quality of the teachers and principals that they hire use such definitions to focus recruitment, screening, and selection processes, and they frequently use performance tasks (such as teaching a sample lesson) to gauge how well a candidate performs in relation to those targets. In so doing, these districts not only set themselves up to hire teachers who perform at a relatively high level at the outset, but they also get to know each candidate in ways important to ensuring the right fit with teaching assignments.[29]

Common definitions also help staff of C&I units to design, provide, and assess professional learning opportunities. For example, in one of our partnership districts, C&I staff created a teacher evaluation system that scored teachers on the extent to which their teaching reflected the standards in their instructional framework (i.e., their definition of high-quality teaching); the results informed their decision to target professional development on particular forms of inquiry across the content areas.

Just as important, a common definition of high-quality teaching and principal leadership allows for joint strategic work within and between central office units, since it enables staff to see how they contribute to the district's overall strategy for improving teaching and learning. For example, in one of our partner districts, C&I and HR staff are participating in a series of strategic planning sessions to decide on common data they can use to inform professional development and the reassignment of teachers and principals, especially at their chronically low-performing schools. Staff have commented to us that before they had a shared definition of high-quality teaching, their conversations mainly focused on sharing information about what each unit was doing; now, staff more carefully scrutinize the extent to which each is contributing to an overall approach related to improving teaching quality.

But the extent to which such definitions help anchor performance alignment depends in part on the quality of the definitions themselves, and on the ways in which staff use them.

For example, many definitions of high-quality teaching and leadership are so long that they do not adequately focus teachers, principals, or central office staff on common performance targets. Emerging research reinforces the importance of choosing a manageable number of teaching and leadership practices to anchor observations and improvement efforts. Districts that do so tend to amass detailed information that they can use to provide intensive and useful feedback for teachers and principals.[30] On the other hand, when staff try to use too many elements to guide their work, they risk focusing on none of them at a level deep enough to support improved practice.

Many teachers and principals in our partner districts report that when district staff neglect to prioritize their goals, they tend to resort to checklist-style observations—simply marking off whether or not they see evidence of particular practices. Far more valuable would be collecting detailed information about classroom teaching and principal leadership that would allow them to provide meaningful feedback or assess the value of a particular professional development strategy.

Further, while district frameworks might include some teaching and leadership practices that are supported by research, they might also include some that are not. For instance, they might emphasize the use of complex questions to generate classroom discussion, which has been associated with deeper learning of mathematics, science, and other content. But they could also give priority to teachers' participation in professional development workshops, which have been found to have less-proximate influences on student learning. Similarly, many definitions of high-quality principal leadership include vaguely defined actions such as "providing feedback to teachers," which hardly specifies what principals actually do to contribute to improvement. And some feedback can have a negative impact on teacher learning.[31]

The generic nature of such frameworks also poses problems. For instance, the teaching moves shown to be effective in secondary science instruction are not necessarily the same as those found to promote student learning in elementary mathematics.[32] Similarly, leading a secondary school involves practices that can differ from those associated with elementary school leadership. And while individual principals sometimes have a direct influence on the quality of teaching, a growing strand of research suggests that successful principals often cultivate the leadership of teachers to grow their own and their colleagues' practice.[33] Yet, in coming up with their definitions of high-quality principal leadership, districts often neglect to make these and other important distinctions.

However, while such definitions of high-quality teaching and leadership are necessary, they are hardly sufficient. To see real gains, district leaders need to address the entire central office's performance, asking: What would the office look like if it were truly designed to support instructional leadership, high-quality teaching, and—ultimately—deeper learning? Currently, are staff engaged in work that is not in service of such results? And, beyond simply helping them do their current work more efficiently, what can be done to engage them in the right work?

Ensure That Principal Supervisors Are Truly Focused on Supporting Instructional Leadership

To become true leaders of teaching and learning improvement in their schools, principals often need intensive and personalized supports, which district principal supervisors are in unique positions to provide.[34]

In our work, however, we have found that principal supervisors typically spend the bulk of their time engaged in tasks such as monitoring schools' compliance with federal, state, and district policies, running interference for ineffective central office units, and conducting cursory principal evaluations—none of which supports principals' growth as instructional leaders. Nor does the size of the district seem to matter. In small school systems, one might expect to see more personalized attention to principals' needs. But we have found that principal supervisors in smaller districts (where the role typically falls to superintendents or directors of teaching and learning) also spend their time mainly on operational issues and evaluation. That is the case even among superintendents who say that they have a responsibility to provide principals with feedback and other supports to help them strengthen their instructional leadership.[35]

Viewing principal supervisors as an important but largely untapped resource, districts pursuing performance alignment take deliberate steps to reduce the amount of time supervisors spend on operational and regulatory functions and shift their focus toward improving instruction. In turn, supervisors have the greatest impact on their districts when they dedicate their time to specific teaching strategies such as modeling effective instructional leadership, both in one-on-one settings and in professional learning communities.[36]

Such supervisors are careful not to skip over the principal and instead work directly with teachers, in an effort to have a more immediate impact on the quality of teaching and learning in local schools. We have found that when they do so, they miss important opportunities to support principals, resulting in weaker instructional leadership over the long term, as well as undermining the overall coherence of teachers' professional learning opportunities.[37]

Supervisors can become progressively more capable of helping princi-pals only if they receive ongoing support.[38] We find that it is particularly important that their own district leaders protect their time, taking other tasks off their plates so that they can focus on working intensively with principals. Further, they should be assigned a manageable caseload—we estimate that this consists of eight to twelve principals per supervisor, as-suming that those principals have varying levels of expertise as instruc-tional leaders and need varying amounts of assistance.[39] And we find that it is important for supervisors to receive intensive professional develop-ment as well, in order to perform their role effectively.[40]

Ensure That All Staff Members Focus Their Time and Other Resources on Activities That Support Schools' Pursuit of Deeper Learning

In our research, we have found it to be critical for principal supervisors to have the time and support they need to work intensively with principals, helping them understand what it entails to provide effective instructional leadership. But it is also critical that their efforts align with the work go-ing on across the district. To have a positive impact, they must be working in sync with the rest of the central office, with everybody reaching across traditional silos to pursue a common theory of action about how to realize deeper learning for all students.[41]

As noted earlier, we find it particularly important that principal su-pervision be well aligned with the work of C&I and HR. Misalignment with C&I means that supervisors are unable to draw on other professional learning resources to help principals. And misalignment with HR means that supervisors often end up diverting their attention from supporting principals to performing whatever HR duties are not getting done cor-rectly, efficiently, or at all.

In our most recent district partnerships, we have observed that the stra-tegic movement of principals—either to different schools or out of the principal corps altogether—can be just as impactful as efforts to provide them with high-quality professional development. This underscores just how important HR units are to school improvement. When HR systems make it difficult or impossible to reassign or remove principals, supervi-sors can end up spending an inordinate amount of time trying to help leaders who require far more assistance than they can provide, leaving them with less time to help others.

In central offices aligning to performance, district leaders carefully scrutinize the work of all staff members to ensure that they contribute meaningfully to leadership, teaching, and learning. Particularly in our original study districts, leaders helped every staff member to identify aspects of their work that did nothing to support high-quality teaching and learning—whether directly or indirectly—and helped them find ways to align their work more tightly to that goal.[42] In the process, leaders sought to eliminate systems and tasks that seemed outdated or unnecessary, redirecting the resources to tasks that are more essential to the improvement of teaching and learning.[43] In effect, they found ways to maximize the benefit of central office functions relative to their cost, addressing the familiar concern that districts tend to be top-heavy or bloated.

Based on their experiences, we have compiled a number of lessons for leaders seeking to align their school systems to the goals of deeper learning.

Collect and Use the Right Data

To help them answer questions that are fundamental to system-wide improvement, district leaders must have access to the right data. For example: What is the current capacity of teachers in each school relative to the district's instructional framework, the district's strategic plan, and the individual school's improvement plan? Do our efforts reflect the latest knowledge about how best to support teachers in reaching such goals?

In one district, central office leaders realized that, to answer such questions, they would have to build an entirely new data dashboard. While their existing system provided extensive information about achievement test performance, grades, attendance, and teacher evaluation results, it did little to help them understand the quality of teachers' classroom instruction. For instance, teachers in several schools had received particularly low marks on the teacher evaluation related to using explicit objectives in their teaching. However, when C&I staff more closely examined what teachers were doing in their classrooms, they observed that those teachers actually had different levels of capacity related to this evaluation standard.

Nor could the system help them answer questions important to their strategic decision making, such as: Which of our students are chronically low performing across grades and subject areas? Which teachers and principals, if any, have these students had in common? What other features of these schools might help explain such results?

Having built a new data system, leaders in this district now report to us that they are able to make grounded hypotheses about the root causes of disappointing student outcomes, and they can identify key points of leverage that are likely to improve performance. Having access to better data means they are no longer tempted to blanket their schools with professional development offerings and staffing changes in the hope that some of them might pay off. Instead, they are now careful to target their efforts on the areas of greatest need.

Another district that we work with is now developing a strategy to improve the quality of the data it collects through its annual school improvement planning (SIP) process. The SIP previously required schools to report their goals and strategies for student learning for the coming year. But knowing what schools wanted to achieve did nothing to help district staff figure out which supports might enable them to realize such results. Instead, the new, redesigned SIP will lead schools through a process of assessing their current capacity relative to their performance targets, which will provide better information about the kinds of district support they will need.

Address Teaching and Learning Across Subject Areas

Second, as C&I staff make decisions about which sorts of professional development to provide to schools, they should not confine themselves to the traditional subject-matter silos. Rather, they should consider working collaboratively across professional development areas, guided by relevant data about teaching and leadership quality. For instance, in one district, C&I staff from several subject areas meet regularly to discuss their data about teacher capacity in individual schools. Only then, and in collaboration with their principal supervisors and school principals, do they choose the specific professional development approaches that are most likely to have the greatest impact on teaching.

In other words, leaders of these units do not assume that their own subject areas should be the focus of professional development services. Nor do they restrict their choices to the services they themselves can provide. Rather, they start out by considering the schools' overall needs and priorities.

Build Bridges Within the Central Office—Especially Between C&I and Human Resources

In districts aligning to performance, C&I and HR leaders also collaborate to ensure that professional development aligns with the systems guiding the placement of teacher and principal candidates.

For example, one of our partner districts is building a new system of coordination between C&I and HR in which school-specific decisions about professional development happen in tandem with analyses of the fit between particular teachers and their placements. Beginning with the initial screening of job candidates, HR staff collect information related to their teacher education or leadership programs, prior professional experiences, and scores on performance-based tasks—such as teaching mock or actual lessons—integrated into the hiring process. (Researchers and district leaders have been able to use such information to identify, for example, teacher education programs whose graduates tend to do especially well in a particular district, school, grade level, or subject area.[44]) When questions arise as to the quality of work by individual teachers or principals, HR and C&I staff meet and review that data, using it to inform their decisions as to whether it would be preferable to move those people to new positions or keep them in place while providing them with professional development services.

Leaders in C&I and HR units can also eliminate or streamline existing tasks to maximize the time their staff spend on work that helps improve teaching and learning. For example, by automating various routine processes related to professional leave, payroll, and the verification of continuing education credits, one district was able to redirect staff to an enhanced recruitment team, which reviews school-level data to help identify teaching candidates who seem to fit particularly well with the given position and the local workplace dynamics.

Search Out Additional Opportunities for Alignment

We continue to find that while principal supervision, C&I, and HR play lead roles in district efforts to improve teaching and learning, other aspects of the central office also have important parts to play.

For example, in one study, we observed that administrators and HR staff made a strategic decision to reduce the number of teachers in a given school, but implementation stalled because information technology, payroll, and other systems could not easily process the decision.[45] In another instance, C&I staff found that professional development events were more successful when staff from the facilities and payroll departments were included in the planning.[46]

In another positive example of alignment between noninstructional units and the improvement of teaching and learning, a district's chief of operations decided to engage her bus drivers in a series of conversations about the role they could play in enhancing the quality of student learning and reinforcing the school culture, such as its rules of appropriate conduct. For instance, they could greet students personally every morning, communicate with their adult caregivers at bus stops, and relay any important information to school staff (which can be particularly valuable when those caregivers are unable or unwilling to communicate with school staff directly).

In another district, following complaints by school principals about the lack of responsiveness of buildings and grounds staff, the chief of operations partnered with union leaders to find ways to improve performance. They discovered that principals wasted numerous hours following up on outstanding work orders, but they also found that buildings and grounds staff had not been proactively identifying and addressing issues that could have maximized the use of instructional space. Union leaders believed the staff wanted to improve their performance but had never been invited or supported to do so. In response, the central office established a relationship with a local community college to help raise staff skill levels, and staff built a department performance scorecard to track metrics such as how much time they saved principals when they worked in more responsive and proactive ways.

Given our limited experiences working with units other than principal supervision, C&I, and HR, and given the limited research in this area, we can touch only briefly on the importance of performance alignment throughout the rest of the central office. However, we do find that when district leaders neglect to consider all parts of the central office, they ultimately face a host of predictable problems, including competition among units, lack of coordination, and use of the wrong data to inform change.

CONCLUSION

We have argued that strong, coordinated support from the district central office is essential to realizing deeper learning for all schools and all children. No matter how committed individual district leaders may be to school improvement, their plans will likely be stymied unless they find ways to bring every part of the system into alignment with the goals of excellent teaching and learning for all students.

As we have written elsewhere, the changes we describe here are a far cry from administration as usual. District leaders who are serious about this work do not simply tinker with their central offices but transform them into teaching and learning support systems.[47] Such efforts go well beyond the shifting of boxes and lines on formal organizational charts and reach into the daily work of each and every central office staff person to engage them fully in redesigning their roles and participating in multiple stages of reform.

Our main recommendation to all district leaders—and policy makers and foundation leaders as well—is to heed these lessons and support major improvements in central offices focused on performance alignment. Further, because aligning for performance relies so heavily on remaking the day-to-day work of the central office, district leaders would do well to invest in building the capacity of their own staff to help lead the effort. Our partner districts have done so not only by creating professional learning opportunities for existing staff but also by bringing in new staff whose expertise (in leadership, instruction, finance, and other areas) does not necessarily fit the traditional central office mold.

Going forward, how can district leaders, researchers, policy makers, and others ensure the continued development of central office staff capacity consistent with performance alignment?

One place to start is the creation of new data systems to capture and display information that goes well beyond test scores, and to allow staff in all parts of the central office to better understand the quality of teaching, learning, and principal leadership in their schools—and to see how they might align their work to support improvement. District leaders build such systems not by relying on whatever data sources happen to be available but, rather, by taking proactive steps to collect data that can help them answer their most pressing questions about adult capacity and performance.

Another place to begin may be to enlist researchers to help districts strengthen their understanding—and, in the process, to strengthen the larger knowledge base—of the ways in which central office work practices matter to student outcomes.

Finally, as we noted earlier, care should be taken to create policy frameworks that support these efforts. Historically, state and federal governments, as well as foundations, have contributed to the lack of strategic coordination within central offices by, for example, distributing funding and designing accountability systems in ways that reinforce organizational silos, typically by privileging test score results as performance targets and doing little to help districts build data systems that can drive performance improvements. Going forward, then, the question is: How can policy makers and foundations work together to support districts in ways that enable the creation of integrated district systems in support of deeper learning?

9

Toward Systems of Assessments for Deeper Learning

David T. Conley

IMAGINE THIS SCENARIO: You feel sick, and you're worried that it might be serious, so you go to the nearby health clinic. After looking over your chart, the doctor performs just two tests—measuring your blood pressure and taking your pulse—and then brings you back to the lobby. It turns out that at this clinic the policy is to check patients' vital signs and only their vital signs, prescribing all treatments based on this information alone. It would be prohibitively expensive, the doctor explains, to conduct a more thorough examination.

Most of us would find another health-care provider.

Yet this is, in essence, the way in which states gauge the knowledge, skills, and capabilities of students attending their public schools. Reading and math tests are the primary and, in most cases, exclusive indicators of student achievement that have counted in federal and state accountability systems since 2001.[1] Faced with tight budgets and growing protests, policy makers have demanded that the costs and time associated with such testing be minimized.[2] And, based on the quite limited information that these tests provide, state officials and educators have drawn a wide range of inferences, some appropriate and some not, about students' overall academic performance and progress and the efficacy of the public schools they attend.[3]

One would have to travel back in time to the agrarian era of the 1800s to find educators who still seriously believe that their only mission should be to get students to master the basics of reading and math. During the industrial age, the curriculum expanded to include core subjects such as science, social studies, and foreign languages, along with exploratory electives and vocational education. And in today's postindustrial society, it is commonly argued that all young people need the sorts of advanced content knowledge, thinking skills, communication capabilities, and human relation dispositions that used to be taught to an elite few.[4] So why do the schools continue to rely overwhelmingly on assessments that do not go beyond the "three Rs"?[5]

That's a question that countless Americans have come to ask. Increasingly, educators and parents alike are voicing their dismay over current approaches to testing and school accountability.[6] Indeed, we may now be approaching an important crossroads in American education, as growing numbers of critics call for a fundamental change of course in assessment policy and practices.[7]

In this chapter, I draw upon recent research findings and policy analyses to argue that the time is ripe for a major shift in educational assessment. Thanks to advances in cognitive science—as well as analyses of syllabi, assignments, assessments, and student work from entry-level college courses—we now have a much more detailed picture of what students need to do to be fully college and career ready.[8]

Over the next several years, will educational stakeholders remain satisfied with the tests they have been using, or will they demand new forms of assessment? The Every Student Succeeds Act (ESSA) dramatically reins in the federal government's influence over local educational policy making, but will states and districts take advantage of this flexibility to adopt measures of student learning that address more than just reading and math?[9] Will state policy makers demand evidence that students can apply knowledge in novel and nonroutine ways, across multiple subject areas and in real-world contexts? Will they be willing to invest in assessments that get at deeper learning, addressing the whole constellation of knowledge and skills that are the outcome of what ESSA refers to as a "well-rounded education"?

The goal of this chapter is to present a vision for a new system of assessments, one designed to support the kinds of ambitious teaching and learning that parents say they want for their children, and which federal policy now seems to endorse.

HISTORICAL OVERVIEW

Ironically, due to the decentralized nature of educational governance in the United States, the nation's educators already have access to a vast array of assessment methods and tools that they can use to gain a wide range of insights into students' learning across multiple subject areas. Those methods run the gamut from individual classroom assignments and quizzes, to capstone projects, to state tests, to college admissions exams and results from Advanced Placement and International Baccalaureate exams. Many measures are homegrown, reflecting the boundless creativity of American educators and researchers. Others have been produced professionally and have long development histories and well-documented technical pedigrees. Some measures draw upon and incorporate ideas and techniques from other sectors—such as business and the military—and from other countries, where a wider range of methods have solid, long-term track records.

The problem is that not all, or even most, schools or states have taken advantage of this wealth of potential resources. By focusing so intently on reading and math scores, federal and state policy since 2001 has forced underground many of the assessment approaches that could be used to promote and measure more complex student learning outcomes.

A Historical Tendency to Focus on Bits and Pieces

The current state of educational assessment has much to do with a long-standing preoccupation in the United States with reliability (the ability to measure the same thing consistently) over and above a concern with validity (the ability to measure the right things).[10] To be sure, psychometricians—the designers of educational tests—have always considered validity to be critical, at least in theory.[11] In practice, though, validity itself has been defined largely in terms of the test's reliability. Measurement experts have had far more success assuring the reliability of individual test forms than in dealing with messier and more complex questions about what should be tested, for what purposes, and with what consequences for the people involved.[12]

Over the past century, this emphasis on reliability has led to the creation of tests made up of lots of discrete questions, each one pegged to a very particular skill or bit of knowledge. The more specific the skill, the easier it becomes to create additional test items that get at the same skill at the same level of difficulty across multiple forms of the test, which translates to more consistent results.

This focus on particulars has had a clear impact on instruction.[13] To prepare students to do well on such tests, schools have been encouraged to treat literacy and numeracy as a collection of distinct, discrete pieces to be mastered, with little attention to students' ability to put those pieces together or to apply them to other subject areas or real-world problems.[14]

Further, if the fundamental premise of educational testing in the United States is that any type of knowledge can be disassembled into discrete pieces to be measured, then the corollary assumption is that, by testing students on just a sample of these pieces, one can get an adequate representation of the student's overall knowledge of the given subject.

It's a bit like the old connect-the-dots puzzles, with each item on a test representing a dot. Connect enough items and you get the outline of a picture or, in this case, an outline of a student's knowledge that, via inference, can be generalized to untested areas of the domain to reveal the "whole picture," even if that line drawing is a far cry from a true portrait.

This certainly makes sense in principle, and it lends itself to the creation of very efficient tests that do what they're designed to do. But what if the assumptions we make about what these tests are telling us aren't true in a larger sense? What if knowing the parts is not the same as understanding the whole? What if knowing isolated pieces of the subject doesn't mean that students can apply this knowledge, or, perhaps most important, transfer it to new situations or other subject areas?

Assessment Built on Intelligence Tests and Social Sorting Models

Another reason for the focus on measuring literacy and numeracy this way has to do with the unique evolution of assessment in this country. A very different approach—what would now be called "performance assessment" (referring to activities that allow students to show what they can do with what they've learned)—was common in schools throughout the early 1900s, although perhaps not in a form readily recognizable to today's educator. For example, written examinations developed, administered, and scored locally were the primary means for gauging student learning and determining college admission. Oral presentations in the form of recitations were also important.[15]

However, these types of assessment were not considered particularly "scientific," an important criticism in an era when science was being applied to the management of schools. Events in the field of psychological measurement from the 1900s to the 1920s exerted an outsized influence on educational assessment. The nascent research on intelligence testing gained favor rapidly in education and led to "scientific" ways to group and sort students. Tests administered to all World War I conscripts showed that "intelligence" was distributed in the form of a normal curve (hence "norm-referenced testing"): immigrants and people of color scored poorly, whites scored better, and upper-income individuals scored the best. This confirmed the social order of the day.[16]

At the same time, public education in the United States was experiencing a meteoric increase in student enrollment, along with rising expectations for how long students would stay in school. To be more "efficient," schools chose to categorize, group, and distribute students according to their presumed abilities.[17] Children of differing ability should surely be prepared for differing futures, the thinking went, and "scientific" tests could determine abilities and likely futures cheaply and accurately. All of this would be done in the best interest of all children, they argued, to help them avoid frustration and failure.[18]

Unfortunately, the available testing technologies then and now have never been sufficiently complex or nuanced enough to make these types of predictions. In fact, no assessment can take into account all the factors associated with individual success. So assessment derived from intelligence testing has been used (or misused, really) throughout much of the past century to categorize students and assign them to different tracks, each assumed to lead to a particular life pathway.[19]

Moreover, additional problems with norm-referenced testing—designed to see how students stack up against one another—are readily apparent. In the first place, it is not clear how to interpret the results. By definition, some students will come out on top and others will rank at the bottom. But this is no reason to assume that top scorers have mastered the given material (since they may just have scored a little less poorly than everybody else). Nor can it be assumed that low scorers are not capable of learning the material (since, depending on where they happen to go to school, they may never have been taught the given material at all). And, finally, these tests fail to provide much actionable information telling students what to do to improve their scores, so they tend to perpetuate the results they get.[20]

Assessment to Guide Improvement

Since the late twentieth century, the use of intelligence tests and academic exams to sort students into tracks has been largely discredited.[21] Moreover, in today's economy, where everyone needs to be capable of learning throughout their careers and lives, it would be socially and economically counterproductive to keep sorting students in this way. It's far better to try to educate all children to a high level than to label some as losers and anoint others as winners.

Criterion-referenced tests are one alternative. They measure how well students perform in relation to a set of criteria or standards. In principle, all students could do well (or poorly) on a criterion-referenced test. This type of assessment doesn't require a normal distribution.[22]

The first, limited manifestation of criterion-referenced testing was the mastery learning movement of the late 1970s.[23] Mastery learning focused entirely on basic skills in reading and math, and it reduced those skills down to the smallest testable units possible. However, it did represent a real departure from the status quo, since it argued that individual students should continue to receive instruction and opportunities to practice until they "mastered" the relevant content. In theory, everyone could succeed, given enough time and instruction. The purpose of assessment was not to sort students into winners and losers, but simply to generate information about their performance in order to help them improve.

One of the problems with mastery learning, though, was that it was limited to content that could be broken up into dozens of distinct subcomponents that could be tested in detail.[24] As a result, educators and students were quickly overwhelmed trying to keep track of progress on all the elements. Equally vexing was the fact that mastering those elements didn't necessarily lead to proficiency in the larger subject area, or the ability to transfer knowledge and skills to new contexts.[25] Students could pass reading tests only to be unable to read new kinds of material, and they could ace math tests only to be stumped by problems that did not fit familiar patterns. Students also often failed to retain much of what they had "mastered." To critics of mastery learning, the approach highlighted the limitations of shallow learning models.[26]

Early Statewide Performance Assessment Systems

Initially referred to as outcomes-based education, the first wave of academic standards emerged in the late 1980s and early 1990s.[27] As with mastery learning, the goal was for all students to succeed. But these standards were more expansive, designed to produce a well-educated, well-rounded student, not just one who could demonstrate discrete literacy and numeracy skills. Thus, for example, they included not just academic content knowledge, but also outcomes that related to thinking, creativity, problem solving, and the interpretation of information.

These more complex standards created a demand for assessments that went well beyond measuring bits and pieces of information. Thus, the early 1990s saw the bloom of statewide performance assessment systems that sought to gauge student learning in a much more ambitious and integrated fashion. Vermont and Kentucky required students to collect their best work in "portfolios," which they could use to demonstrate their full range of knowledge and skills. Connecticut, Maryland, and California introduced performance assessments.[28] Oregon created an elaborate system that included classroom-based performance tasks, along with certificates of mastery at the ends of grades 10 and 12, requiring what amounted to portfolio evidence that students had mastered a set of content standards.[29]

These assessments represented a radical departure from previous achievement tests and mastery learning models. They were also quite difficult to manage and score—requiring more classroom time to administer, more training for teachers, and more support by state education agencies. They quickly encountered a range of technical, operational, and political obstacles.

Vermont, for example, ran into problems establishing reliability, the holy grail of U.S. psychometrics, as teachers were initially slow to reach a high level of consistency in their ratings of student portfolios (although reliability did improve to acceptable levels as teachers became more familiar with the scoring process).[30] In California, parents raised concerns that students were being asked inappropriately personal essay questions.[31] (Also, one year, the fruit flies shipped to schools for a science experiment died en route, jeopardizing a statewide science assessment.) In Oregon, some assessment tasks turned out to be too hard, and others were too easy. And everywhere, students who had excelled at taking the old tests struggled with the new assessments, leading to a backlash among angry parents.

In the process, a great deal was learned about the dos and don'ts of large-scale performance assessment. Inevitably, though, political support for the new assessments weakened, particularly as standards were revised again and again in many states. This often resulted in a renewed emphasis on testing students on individual bits and pieces of academic content, particularly in reading and mathematics. While a number of states continued their performance assessment systems throughout the 1990s, most came under increasing criticism due to their costs, their scoring challenges, the amount of time required to administer them, and the professional development challenges involved in preparing teachers to teach to them.

The final nail in the coffin for most large-scale state performance assessment systems was the federal No Child Left Behind law passed in 2001, which mandated testing in English and mathematics in grades 3–8 and once in high school. The technical requirements of NCLB (as interpreted in 2002 by Department of Education staff) could most easily be met with standardized tests using selected-response (i.e., multiple-choice) items.[32]

The designers of NCLB were not necessarily opposed to performance assessment. First and foremost, however, they were intent on using tests to hold educators accountable for how well they educated all student popula-tions.[33] Thus, although the law was not specifically designed to curtail per-formance assessment, this was one of its consequences. A few states (most notably Maryland, Kentucky, Connecticut, and New York) were able to hold on to performance elements of their tests for varying lengths of time, but most states retreated from almost all forms other than multiple-choice items and short essays.

Fast-forward to the present, however, and things may be poised to change once more.

WHY IT'S TIME FOR ASSESSMENT TO CHANGE

An important force to consider when viewing the current landscape of assessment in U.S. schools is the rising weariness with test-based account-ability systems of the type that NCLB mandated. The expectations con-tained in NCLB were both laudable and crystal clear—that all students become competent readers and capable quantitative thinkers. The means by which these qualities were to be judged, however, led to an overem-phasis on test scores derived from assessments that inadvertently deval-ued conceptual understanding and deeper learning. Thus, even though student test scores rose in some areas, many educators and researchers were doubtful that this represented real improvements in learning.[34] Fur-ther, a desire to increase test scores and avoid federal sanctions, including reduced funding, led many schools to devote precious class time to test-preparation techniques and to narrow the curriculum to focus, sometimes exclusively, on the content tested on state assessments.[35]

At least two other important reasons help explain why the time may be ripe for a major shift in educational assessment: First, recent research has clarified what it means to be college and career ready, making it increasingly difficult to defend the argument that NCLB-style tests are all that is needed to predict student success. Second, recent advances in cognitive science have yielded new insights into how humans orga-nize and use information, making it difficult to defend tests that treat knowledge and skills as nothing more than a collection of discrete bits and pieces.

What Does It Mean to Be College and Career Ready?

Until the mid-2000s, education in most high schools was geared toward making at least some students eligible to attend college, but not necessarily making them ready to succeed.

For students hoping to attend a selective college, eligibility was achieved by taking required courses, getting sufficient grades and admission test scores, garnering a positive letter of recommendation, and perhaps participating in community activities. For most open-enrollment institutions, it was sufficient simply for applicants to have a high school diploma, and then apply, enroll, and pay tuition. Whether students could succeed once admitted was largely beside the point. Access was paramount.

The new economy has changed all of that. Being admitted to college does not mean much if the student is not prepared to complete a program of study. A certificate or degree is the new ticket to full economic participation. A college education has to improve a student's future economic prospects, if for no other reason than to enable repayment of the increasingly crushing debt load students accumulate.

Why have high school educators been focused on students' eligibility for college and not on their readiness to succeed there? A key reason is that no one was entirely sure what college readiness entailed. Until the 2000s, essentially all the research in this area used statistical techniques that involved collecting data on factors such as high school grade-point average, admission tests, and the titles of high school courses taken, and then trying to determine how those factors related to first-year college grades or retention beyond the first term.[36] These results produced broad generalizations, such as "take challenging courses in high school." However, this line of research could not zero in on what, specifically, enabled some students to succeed while others with similar preparation struggled.

In recent years, however, researchers have been able to identify a number of very specific factors that, in combination, maximize the likelihood that students will make a successful transition to college. Drawing upon analysis of course-content data from tens of thousands of courses at a wide range of postsecondary institutions, we now have a much better understanding of the demands, expectations, and requirements students must meet to succeed in entry-level college courses.[37]

For clarity's sake, I have highlighted four main factors—I call them "keys"—that research has identified as contributing to college readiness:

- *Key cognitive strategies.* The thinking skills students need to learn material at a deeper level and to make connections among subjects.
- *Key content knowledge.* The big ideas and organizing concepts of the academic disciplines that help structure all the detailed information and nomenclature that constitute the subject area, along with the attitudes students have toward learning content in each subject area.
- *Key learning skills and techniques.* The student ownership of learning that connects motivation, goal setting, self-regulation, metacognition, and persistence with study skills, note taking, online record keeping, and other capabilities.
- *Key transition knowledge and skills.* The aspiration to attend college, the ability to choose the right college and to apply and secure necessary resources, an understanding of the expectations and norms of postsecondary education, and the capacity to advocate for oneself in a complex institutional context.

In turn, each of these keys has a number of components, all of which are things that can be assessed, taught, and learned successfully (see figure 9.1). (Note that the model does not include certain factors, such as parental income and education level, that are strongly associated statistically with college success but which are not actionable by schools, teachers, or students.)

Advances in Cognitive Science

Recent research in cognitive science provides a second major impetus for shifting the nation's schools away from a single-minded focus on current testing models and toward a wider range of assessments that gauge deeper learning.

Of particular importance is research into the malleability of the human brain, which has provided strong evidence that individuals are capable of improving many skills and capacities previously thought to be fixed.[38] Intelligence was long assumed to be a unitary, unchanging attribute, one that can be measured by a single test. However, that view has come to be replaced by the understanding that intellectual capacities are varied and

FIGURE 9.1 The four keys to college and career readiness

Key Cognitive Strategies	Key Content Knowledge	Key Learning Skills & Techniques	Key Transition Knowledge & Skills
Think	**Know**	**Act**	**Go**
Problem formulation Hypothesize Strategize **Research** Identify Collect **Interpretation** Analyze Evaluate **Communication** Organize Construct **Precision and accuracy** Monitor Confirm	**Structure of knowledge** Key terms and terminology Factual information Linking ideas Organizing concepts **Attitudes toward learning content** Content Challenge level Value Attribution Effort **Foundation knowledge and skills** Specific college and career readiness standards	**Ownership of learning** Motivation High aspirations Self-efficacy Self-monitoring Persistence **Learning techniques** Time management Test-taking skills Note-taking skills Memorization/recall Strategic reading Collaborative learning Technology Help seeking	**Contextual** Aspirations Norms/culture **Procedural** Institution choice Admission process **Financial** Tuition Financial aid **Cultural** Postsecondary norms **Personal** Self-advocacy in an institutional context

multidimensional and can be developed over time, if the brain is stimulated to do so.

One critical finding is that students' attitude toward learning academic material is at least as important as their aptitude.[39] For generations, test designers have used "observed" ability levels based on test scores to steer young people into academic and career pathways that seem to match their natural talents and capabilities. But the reality is that, far from helping students, such a use of test results discourages many from engaging in the sustained, productive effort that would allow them to succeed in a more challenging course of study more closely associated with their interests.

Recent research also challenges the commonly held belief that the human brain is organized like a library, with discrete bits of information grouped by topic in a neat and orderly fashion, to be recalled on demand.[40] In fact, evidence reveals that the brain is quite sensitive to the *importance* of information, and it makes sense of sensory input largely by determining its relevance.[41] Thus, the long-standing American preoccupation with breaking down subject-area knowledge into small bits and testing the ability to recall those bits may in fact be counterproductive.

When confronted by a torrent of bits and pieces presented one after the other, without a chance to form strong links among them, the brain tends to forget some, connect others in unintended ways, experience gaps in sequencing, and miss whatever larger purpose and meaning might have been intended. The net result is that little is retained over time.[42] Likewise, when tests are designed to measure students' mastery of discrete bits, they provide few useful insights into students' understanding of how any particular piece of information connects to the larger structure of knowledge in the subject area.

Having received few cues about the relative importance of the given content, and having few opportunities to fit it into a larger framework, it's no wonder that students often forget much of what they have learned, from one year to the next. Or that even though they can answer test questions focusing on the details of a topic, they struggle to demonstrate understanding of the larger relevance or meaning of the material. Indeed, this is one possible explanation for why scores at the high school level on tests such as the National Assessment of Educational Progress—which gets at students' conceptual understanding, along with their content knowledge—have flatlined over the past two decades, a period when the emphasis on basic skills increased dramatically.

Ideally, K–12 curriculum and instruction should guide students through learning progressions that increase in complexity over time, moving toward larger and more integrated structures of knowledge. Rather than being taught skills and facts in isolation, students should be deepening their mastery of key concepts and skills at each subsequent grade level, and learning to apply and extend knowledge to new topics, subjects, problems, tasks, and challenges. Teachers require tests and tools that challenge students to demonstrate their conceptual understanding, relate smaller ideas to bigger ones, and show that they grasp and retain what they have learned.

MOVING TOWARD A BROADER RANGE OF ASSESSMENTS

Assessments can be described as falling along a continuum (see figure 9.2), ranging from those that measure bits and pieces of student content knowledge to those that seek to capture student understanding in more integrated and holistic ways. But it is not necessary or even desirable to choose just one approach and reject all others. As I describe in this section, a number of states previously used, or are now creating, school assessment models that combine elements from multiple approaches. These approaches generate a much more detailed and useful picture of student learning than does a single test.

Traditional Multiple-Choice Tests

Traditional multiple-choice tests, whatever their flaws, are a mature technology that offers some distinct advantages. They tend to be reliable, as noted. Also, in comparison to some other forms of assessments, they do not require a lot of time or money to administer, and they generate scores that are familiar to educators. Thus, it is not surprising that a number of states, when given the option of using more sophisticated tests, chose instead to remain with or reinstitute multiple-choice tests with which they were already familiar. One recent advancement in this area is the design and use of computer-adaptive tests, which add a great deal of efficiency to multiple-choice testing. Depending on the student's responses,

FIGURE 9.2 Continuum of assessments

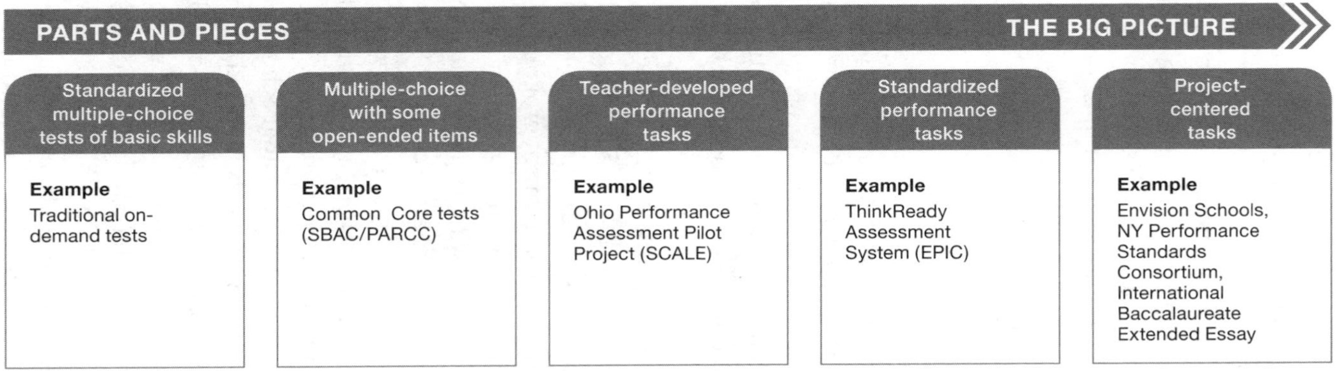

PARTS AND PIECES			THE BIG PICTURE	
Standardized multiple-choice tests of basic skills	Multiple-choice with some open-ended items	Teacher-developed performance tasks	Standardized performance tasks	Project-centered tasks
Example Traditional on-demand tests	**Example** Common Core tests (SBAC/PARCC)	**Example** Ohio Performance Assessment Pilot Project (SCALE)	**Example** ThinkReady Assessment System (EPIC)	**Example** Envision Schools, NY Performance Standards Consortium, International Baccalaureate Extended Essay

the software automatically adjusts the level of difficulty of the questions it poses (after a number of correct answers, it moves on to harder items; too many incorrect responses, and it moves back to easier ones), quickly zeroing in on the student's level of mastery of the given material. Further, the technology makes it a simple matter to include items that test content from previous and subsequent grades, which allows measurement of a very wide distribution of knowledge and skills (from below grade level to far above it) that might exist in any given class or testing group. This method has its own issues as well, but, when used properly, can provide useful information back to schools in a short period of time.

Performance Tasks

Performance tasks today encompass a wide range of formats, requiring students to complete activities that can take anywhere from twenty minutes to two weeks, and that ask them to engage with content that can range from a two-paragraph passage to a whole collection of source documents. Generally speaking, though, most performance tasks can be completed in a few class periods at most.

A number of prominent examples deserve mention.

In 1997, the New York Performance Standards Consortium, a group of New York schools with a history of using performance tasks as a central element in their school-based assessment programs, successfully sued the state of New York to allow the use of performance tasks in lieu of Regents Examinations to meet state testing requirements.[43] Most notable among these schools was Central Park East Secondary School, which had a long and distinguished history of having students present their work to panels consisting of fellow students, teachers, and community members with expertise in the subject matter being presented. Most of these schools were also members of the Coalition of Essential Schools, which advocated for these types of assessment at its over six hundred member schools.

More recently, my colleagues at the Educational Policy Improvement Center (EPIC) and I developed ThinkReady, an assessment of the key cognitive strategies.[44] Its performance tasks—which take anywhere from a few class periods to several weeks (with out-of-class work) to complete—require students to demonstrate skills throughout the assessment in problem formulation, research, interpretation, communication, precision, and accuracy. Teachers use a novice-to-expert scoring guide that tells them where students stand on thinking skills associated with college readiness. The system spans grades 6 through 12 organized around four benchmark levels that represent cognitive skill progression rather than grade level.

The Ohio Performance Assessment Pilot Project created performance-based assessments for use by Ohio educators in grades 3 through 12. Teachers developed tasks in English, mathematics, science, social studies, and career and technical pathways. The tasks were field tested and piloted and then refined. Tasks were scored online and at in-person scoring sessions. They were then made publicly available online.[45]

New Hampshire is in the process of developing common statewide performance tasks that will be included within a comprehensive state assessment system in combination with standardized assessments from the Smarter Balanced Assessment Consortium (SBAC).[46] The tasks will be based on college- and career-ready competencies across major academic disciplines, including the Common Core–aligned competencies for English language arts, literacy, and mathematics, as well as New Hampshire's K–12 Model Science Competencies. Performance tasks are being developed for elementary, middle, and high school grade spans. They will be used to compare student performance across the state in areas not tested by SBAC, such as the ability to apply learning strategies to complex tasks.

Each performance task will be a complex curriculum-embedded assignment involving multiple steps that require students to use metacognitive learning skills. As a result, student performance will reflect the depth of what students have learned and their ability to apply that learning as well. Work with pilot districts is entering its second year with plans to scale up statewide in subsequent years.

New Hampshire also partnered with the Center for Collaborative Education and the National Center for the Improvement of Educational Assessment to develop the Performance Assessment for Competency Education, or PACE, designed to measure student mastery of college- and career-ready competencies.[47] PACE includes a web-based bank of common and locally designed performance tasks, to be supplemented with regional scoring sessions and local district peer-review audits.

Colorado, Kansas, and Mississippi have partnered with the Center for Educational Testing and Evaluation at the University of Kansas to form the Career Pathways Collaborative. The partnership's Career Pathways Assessment System tests general work-readiness skills such as problem solving and critical thinking, as well as the skills needed in specific career pathways.[48] It uses a mix of multiple-choice questions and classroom-based performance tasks to identify student competency in a chosen career pathway and the students' readiness for postsecondary education, an apprenticeship, or an entry-level job in that area of interest.

Project-Centered Assessment

Much like performance tasks, project-centered assessment engages students in open-ended, challenging problems.[49] The differences between the two approaches have to do mainly with their scope, complexity, and the time and resources each requires. Projects tend to involve lengthier, multistep activities, such as the extended essay required for the International Baccalaureate diploma, or assignments that conclude with a major student presentation of a significant project or piece of research.

An example of this longer-term project can be found at Envision Schools, a secondary-level charter school network in the San Francisco area, where this kind of assessment is a central feature of its instructional program. The school requires students to conduct semester- or year-long projects that culminate in a series of products and a presentation that undergoes formal review by teachers and peers.[50] A student or team of students might undertake an investigation of, say, locally sourced food. This might involve researching where the food they eat comes from, what proportion of the price represents transportation, how dependent they are on other parts of the country for their food, what choices they could make if they wished to eat more locally produced food, what the economic implications of doing so would be, whether doing so could cause economic disruption in other parts of the country as an unintended consequence, and so on. The project would then be presented to the class and evaluated by the teacher using a scoring guide that includes ratings for content knowledge in mathematics and economics; the quality of argumentation; the appropriateness of information sources cited; the quality and logic of the conclusions reached; and overall precision, accuracy, and attention to detail.

Another well-known example is the Summit Public Schools network of charter schools, also located in the Bay Area.[51] While Summit requires students to master high-level academic standards and cognitive skills, the specific topics they study and the particular ways in which they are assessed are personalized, planned out according to their needs and interests. The school's schedule provides students ample time to work individually and in groups on projects that address key content in the core subject areas. In the process, students assemble digital portfolios of their work, providing evidence that they have developed important cognitive skills (including specific "habits of success," the metacognitive learning skills associated with readiness for college and career), acquired essential content knowledge, and learned how to apply that knowledge across a range of academic and real-world contexts. Ultimately, the goal is for students to present projects and products that can withstand public critique and are potentially publishable.

Collections of Evidence

Strictly speaking, collections of evidence are not assessments at all. Rather, they are a way to organize and review results of a broad range of assessments, so that educators can make accurate decisions about student readiness for academic advancement, high school graduation, or postsecondary programs of study.[52]

For example, New Hampshire recently introduced a technology portfolio for graduation that allows students to collect evidence to show how they have met standards in this field. The New York Performance Standards Consortium received a state-approved waiver allowing its students to complete a graduation portfolio in lieu of some of New York's Regents Examination requirements. Students must compile a set of ambitious performance tasks, including a scientific investigation, a mathematical model, a literary analysis, and a history/social science research paper, sometimes augmented with other tasks such as an arts demonstration or analyses of a community service or internship experience. All of these are measured against academic standards and are evaluated using high-quality scoring rubrics.

The state of Kentucky implemented a similar approach in 1992. The Kentucky Instructional Results Information System incorporated information from several assessment sources, including multiple-choice and short-essay questions, performance "events" requiring students to solve applied problems, and collections of students' best work in writing and mathematics.[53] (Students were also assessed in reading, social science, science, arts and humanities, and practical living/vocational studies.) The writing assessment, which continued until 2012, was especially rigorous: in grades 4, 7, and 12, students submitted three or four pieces of written work to be evaluated, and in grades 5, 8, and 12 they completed on-demand writing tasks, with teachers assessing their command of several genres, including reflective essays, expressive or literary work, and writing that uses information to persuade an audience.

Such approaches demonstrate the feasibility of a richer and more nuanced system of assessments. States learned many lessons over the past two decades that can now support multiple-measure approaches, and these lessons ought to be remembered and incorporated into the assessment development activities occurring in states as a result of ESSA.

Other Assessment Innovations

Earlier this decade, the Asia Society commissioned the RAND Corporation to produce an overview of models and methods for measuring twenty-first-century competencies.[54] The resulting report describes a number of models that closely map onto the range of assessments described in figure 9.2. However, it also describes "cutting-edge measures" such as assessments of higher-order thinking used by the Program for International Student Assessment (PISA).

First administered in 2000, PISA is designed to compare student performance among member countries. Coordinated by the Organization for Economic Cooperation and Development and administered every three years to randomly selected fifteen-year-olds, it assesses knowledge and skills in mathematics, reading, and science. It is perhaps best known for its emphasis on problem-solving skills and other more complex (sometimes referred to as "hard-to-measure") cognitive processes, which it gauges through the use of innovative types of test items.[55]

In 2015, for example, PISA introduced an online assessment of performance on tasks that require collaborative problem solving. Through interactions with a digital avatar (simulating a partner the student has to work with on a project), test takers demonstrate their skills in establishing and maintaining a shared understanding of a problem, taking appropriate action to solve it, and establishing and maintaining team organization. Students encounter multiple scenarios, in which the problem type, the context, the information available, and the relationships among group members all vary. Scores are based on responses to the computer program's prompts and actions. Early evidence suggests that this method is quite effective in distinguishing different collaborative problem-solving skill levels and competencies.

Further, national testing organizations such as ACT and the College Board, makers of the SAT, have updated their systems of exams to keep them in step with recent research on the knowledge and thinking skills that students need to succeed in college.[56] However, these tests do not involve student-generated work products beyond an optional essay. ACT has introduced Aspire, a series of summative, interim, and classroom exams and optional measures of metacognitive skills that are designed to determine whether students are on a path to college and career readiness from third grade on.[57] And the redesigned SAT, which rolled out in spring 2016, incorporates a series of changes that require test takers to cite evidence to a greater degree when making claims, as well as to more deeply understand what they are reading.[58]

Metacognitive Learning Strategies Assessments

Metacognitive learning strategies are the things students do to enable and activate thinking, remembering, understanding, and information processing more generally.[59] Metacognition occurs when learners demonstrate awareness of their own thinking, then monitor and analyze their thinking, recognize when they are having trouble, and adjust their learning strategies.

Metacognitive skills often contribute as much or even more than subject-specific content knowledge to student success in college. When faced with challenging new coursework, students with highly developed learning strategies tend to have an important advantage over peers who can only learn procedurally (i.e., by following directions). Therefore, it is important to assess learning skills as well as content knowledge. Ideally, results from learning-skill assessments can provide teachers with useful insights into why students might be having trouble learning certain material or completing a particular assignment.

However, measures of these skills are subject to their own set of criticisms. For example, many rely on student self-reports (e.g., questionnaires asking what was easy or difficult about an assignment or surveying a student's attitude toward the content). Measurement experts also point out that, while they may not be intended for this purpose, self-reports can easily lead teachers to make character judgments about students, bringing an unnecessary source of bias into the classroom.[60] Finally, the measurement properties of many early instruments in this area have been somewhat suspect, particularly when it comes to reliability. In short, while assessments of metacognition can be useful, educators and policy makers have good reason to take care in their use and in the interpretation of results.

Still, it is beyond dispute that many educators and, increasingly, policy makers are taking a closer look at such measures, excited by their potential to help narrow the achievement gap for underperforming students. For example, public interest in the role that perseverance, determination, tenacity, and grit can play in learning has surged.[61] Similarly, the notion of academic mind-set has struck a chord with many practitioners who see evidence daily that students who can rely on sustained effort more than innate aptitude in a subject are able to perform better.[62] And researchers are now pursuing numerous studies of students' use of study skills, time-management strategies, and goal-setting capabilities.

In large part, what makes these metacognitive skills so appealing is the recognition that such things can be taught and learned, while the evidence suggests that all are important for success in and beyond school.[63]

One of the best-known assessment tools in this area is Angela Duckworth's Grit Index, which consists of a dozen questions that students can quickly complete.[64] These questions help predict the likelihood of completing high school or doing well in situations that require sustained focus and effort. While Duckworth herself is quick to point out the limitations of the index and of the notion of grit in isolation from other factors, many educators have nonetheless been drawn to the concept as a potential tool to help enhance student success.[65] Another tool, Carol Dweck's Growth Mindset program, helps learners understand and change the way they think about how they approach learning.[66] The program focuses on teaching students that their attitude toward a subject is as important as any native ability they have in it.

EPIC's CampusReady instrument is designed to assess self-perceptions of college and career readiness in each of the four keys described previously.[67] It touches on many metacognitive learning skills and mind-sets, as well as a number of other attitudes, habits, behaviors, and beliefs necessary to succeed at postsecondary studies.

The California Office to Reform Education (CORE) districts began incorporating measures of social/emotional learning into their accountability systems in the 2014–15 academic year.[68] Four measures were piloted across twenty CORE schools to measure growth mind-set, self-efficacy, self-management, and social awareness. For each metacognitive assessment, one version was selected from existing measures, while the other was developed in partnership with methodological experts in an effort to improve upon existing measures. Early results suggest these measures contribute to predicting academic performance.[69]

While metacognitive measures are now receiving a great deal of attention, they still face a range of challenges to widespread use. Perhaps the greatest obstacle is that most rely on self-reported information, which is subject to social desirability bias. In other words, even if no stakes are attached to the assessment, respondents tend to give answers they believe people want to see.

Over time, however, students can be encouraged to provide more honest self-assessments, particularly if they know they will not be punished or rewarded exclusively based on their responses, and self-reported data can also be triangulated against test scores to provide more insight into why students performed as they did.[70] Information of this sort is best used longitudinally, to determine if students are developing the learning strategies and mind-sets necessary to be successful lifelong learners. Such assessments can help enhance learner success and enable deeper learning, but they should not be overemphasized or misused for high-stakes purposes.

TOWARD A SYSTEM OF ASSESSMENTS

Under ESSA, it may be possible for states and districts to implement a combination of measures that not only meet their accountability needs but also provide students, teachers, schools, and postsecondary institutions with valid information that empowers them to make wise educational decisions.[71]

Today's resurgent interest in multiple measures, coupled with new attention to the value of metacognitive learning skills, invites progress toward what I call a "system of assessments"—a comprehensive approach that draws from multiple sources to develop a holistic picture of student knowledge and skills in all of the areas that make a real difference for college, career, and life success.[72]

For example, such a system might include some use of the kinds of standardized achievement tests and college admission tests that dominated the NCLB era, as well as familiar data such as high school grades and GPA. But it would also incorporate other sources of data with stronger validity, such as assessment of research papers and capstone projects; students' assessments of their own key learning skills over multiple years; indicators of perseverance and goal focus as evidenced by completion of complex projects; and teachers' judgments of student progress in developing a range of key learning skills.

Of course, there will be challenges involved in assessing deeper learning.

Although today's information technologies are sophisticated and efficient enough to manage the complex information generated by a system of assessments, it will be no easy task to do so successfully. And while some states, researchers, and testing organizations are seeking to develop new methods to assess deeper learning skills on a large scale, none have yet cracked the code to produce an assessment that can be scored in an automated fashion, at costs that are in line with what states now spend on testing.

Indeed, scoring may be the holy grail of performance assessment of deeper learning. Until and unless designers can devise better ways to score complex student work, either by teachers or externally, higher-order and deeper learning skills will continue to be neglected by the designers of large-scale statewide assessments, at least those used for high-stakes accountability purposes.

As long as the primary purpose of assessments is to reach judgments about students, schools, and teachers' performance, the desire for reliable and efficient tests will continue to trump concerns about validity and value. Thankfully, though, one important lesson to emerge from No Child Left Behind—and its decade-long rush to judge the quality of individual schools—is that not all assessments are, or should be, summative. In fact, the majority of the assessment that goes on every day in schools is designed not to hold anybody accountable but to help people make immediate decisions about how to improve student performance and teaching practice.

While it will always be important to know how well schools are teaching foundational skills in English language arts and mathematics, the pursuit of deeper learning will require a much greater emphasis on formative assessments. These signal what students must do to become ready for college and careers, including the development of metacognitive learning skills—about which selected-response tests provide no information at all.

In fact, skills such as persistence, goal focus, attention to detail, investigation, and information synthesis are likely to be the most important for career success in the coming decades. It will become increasingly critical for young people to learn how to cope with college assignments or work tasks that do not have one right answer, that require them to gather new information and make judgments, and that may have no simple or obvious solution. Such integrative and applied skills can be assessed, and they can be assessed most usefully by way of a system of assessments. They neither can nor should be measured at the granular level that is the focus of most standardized tests.

10

Deeper Learning in the Age of ESSA

Ideas and Recommendations

Rafael Heller, Rebecca E. Wolfe,
and Adria Steinberg

WHEN THE EVERY STUDENT SUCCEEDS ACT (ESSA) was signed into law, its most immediate effect was to shift the balance of power in educational policy making, reining in much of the federal government's authority in this area and returning it to the state level.

To many of us working to promote deeper learning in K–12 education, that came as welcome news. No longer are states obligated to pursue the narrow set of educational goals and reform strategies that federal officials established on their behalf, first with No Child Left Behind (NCLB), under President Bush, and then with Race to the Top (RTTT), under President Obama. Now they can adopt more ambitious and equitable agendas for school improvement, deciding for themselves how best to prepare young people for college, careers, and civic life.

However, if the present moment holds great promise, so too does it pose great challenges. Whatever the flaws of NCLB and RTTT, those initiatives also created a sense of predictability in the world of school reform. For more than a dozen years, they made it clear who held the greatest influence over educational policy making (i.e., the leaders and staff of the House and Senate education committees and the top brass at the U.S. Department of Education), and they guaranteed that, in every part of the country, policy debates would be dominated by the same few topics (standards, testing, accountability, and a handful of others).

But now that the power to direct the course of school reform has been thrown open to fifty states, those certainties have evaporated. Each state has its own large and complex cast of players (including state superintendents, governors, legislatures, boards of education, big-city mayors, local school committees, university presidents, business leaders, local philanthropists, community activists, and others). Further, each is focused on its own local priorities (anything from strengthening standards and accountability systems to recruiting new teachers, improving rural schools, funding afterschool programs, and addressing crises such as the recent rise in opiate addiction among teenagers).

It could take months, if not years, for local educators and policy makers to create the kinds of political coalitions, find the kinds of resources, and identify the kinds of reforms that will allow them to take full advantage of the authority that ESSA provides. Similarly, it will take time for policy groups—Jobs for the Future (JFF) included—to figure out how best to assist states as they chart a new course for school improvement.

If each state has its own political culture, key policy players, and distinct needs and priorities, then how might supporting organizations provide useful guidance? Under NCLB and RTTT, policy advocates could focus on crafting and advocating for a small set of federal recommendations, and if those ideas made it into law, the effects would be felt in every part of the country. But what kinds of recommendations can and should we offer today, now that every state and district appears to be a policy island unto itself?

Even in the post-NCLB era, the federal government still wields significant influence over state policy making, given the funding it provides, the guidelines and conditions it attaches to that funding, and its regulatory powers. Thus, a few of the following recommendations focus on things that Congress and the U.S. Department of Education can do to support the goals of deeper learning. For the most part, though, we take our audience to be made up of people working at the state and district levels—such as state chiefs, governors, teachers and administrators, board of education members, and mayors—who may be looking for recommendations that they can adapt to fit their local needs and contexts. With that in mind, we have tried to frame these ideas in ways that are general enough to be relevant across many states but specific enough to be useful to individual policy makers and educational leaders as they decide how best to promote deeper learning.

Many of these ideas were contributed by the authors of the preceding chapters, and we developed the rest through consultations with dozens of other researchers, policy makers, and practitioners across the country. All of them are ideas that we find to be supported by the current knowledge base in fields such as cognitive and developmental psychology, the sociology of education, and the history of public schooling in the United States, as well as by recent research into topics covered in this volume—such as work-based learning, civic education, educational equity, the teaching of English learners, the teaching of students with disabilities, teacher development, organizational change, and the assessment of student learning. And all of them are meant to help answer this question: To provide all students with meaningful opportunities to learn deeply, what strategies for high school improvement should education leaders consider moving to the top of the policy agenda?

We have arranged our recommendations into the three themes that organize this book.

THE PURPOSES AND GOALS OF SECONDARY EDUCATION

As Jal Mehta and Sarah Fine discuss in chapter 1, the goals of deeper learning are not new to American education. For at least a century, reformers have wrestled back and forth over the academic, civic, and economic purposes of public schooling, as well as the responsibility to support young people's individual and social development, their physical and mental health, and even their personal hygiene.

What does strike Mehta and Fine as new is the concerted effort now under way—often under the banner of deeper learning—to marry the equity-driven mission implied by phrases like "No Child Left Behind" and "Every Student Succeeds" with a set of educational goals and practices that have long been reserved for a small, relatively affluent portion of the student population. Some young people—including many of those lucky enough to attend elite private schools or public high schools located in wealthy districts—have always enjoyed opportunities to engage in sophisticated classroom discussions and debates; investigate complex topics of their own choosing; receive thoughtful feedback on their projects, presentations, and written work; express themselves through music and art; explore their college and career options; and so on. But if school reformers can make significant progress in scaling up these sorts of opportunities and extending them to all students, then that truly will be something new and wonderful under the sun.

We recommend that states and districts:

1. *Define clear and specific goals for college, career, and civic readiness.*

In recent years, a number of states have created or revised their definitions of college and career readiness, and, in a few cases, civic readiness as well. For those that have not done so, it will likely be worth the modest investment that such efforts tend to require. States' academic standards documents often highlight the specific knowledge and skills (particularly in math and the English language arts) that students will need in order to prepare for the academic demands of first-year college courses. However, to have a well-informed debate about local priorities for school reform, policy leaders should start from a comprehensive definition of what it means to become ready for life after high school—with attention to the broad range of academic, personal, and social skills that researchers have found to be important.

2. *Create stronger partnerships and smoother transitions between high school and higher education.*

For individual students to be truly "college ready" by the time they leave high school, they need to be able to make a smooth and successful transition from secondary to postsecondary education. One promising way to facilitate that transition is to bring together high school and college faculty to co-design courses, ensuring that the material studied in twelfth grade aligns well with the material studied in the first year of college. Another is to invest in advising programs that start preparing students (particularly first-generation college students) for college-going long before senior year and that continue into students' first year on campus. Also promising are early assessment systems, run by higher education, that let students in grades 9 through 12 know where they stand in relation to college entrance standards. Finally, early college and dual enrollment options have been found to be effective in boosting college degree completion. (In some states, though, policies and funding formulas will need to be revised to facilitate such agreements and make them attractive to both the secondary and postsecondary sectors.)

3. *Create incentives for employers and school systems to focus on career readiness.*

Today, work-based learning is enjoying a renaissance in much of the United States, with strong support not only from the business community but also from the federal government and state policy makers, both Democratic and Republican. Advocates for deeper learning should understand that the current generation of investments in career readiness is designed to provide students with meaningful opportunities to work and/or pursue higher learning, and not to steer them into purely vocational tracks. And as Nancy Hoffman argues in chapter 2, preparing for working life can be one of the most powerful ways for young people to learn deeply. We strongly recommend that states and the federal government create incentives for employers and the education sector to invest in work-based deeper learning, helping it to gain a stronger foothold throughout the country. Numerous strategies appear to be promising, such as providing tax credits to businesses that offer high-quality internships and apprenticeships; providing subsidies to schools and industries that share state-of-the-art equipment and training facilities; offering academic credit for internships; and designing new career education programs based on the analysis of regional labor market trends.

4. *Give equal weight to the civic mission of public schooling.*

With political discourse more polarized than it has been in decades, it is particularly important today to empower young people to follow current events, evaluate the quality of news sources, engage in reasoned debate, analyze competing views on controversial topics, serve responsibly on juries, and otherwise contribute to the public good. Specifically, states and districts should develop improved civics curricula and assessments of civic learning. A number of states have required (or have considered requiring) all high school students to pass a civics test, perhaps modeled after the citizenship test administered by the Immigration and Naturalization Service. However, requiring just the memorization of laws, Constitutional amendments, the branches of government, and such—culminating in fact-heavy, multiple-choice tests—is unlikely to have a significant effect on civic knowledge and participation, as Peter Levine and Kei Kawashima-Ginsberg argue in chapter 3. A more useful approach would be for states to create more sophisticated curricula that encourage interdisciplinary work, community service learning projects, and internships focused on public service, for example, as well as related assessments, encouraging students not only to learn critical content but also to demonstrate their understanding through authentic performance tasks such as debating an issue of public importance, analyzing a legal controversy, or participating in a mock jury.

ACCESS AND OPPORTUNITY

During the NCLB era, enormous amounts of attention were devoted to standards, accountability, teacher quality, and a handful of other topics in K–12 education. In turn, that left relatively little funding or space on the policy agenda for other means of promoting equity, such as efforts to create new school and community services in distressed neighborhoods, to reinvest in college and career advising, and to ensure that basic skills instruction does not crowd out opportunities to learn higher-order skills and advanced content. Under ESSA, however, states and districts have an opportunity to rethink their priorities and, if they choose, to direct targeted attention and resources to the students who need them most, including youth from low-income backgrounds, English language learners, and individuals with disabilities. We urge federal, state, and district leaders to:

1. *Provide the supports that* all students *need in order to learn deeply.*
    In 2013, as Pedro Noguera, Linda Darling-Hammond, and Diane Friedlaender note in chapter 4, the National Commission on Excellence and

Equity recommended that states and districts take a number of steps to strengthen the educational opportunities available to underserved children. These include, for example, changing salary structures and working conditions to encourage more seasoned and effective teachers to work in low-income neighborhoods, as well as revising state accountability systems to hold policy makers responsible for ensuring that every school has sufficient resources to carry out its core functions. However, as the authors argue in this volume, states and districts should go farther, taking many other proactive steps to make schooling more equitable. For example, states should adopt strategies, such as weighted student formulas, that fund schools on the basis of realistic estimates of the costs of educating students who live in poverty and/or have other risk factors. And states and the federal government should ramp up funding for school models that ensure students in high-need communities receive so-called "wraparound" services, including health and mental health care, summer learning opportunities, college and career advising, and more.

2. *Provide the specific kinds of support that* students with disabilities *need in order to learn deeply.*

Students with disabilities sometimes require specialized instruction and social, emotional, or behavioral supports that general education teachers cannot provide in mainstream classrooms. But when schools make modest investments in particular kinds of professional development, diagnostic tools, and assessment resources, teachers can help most students with disabilities—including the nearly four million enrolled in general education classes in regular public schools—to meet the goals of deeper learning. (Further, these supports tend to benefit all learners, given how common it is for all students, with or without identified disabilities, to struggle with some aspect of cognitive processing, such as memory or attention.) Relevant policy strategies have been endorsed widely by researchers and practitioners in the field of special education, note Sharon Vaughn, Louis Danielson, Rebecca Zumeta Edmonds, and Lynn Holdheide—the coauthors of chapter 5. They urge local and state policy makers to ensure that teacher licensure requirements, professional standards, and job descriptions assign clear responsibility to general education teachers for providing effective instruction to students with disabilities, and to ensure that those teachers receive the training and support they need to do so. State and local policy also can create helpful incentives, such as evaluation systems that reward teachers for differentiating instruction. In addition, states should implement college- and career-readiness assessments that address the full range of deeper learning competencies and include accommodations that enable students with disabilities to show what they know and can do.

3. *Provide the specific kinds of support that* English language learners *need in order to learn deeply.*

As Patricia Gándara notes in chapter 6, research findings strongly suggest that if the goal is to help these students achieve at high levels—and also become proficient in English—then bilingual and dual language instruction tend to be the most effective approaches. Federal incentives would do much to help: the federal government should declare once and for all that immigrant children are a net asset to the nation and their strengths should be celebrated. For example, a national "seal of biliteracy" could be awarded to students who demonstrate high proficiency in two or more languages upon high school or college graduation—a skill of great interest to college admissions officers and employers. (Twenty-three states already have such a certification, and several more are considering it.) Perhaps most important, policy makers can support efforts to recruit highly trained, highly skilled, bilingual teachers, particularly in states and districts that enroll significant numbers of English language learners. Further, it is critically important that states and districts discontinue the use of English-language tests to assess the academic skills of students who are not yet fluent in that language. Alternatives include giving students more time to acquire English before testing them in English, reducing the stakes attached to such tests, assessing students' academic skills in their native language, and/or offering alternative assessments while students are still learning English.

SCHOOL IMPROVEMENT FOR DEEPER LEARNING

Under NCLB and the education reform approach embodied by initiatives like Race to the Top, the federal government invested more than a dozen years and many billions of dollars on efforts to change the incentive systems that drive educators' behavior, by creating new pressures on them to improve their performance (as measured by gains on student test scores) and by rewarding them for implementing specific reforms. But as critics often note, the government made comparatively few investments during those years in efforts to strengthen educators' *capacity* to do these things.

ESSA provides states with far greater flexibility to define their own strategies for school improvement. Reformers everywhere are calling for new efforts to build educators' capacity to provide effective instruction, leadership, mentoring, professional development, student support services, and more. And yet, the question remains: What can states *do* to improve their school systems in tangible, effective ways?

None of the authors of the previous chapters is a Pollyanna. All of them recognize that educational change (whether at the level of the state, district, school, or classroom) is tough work. But—along with many of the dozens of others with whom we've consulted in recent months—they do tend to make similar and overlapping recommendations about the kinds of professional and institutional capacity building that are needed, as well as the most promising ways for policy makers and education leaders to proceed:

1. *Create the conditions under which teachers can learn and improve.*

Teacher performance incentives may have a useful place in public education. However, after years of investment in teacher evaluation systems, merit-pay programs, and related reform strategies with mixed or limited results, states and districts ought to shift the balance toward efforts to help teachers build the kinds of professional knowledge and skill that Magdalene Lampert describes in chapter 7. For example, they should invest in the creation of high-quality teacher preparation, induction, and residency programs, exposing new teachers whenever possible to classrooms and schools that provide powerful examples of deeper teaching and learning. To make such training affordable, federal, state, and district policy makers should invest in service scholarships for a diverse pool of talented recruits who can commit to working in high-need schools and fields for a significant length of time, and they should support release time for accomplished mentors to coach beginning teachers. Equally important as improving preservice training is providing real support for ongoing professional development, such as participation in professional networks, career ladders, peer evaluation programs, and instructional coaching that focuses on deeper teaching within and across content areas. Policy makers also should make it a high priority to redesign schedules and staffing patterns in ways that carve out more time for teachers to engage in common planning, peer observations, and the other activities described above.

2. *Invest in the capacity of school districts.*

While policy makers and foundation leaders may have good reason to fund the development of new school models and individual charter schools and networks, they should not overlook the critical roles that district offices play in empowering schools to improve (or, for that matter, blocking their efforts to do so). Increasingly, over the past few decades, districts have been called upon to provide services (in support of teaching, professional development, and instructional leadership, for example) that go well beyond the sorts of record-keeping and compliance functions they were originally designed to manage, as Meredith Honig and Lydia Rainey explain in chapter 8. However, most central offices are starved for the resources needed to hire staff with the relevant expertise, much less to hire enough staff to do the given work. At a time when few states and districts have funds to spare, it may be tempting to direct scarce resources elsewhere. However, policy makers should understand that, if they continue to neglect district offices, they will undermine whatever improvements they hope to make at the school and classroom levels.

3. *Create assessment and accountability systems that support deeper teaching and learning.*

Recent years have seen a surge in public and political opposition to frequent high-stakes testing in the nation's schools. Today, "opt-out" movements are active across the country, and several states have seen significant declines in the numbers of students showing up for annual standardized exams. But amid the uproar over test-based accountability, some promising signs of bipartisan consensus have emerged as well. In particular, many recognize the value of formative, low-stakes assessments to help students keep track of their own progress and to let teachers know how best to help them. To the extent that assessments are used for summative purposes—for example, to determine grades and award diplomas—many reformers now advocate for a renewed focus on the sorts of performance assessments that a number of states developed and piloted in the 1990s and early 2000s, before NCLB created a market for simpler, standardized tests. Currently in development in numerous districts and many states, such assessments call upon students to demonstrate their knowledge and skills by writing papers, giving presentations, solving problems, making and defending arguments, and so on. These kinds of systems can be complicated to set up, and they require up-front and ongoing investments to ensure that teachers score them fairly and reliably. And yet, as David Conley describes in chapter 9, they also tend to push students to do high-quality work and present valuable professional development opportunities for the teachers involved in designing and evaluating the assessments.

Today, assessment and accountability remain perhaps the hottest topics in educational policy, both on Capitol Hill and in state capitals across the country, and we expect that debates in this area will evolve considerably over the coming months. Hence, we have refrained from giving highly specific recommendations, which would likely become obsolete by the time this book hits the shelves. In this area, our only advice is this: If—as we hope—school systems become less reliant on standardized, multiple-choice achievement tests, and if they turn to a broader range of measures, including formative and performance assessments, then patience will be school reformers' greatest virtue. Nothing will matter more to the quality of K–12 education than to figure out ways to improve assessments and accountability; but those efforts will not be easy, and they cannot be rushed.

A FINAL WORD

As we said in the introduction to this book, our goal is not to promote a particular school model, or to trumpet a particular set of instructional practices, or to persuade readers to adopt the terminology of deeper learning. After a decade and a half of NCLB, we know this is no time for top-down mandates or blanket recommendations. We also know that schools and classrooms function best when they are governed by the intelligence and good sense of well-prepared educators. And we know that states and districts tend to make better decisions when compelled to respond to local interests and needs, and not to regulations imposed from above.

Like many others in K–12 education, we also worry that by returning so much authority to the states, ESSA could do more harm than good. Now that the federal government has less power to peer into individual schools and classrooms and to insist that all children be accounted for, there is real danger once again that many students—especially poor children and children of color—will become invisible to state and district leaders, as they often were prior to NCLB. Moreover, many of the state and district agencies that ESSA relies on to lead the next generation of school improvement efforts have spent the past decade and a half scrambling to comply with federal requirements, even while coping with staff shortages and budget cuts. They may be well positioned to implement bold new educational strategies, but they are not necessarily well *equipped* to do so.

But we take comfort in the argument that Jal Mehta and Sarah Fine advance in chapter 1: in the long run, educational decision making at the state and local levels will be shaped more powerfully by the demands of the contemporary world than by the lingering bigotries of the previous century. And it is clear today that economic and social conditions are pushing very strongly toward higher expectations for all children and toward more equal opportunities for them to learn deeply. We are optimistic that the public demand for such an education will only increase, educators' capacity to provide it will only grow, and political support for it will only strengthen.

NOTES

Foreword

1. J. W. Pellegrino and M. Hilton, eds., *Education for Life and Work: Developing Transferable Knowledge and Skills in the 21st Century* (Washington, DC: National Academies Press, 2012).

Introduction

1. See, for example, "What Parents Should Know," Common Core State Standards Initiative, www.corestandards.org/what-parents-should-know; also see *Making College and Career Readiness the Mission for High Schools: A Guide for State Policymakers* (Washington, DC: Achieve and the Education Trust, 2008).

2. D. T. Conley, *Four Keys to College Readiness* (New York: John Wiley & Sons, 2017); D. T. Conley, *College Knowledge: What It Really Takes for Students to Succeed and What We Can Do to Get Them Ready* (New York: John Wiley & Sons, 2008).

3. A. Carnevale, A. Hanson, and A. Gulish, *Failure to Launch: Structural Shift and the New Lost Generation* (Washington, DC: Georgetown University Center on Education and the Workforce, 2013); R. Halpern, *Youth, Education, and the Role of Society: Rethinking Learning in the High School Years* (Cambridge, MA: Harvard Education Press, 2013); J. Heckman et al., "The Effects of Cognitive and Noncognitive Abilities on Labor Market Outcomes and Social Behavior," *Journal of Labor Economics* 24, no. 3 (2006); R. Murnane and F. Levy, *Teaching the New Basic Skills: Principles for Educating Children to Thrive in a Changing Economy* (New York: The Free Press, 1996).

4. J. D. Bransford, A. L. Brown, and R. R. Cocking, *How People Learn: Brain, Mind, Experience, and School* (Washington, DC: National Academy Press, 1999); J. A. Durlak et al., "The Impact of Enhancing Students' Social and Emotional Learning: A Meta-Analysis of School-Based Universal Interventions," *Child Development* 82 (2011): 405–32; C. Dweck, G. Walton, and G. Cohen, *Academic Tenacity: Mindsets and Skills That Promote Long-Term Learning* (Seattle, WA: Gates Foundation, 2011); C. Farrington et al., *Teaching Adolescents to Become Learners: The Role of Noncognitive Factors in Shaping School Performance* (Chicago, IL: Consortium on Chicago School Research, 2012); J. Pellegrino and M. Hilton, eds., *Education for Life and Work: Developing Transferable Knowledge and Skills in the 21st Century* (Washington, DC: National Academies Press, 2012).

5. G. Duncan and R. Murnane, *Restoring Opportunity: The Crisis of Inequality and the Challenge for American Education* (Cambridge, MA: Harvard Education Press, 2013); R. D. Putnam, *Our Kids: The American Dream in Crisis* (New York: Simon & Schuster, 2015); M. Leachman et al., *Most States Have Cut School Funding, and Some Continue Cutting* (Washington, DC: Center on Budget and Policy Priorities, 2016); D. Sciarra and M. Hunter, "Resource Accountability: Enforcing State Responsibilities for Sufficient and Equitable Resources Used Effectively to Provide All Students a Quality Education," *Education Policy Analysis Archives* 23, no. 21 (2015); N. Ushomirsky and D. Williams, *Funding Gaps 2015: Too Many States Still Spend Less on Educating Students Who Need the Most* (Washington, DC: The Education Trust, 2015).

6. D. Tyack, *The One Best System: A History of American Urban Education* (Cambridge, MA: Harvard University Press, 1974).

Chapter 1

1. R. Kegan, "Hidden Curriculum of Adult Life: An Adult Development Perspective," in *Stockholm Lecture Series in Educology: Adult Development in Post-Industrial Society and Working Life*, ed. T. Hagstrom (Stockholm: Stockholm University, Department of Education, 2003).

2. M. Levinson, *No Citizen Left Behind* (Cambridge, MA: Harvard University Press, 2012).

3. R. Murnane and F. Levy, *Teaching the New Basic Skills* (New York: Free Press, 1996); B. Trilling and C. Fadel, *21st Century Skills: Learning for Life in Our Times* (San Francisco, CA: Jossey-Bass, 2009).

4. D. K. Cohen, "Teaching Practice: Plus Ça Change," in *Contributing to Educational Change: Perspectives on Research and Practice*, ed. P. W. Jackson (Berkeley,

CA: McCutchan, 1988); R. S. Lynd and H. M. Lynd, *Middletown: A Study in American Culture* (New York: Harcourt, Brace & Company, 1929); J. M. Rice, *The Public School System of the United States* (New York: The Century Co., 1893).

5. J. Anyon, "Social Class and School Knowledge," *Curriculum Inquiry* 1, no. 1 (1981); J. Oakes, *Keeping Track: How Schools Structure Inequality* (New Haven, CT: Yale University Press, 1985).

6. *Middle Class or Middle of the Pack? What Can We Learn from Benchmarking U.S. Schools Against the World's Best?* (New York: America Achieves, 2013); H. L. Fleischman et al., *Highlights from PISA 2009: Performance of U.S. 15-Year-Old Students in Reading, Mathematics, and Science Literacy in an International Context* (Washington, DC: U.S. Department of Education, National Center for Education Statistics, 2010).

7. E. Yazzie-Mintz, *Charting the Path from Engagement to Achievement: A Report on the 2009 High School Survey of Student Engagement* (Bloomington, IN: Center for Evaluation and Education Policy at Indiana University, 2010).

8. V. Perrone, "Why Do We Need a Pedagogy of Understanding?" in *Teaching for Understanding*, ed. M. Stone Wiske (San Francisco, CA: Jossey-Bass, 1998), 14.

9. Cisco Systems, Inc., *Equipping Every Learner for the 21st Century* (San Jose, CA: Cisco Systems, 2008).

10. L. Cuban, *How Teachers Taught: Constancy and Change in American Classrooms 1890–1990*, 2nd ed. (New York: Teachers College Press, 1993); F. Wirt and M. Kirst, *Schools in Conflict: The Politics of Education* (Berkeley, CA: McCutchan, 1982).

11. P. Graham, *Schooling America: How the Public Schools Meet the Nation's Changing Needs* (New York: Oxford University Press, 2007).

12. R. Elmore and E. City, "Beyond Schools," *Education Week* 30, no. 31 (2011).

13. J. Mehta, R. Schwartz, and F. Hess, *The Futures of School Reform* (Cambridge, MA: Harvard Education Press, 2012).

14. The William and Flora Hewlett Foundation, *Deeper Learning Defined* (Menlo Park, CA: Hewlett Foundation, 2013).

15. J. Pellegrino and M. Hilton, eds., *Education for Life and Work: Developing Transferable Knowledge and Skills in the 21st Century* (Washington, DC: National Academies Press, 2012); J. D. Bransford, A. L. Brown, and R. R. Cocking, *How People Learn: Brain, Mind, Experience and School* (Washington, DC: National Academy Press, 1999); M. S. Wiske, ed., *Teaching for Understanding* (San Francisco, CA: Jossey-Bass, 1998).

16. This idea relates to Jerome S. Bruner's notion that to truly understand a domain one must understand the structure of how that field organizes its

knowledge. This kind of epistemological understanding, he argues, is critical to building the conceptual schemas that enable transfer within a domain. See J. S. Bruner, *The Process of Education* (Cambridge, MA: Harvard University Press, 1960).

17. H. Borko and C. Livingston, "Cognition and Improvisation: Differences in Mathematics Instruction by Expert and Novice Teachers," *American Educational Research Journal* 26, no. 4 (1989).

18. E. Wexler, "Gallup: Student Engagement Declines with Every Grade," *Education Week*, January 14, 2013, http://blogs.edweek.org/teachers/teaching_now/2013/01/gallup_student_engagement_drops_with_each_grade.html.

19. B. S. Bloom, *Developing Talent in Young People* (New York: Ballantine Books, 1985); D. Coyle, *The Talent Code* (New York: Bantam Books, 2009).

20. This idea of a spiral came from a group of students in our deeper learning class, as part of a class assignment to analyze data we collected through interviews with deep learners. The students in that group were Meredith Innis, Ben Johnson, Jessica Lander, David Sabey, Jesse Tang, Julia Tomasko, Tat Chuen Wee, and Olivia Werby. It was also influenced by reading Bloom, *Developing Talent in Young People*.

21. J. Lave and E. Wenger, *Situated Learning: Legitimate Peripheral Participation* (New York: Cambridge University Press, 1991).

22. A. Collins, J. S. Brown, and S. E. Newman, "Cognitive Apprenticeship: Teaching the Craft of Reading, Writing and Mathematics," *Thinking: The Journal of Philosophy for Children* 8, no. 1 (1988): 2–10. While these subject areas might be disciplinary communities, there is also an argument that the most appropriate educational goal at the secondary level should focus on general skills like reading and writing, critical thinking, and scientific reasoning (see R. Heller, "In Praise of Amateurism: A Friendly Critique of Moje's 'Call for Change' in Secondary Literacy," *Journal of Adolescent and Adult Literacy* 54, no. 4 [2010]). Others have argued that these general skills may emerge only through deep immersion in particular classes or fields (see E. Moje, "Response to Heller's 'In Praise of Amateurism: A Friendly Critique of Moje's "Call for Change" in Secondary Literacy,'" *Journal of Adolescent and Adult Literacy* 54, no. 4 [2010]). Settling this debate is beyond the scope of this paper, but we would note that many teachers seek to impart these more general skills by modeling them and by inducting students into a community of adults who have these abilities and dispositions.

23. Cuban, *How Teachers Taught*.

24. D. Tyack, *The One Best System: A History of American Urban Education* (Cambridge, MA: Harvard University Press, 1974); Rice, *Public School System*.

25. Lynd and Lynd, *Middletown*.

26. Tyack, *One Best System*; Graham, *Schooling America*.

27. R. Callahan, *Education and the Cult of Efficiency: A Study of the Social Forces That Have Shaped the Administration of the Public Schools* (Chicago, IL: University of Chicago Press, 1962); J. Mehta, *The Allure of Order: High Hopes, Dashed Expectations, and the Troubled Quest to Remake American Schooling* (New York: Oxford University Press, 2013).

28. J. Dewey, *The School and Society; the Child and the Curriculum* (Chicago, IL: University of Chicago Press, 1956).

29. Cohen, "Teaching Practice: Plus Ça Change."

30. J. M. Brewer, *The Vocational Guidance Movement* (New York: Macmillan, 1918); L. A. Cremin, *The Transformation of the School: Progressivism in American Education 1876–1957* (New York: Vintage, 1961).

31. S. F. Semel and A. R. Sadovnick, eds., "Schools of Tomorrow," in *Schools of Today: What Happened to Progressive Education* (New York: Peter Lang International Academic Publishers, 2005), 14. More recent work by Cuban—L. Cuban, *Hugging the Middle: How Teachers Teach in an Era of Testing and Accountability* (New York: Teachers College Press, 2008)—has emphasized that teachers now often alternate between more teacher-centered practices, which efficiently move students to meet district pacing guides, and student-centered activities, which are more engaging and facilitate student cooperation with the goals of school. This hybrid mix is a departure from the more teacher-centered approach of the past, but is not necessarily "deeper" in terms of creating powerful experiences for students.

32. P. Dow, *Schoolhouse Politics: Lessons from the Sputnik Era* (Cambridge, MA: Harvard University Press, 1991).

33. National Commission on Excellence in Education, *A Nation at Risk: The Imperative for Educational Reform—a Report to the Nation and the Secretary of Education, United States Department of Education* (Washington, DC: National Commission on Excellence in Education, 1983).

34. Cuban, *How Teachers Taught*.

35. R. Hofstadter, *Anti-Intellectualism in American Life* (New York: Knopf, 1963).

36. Dow, *Schoolhouse Politics*.

37. W. J. Wilson, *The Truly Disadvantaged: The Inner City, the Underclass, and Public Policy* (Chicago, IL: University of Chicago Press, 1987); D. Massey and

N. Denton, *American Apartheid: Segregation and the Making of the Underclass* (Cambridge, MA: Harvard University Press, 1993).

38. Anyon, "Social Class and School Knowledge"; J. Oakes, *Keeping Track: How Schools Structure Inequality* (New Haven, CT: Yale University Press, 1985). Some scholars have argued that there is a correspondence between the ways in which students are treated in school and the occupational positions they are expected to hold, with upper-middle-class students learning the managerial skills of how to assess information, weigh options, and make decisions, whereas working-class and high-poverty students learn how to follow directions compliantly. S. Bowles and H. Gintis, *Schooling in Capitalist America* (New York: Basic Books, 1976); M. Kohn, *Class and Conformity* (Chicago, IL: University of Chicago Press, 1977).

39. Elite private schools, such as Exeter, Andover, Fieldston, Dalton, and many others, benefit considerably from significant financial resources as well as the social and cultural capital of their students, but they built on these assets in ways that have created some of the most developed examples of deeper learning that exist in the country. See A. Powell, *Lessons from Privilege: The American Prep School Tradition* (Cambridge, MA: Harvard University Press, 1996).

40. See J. Mehta and S. Fine, *In Pursuit of Deeper Learning* (forthcoming); J. Mehta and S. Fine, *The Why, What, Where, and How of Deeper Learning in American Secondary Schools* (Boston, MA: Jobs for the Future, 2015).

41. S. L. Lightfoot, *The Good High School: Portraits of Character and Culture* (New York: Basic Books, 1983); T. Sizer, *Horace's Compromise: The Dilemma of the American High School* (Boston, MA: Houghton Mifflin, 1984); and M. Rose, *Possible Lives: The Promise of Public Education in America* (Boston, MA: Houghton Mifflin, 1995) were all, in different ways, models and inspirations for our initial study.

42. Sizer, *Horace's Compromise*; J. I. Goodlad, *A Place Called School* (New York: McGraw-Hill, 1984); A. G. Powell, E. Farrar, and D. Cohen, "The Shopping Mall High School: Winners and Losers in the Educational Marketplace," *NASSP Bulletin* 69, no. 483 (1985): 40–51; T. Kane and D. Staiger, *Gathering Feedback for Teaching: Combining High-Quality Observations with Student Surveys and Achievement Gains* (Seattle, WA: Bill & Melinda Gates Foundation, 2012).

43. Mehta and Fine, *In Pursuit of Deeper Learning*. J. Mehta and S. Fine, "Bringing Values Back In: How Purposes Shape Practices in Coherent School Designs," *Journal of Educational Change* 16, no. 4 (November 2015): 483–510, provides greater detail on exactly what elements need to be aligned for more

consistent realization of instructional priorities. There is also a connection here to the literature on different kinds of school networks, including Montessori, International Baccalaureate, and more recent comprehensive school reform providers that have developed integrated systems to support instructional practice. For one account, see D. K. Cohen et al., *Improvement by Design: The Promise of Better Schools* (Chicago, IL: University of Chicago Press, 2013).

44. Cuban, *How Teachers Taught.*

45. T. Wagner, *The Global Achievement Gap* (New York: Basic Books, 2008).

46. Whether Advanced Placement courses are moving students toward "deeper learning" is a quite complex question. In some subjects and in some teachers' hands, AP can result in rapid coverage of content at the expense of deeper or more developed explorations of fewer topics and, for that reason, some of the most elite schools (public and private) have moved away from AP. At the same time, AP courses are intended to mirror college courses in similar subjects and, as such, often require a command of and an ability to reason about the content that is significantly higher than in most high school courses. There also has been some revision of AP exams in recent years, particularly in the sciences, as the College Board has responded to criticisms that the tests are wider than they are deep, and has refocused some of its exams on fewer topics with more reasoning. Thus we argue that AP can be either an asset for, or a constraint on, deeper learning, depending on the field and the way in which the teacher prepares students for the exam. D. Perkins, *Making Learning Whole* (San Francisco, CA: Jossey-Bass, 2010).

47. Kane and Staiger, *Gathering Feedback for Teaching.*

48. R. Halpern, *The Means to Grow Up* (New York: Routledge, 2009); S. Intrator and D. Siegel, *The Quest for Mastery: Positive Youth Development Through Out-of-School Programs* (Cambridge, MA: Harvard Education Press, 2014).

49. D. Tyack and L. Cuban, *Tinkering Toward Utopia: A Century of Public School Reform* (Cambridge, MA: Harvard University Press, 1995).

50. S. Fine, "A Slow Revolution: Toward a Theory of Intellectual Playfulness in High School Classrooms," *Harvard Education Review* 84, no. 1 (2014); Anyon, "Social Class and School Knowledge."

51. M. Gordon, "The Misuses and Effective Uses of Constructivist Teaching," *Teachers and Teaching: Theory and Practice* 15, no. 6 (2009).

52. Cuban, *How Teachers Taught*; Kane and Staiger, *Gathering Feedback for Teaching.* The Common Core, with its emphasis on fewer topics with more depth, has been an attempt to change this pattern. Whether it—or similar state

standards—succeeds will depend largely on whether the systems are built that would enable these policy aspirations to enable changes in practice.

53. A. Levine, *Educating School Teachers* (Washington, DC: The Education Schools Project, 2006).

54. D. C. Lortie, *Schoolteacher: A Sociological Study* (Chicago, IL: University of Chicago Press, 1975); J. McLaughlin and J. Talbert, *Professional Communities and the Work of High School Teaching* (Chicago, IL: University of Chicago Press, 2001).

55. M. Tucker, *Standing on the Shoulders of Giants: An American Agenda for Education Reform* (Washington, DC: National Center on Education and the Economy, 2011); E. C. Lagemann, *An Elusive Science: The Troubling History of Education Research* (Chicago, IL: University of Chicago Press, 2000); P. B. Walters, "The Politics of Science: Battles for Scientific Authority in the Field of Education Research," in *Education Research on Trial: Policy Reform and the Call for Scientific Rigor*, ed. P. B. Walters, A. Lareau, and S. H. Ranis (New York: Routledge, 2009); H. Burkhardt and A. H. Schofield, "Improving Educational Research: Toward a More Useful, More Influential, Better Funded Enterprise," *Educational Researcher* 32, no. 9 (2003); Cohen et al., *Improvement by Design*.

56. Cohen et al., *Improvement by Design*; Mehta and Fine, *In Pursuit of Deeper Learning*.

57. Mehta and Fine, *In Pursuit of Deeper Learning*; M. M. Brown and A. Berger, *How to Innovate: The Essential Guide to Fearless School Leaders* (New York: Teachers College Press, 2014).

58. J. Herman and R. Linn, *On the Road to Assessing Deeper Learning: The Status of Smarter Balanced and PARCC Assessment Consortia* (Los Angeles, CA: National Center for Research on Evaluation, Standards, and Student Testing, 2013).

59. M. Lampert, T. Boerst, and F. Graziani, "Organizational Resources in the Service of School-Wide Ambitious Practice," *Teachers College Record* 113, no. 7 (2011); J. Mehta, "Unlearning Is Critical for Deep Learning," *Education Week*, January 6, 2015, http://blogs.edweek.org/edweek/learning_deeply/2015/01/unlearning_is_critical_for_deep_learning.html; W. Bridges, *Managing Transitions: Making the Most of Change* (Boston, MA: Da Capo Lifelong Books, 2009).

60. J. Mehta and R. Schwartz, "Building a Twenty First Century School System: Creating a Teaching Profession and Multiple Student Pathways," in *Improving the Odds for America's Children: Future Directions in Policy and Practice*, ed. K. McCartney, H. Yoshikawa, and L. B. Foricier (Cambridge, MA: Harvard Education Press, 2014).

61. A. Lieberman, "Practices That Support Teacher Development: Transforming Conceptions of Professional Learning," in *Teacher Learning: New Policies, New Practices*, ed. M. W. McLaughlin and I. Oberman (New York: Teachers College Press, 1996).

62. A more sensible accountability system might emulate the inspectorate model utilized by the United Kingdom, by many American private schools, and most recently by New York City in the form of school quality reviews. In such a system, schools are periodically visited by an expert team of educators who rely on a diverse array of evidence—including interviews, student surveys, and parental surveys as well as test scores—to make holistic determinations about strengths and areas for improvement.

The United States could also follow the models of the International Baccalaureate program as well as examination systems in other countries such as England, Singapore, and Australia, and develop systems of district or state-level assessments that measure deeper learning competencies. In these models, assessments usually feature a culminating "sit down" exam that entails a series of essays or other open-ended problems, and also a series of specified tasks within the classroom that require the learner to demonstrate the variety of skills and knowledge that are important in a domain.

This classroom portion could mean the development of a portfolio of work, as in the English examination system, or it could be a longer investigation of a single problem, such as the Singaporean science exams, which require students to develop a hypothesis, plan an investigation, record reliable data, interpret experimental results, and reflect on the methods used.

The key to any of these systems is that they do not incentivize the narrowing of curricula or reward the ability to take low-level multiple-choice tests, and instead position the accountability system to reward the kind of deeper learning that Barbara Chow describes in the foreword. In building any such system, it would also be wise for federal, state, and district leaders to think carefully about the twin goals of innovation and improvement.

63. R. Heifetz, *Leadership Without Easy Answers* (Cambridge, MA: Belknap Press of Harvard University Press, 1994).

Chapter 2

1. There are numerous estimates for how many hours Americans spend working; ninety thousand is at the low end. See Bjarki, "7 Time Consuming Things an Average Joe Spends on in a Lifetime," *Tempo* (blog), September 5, 2013, http://blog.tempoplugin.com/2013/7-time-consuming-things-an-average-joe-spends-in-a-lifetime/. Other estimates go up to one million hours.

2. And as Peter Levine and Kei Kawashima-Ginsberg argue in chapter 3, "civic readiness," too, has been treated as an afterthought in recent decades.

3. See, for example, J. M. Bridgeland, J. J. Dilulio Jr., and K. B. Morison, *The

Silent Epidemic: Perspectives of High School Dropouts (Washington, DC: Civic Enterprises, LLC, 2006), https://docs.gatesfoundation.org/Documents/The SilentEpidemic3- 06Final.pdf. This study found that 47 percent of dropouts claimed that school was boring, and 69 percent said that school didn't motivate or excite them. It is important to note, however, that "boredom" masks what a recent study calls "a cluster of factors," many of which have to do with conditions in students' lives external to school. In addition, many students who stay in school and graduate have questions about relevance but have learned to work through boredom. See also America's Promise Alliance and the Center for Promise, *Don't Call Them Dropouts: Understanding the Experiences of Young People Who Leave High School Before Graduation* (Washington, DC: America's Promise Alliance and the Center for Promise at Tufts University, 2014).

4. Here is a typical statement from the California Department of Education: "As you know, career and technical education (CTE) is a powerful motivator for California's young people and a valuable part of California's economy. When students can see a pathway from classrooms to careers, they are much more likely to graduate high school with the skills and experience they need to succeed and to help our businesses succeed. That is a story we should tell, and I hope you will join me and the California Department of Education in doing just that in February 2013, when we celebrate Career and Technical Education Month." Every Student Succeeds Act, California Department of Education, 2012, http://www.cde.ca.gov/nr/el/le/careerandtechnicaleducationmonth.asp.

5. And the reality is that most schools are missing guidance counselors, too. In much of the country, they're in extraordinarily short supply, due mainly to funding cuts. Nationally, public schools average 1 counselor for every 477 students.

6. Thanks to Rafael Heller for these last sentences—and for astute and copious comments during the writing process.

7. A. Sum et al., *The Plummeting Labor Market Fortunes of Teens and Young Adults* (Washington, DC: Metropolitan Policy Program and the Brookings Institution, 2014), http://www.brookings.edu/research/interactives/2014/labor-market-metro-areas-teens-young-adults.

8. Ibid.

9. A. Carnevale, A. Hanson, and A. Gulish, *Failure to Launch: Structural Shift and the New Lost Generation* (Washington, DC: Georgetown University Center on Education and the Workforce, 2013), https://cew.georgetown.edu/cew-reports/failure-to-launch/.

10. My own post-high-school summer job in a hundred-woman typing pool in the un-air-conditioned Newark, New Jersey, courthouse gave me great impetus to study hard in college and find a career as something other than a typist.

11. D. Metlay and D. Sarawitz, "Decision Strategies for Addressing Complex, 'Messy' Problems," *The Bridge, National Academy of Engineering* 42, no. 3 (fall 2012).

12. In addition, their lifetime earnings will be impaired. A substantial body of economic research concludes that late entry into the labor market tends to result in significant reductions in lifetime earnings.

13. R. Halpern, *Youth, Education, and the Role of Society: Rethinking Learning in the High School Years* (Cambridge, MA: Harvard Education Press, 2013).

14. Ibid., 4.

15. A. Collins, J. S. Brown, and A. Holum, "Cognitive Apprenticeship: Making Thinking Visible," *American Educator* 153 (1991).

16. *Education at a Glance 2014: OECD Indicators* (Paris: OECD Publishing, 2014), 10.1787/eag-2014-en.

17. R. Halpern, *It Takes a Whole Society: Opening Up the Learning Landscape in the High School Years* (Quincy, MA: Nellie Mae Education Foundation, 2012).

18. J. Bishop, *Which Secondary Education Systems Work Best? The United States or Northern Europe* (Ithaca, NY: Cornell University, 2010), http://digital commons.ilr.cornell.edu/workingpapers/105; *KOF Youth Labour Market Index: The Multifaceted Situation of Young Persons in the Labour Market* (Zurich, Switzerland: KOF Swiss Economic Institute, 2014); J. Breiding, *Swiss Made: The Untold Story Behind Switzerland's Success* (London: Profile Books, 2013).

19. For a more comprehensive account of strong vocational systems, see N. Hoffman, *Schooling in the Workplace: How Six of the World's Best Vocational Education Systems Prepare Young People for Jobs and Life* (Cambridge, MA: Harvard Education Press, 2011); N. Hoffman and R. Schwartz, *The Swiss Vocational Education System* (Washington, DC: National Center on Education and the Economy, 2014). This section draws substantially on the latter piece.

20. These observations are based on numerous interviews, conducted mainly in 2014, with Swiss teenagers and parents.

21. Observations based on interviews with human resources directors of apprenticeships at Swiss Com, Credit Suisse, and other major employers.

22. Much of the information in this section comes from personal notes from interviews with a group of executives, representing a number of major Swiss companies, in which I participated at the Swiss Economic Forum, June 2014, in Interlaken, Switzerland. The purpose of the interviews was to solicit their

views on the role played by the country's vocational and professional education system in Swiss economic success. Interview subjects included the president of the Swiss Employer Association as well as CEOs of companies such as Price Waterhouse, UBS, the Swiss postal service, and Alpiq (an electric power provider).

23. These are the averages usually cited. For salaries for each profession, see "Recommandations des associations professionelles, etat 2014" at www .orientation.ch/dyn/show/3231#.

24. See S. Wolter, "Cost and Benefit of Apprenticeship Training: A Comparison of Germany and Switzerland," *Applied Economics Quarterly* 551 (2009). Also see other studies by Stefan Wolter, managing director of the Swiss Coordination Centre for Research in Education and a professor of economics at the University of Bern.

25. In French, the schools' mission statement reads: "l'épanouissement de la personnalité des personnes en formation et les encouragent à prendre des responsabilités dans leur vie professionnelle, privée et sociale," from *Plan de formation relatif à l'ordonnance sur la formation professionnelle initiale*, Version 1.1, November 30, 2010, 11, https://www.swissmem-berufsbildung.ch/fileadmin/ _migrated/content_uploads/PM_Plan_de_formation_V11_101130.pdf.

26. Interview with a student at the Center for Young Professionals Banking, the training and competence center for banking education, Zurich, October 16, 2014.

27. Halpern, *Youth, Education, and the Role of Society*, 30, 39.

28. The career academy movement, the largest "modern" CTE program with some seven thousand schools, helps graduates achieve higher earnings as adults. The academies introduce students to career themes and typically include workplace learning. Project Lead the Way introduces high school students to engineering using a rigorous, uniform curriculum; national assessments; professional development for teachers; and extensive project-based learning. It can be installed within a traditional high school and has now spread to more than three thousand high schools. High Schools That Work, developed by the Southern Regional Education Board, has grown into the nation's largest effort to integrate challenging academics and CTE. Currently, SREB is working to develop new, high-quality, career-focused "programs of study," taking advantage of funding available through a provision in the U.S. Department of Education's Perkins legislation.

29. G. Hoachlander and D. Yanofsky, "Making STEM Real," *Educational Leadership* 68, no. 6 (2011).

30. For an update on the work thus far, see Jobs for the Future and Harvard

Graduate School of Education, *The Pathways to Prosperity Network: A State Progress Report, 2012–2014* (Boston, MA: Jobs for the Future, 2014), http://www.jff.org/sites/default/files/publications/materials/Pathways-to-Prosperity-for-Americas-youth-080514.pdf.

Chapter 3

1. National Commission on Excellence in Education, *A Nation at Risk: The Imperative for Educational Reform—a Report to the Nation and the Secretary of Education, United States Department of Education* (Washington, DC: National Commission on Excellence in Education, 1983).
2. R. W. Larson and R. M. Angus, "Adolescents' Development of Skills for Agency in Youth Programs: Learning to Think Strategically," *Child Development* 82, no. 1 (2011).
3. A. Dávila and M. T. Mora, *An Assessment of Civic Engagement and Educational Attainment* (Medford, MA: Center for Information and Research on Civic Learning and Engagement [CIRCLE], 2007); C. Spera et al., *Volunteering as a Pathway to Employment: Does Volunteering Increase Odds of Finding a Job for the Out of Work?* (Washington, DC: Corporation for National and Community Service, Office of Research and Evaluation, 2013); D. Anderson-Butcher, W. S. Newsome, and T. M. Ferrari, "Participation in Boys and Girls Clubs and Relationships to Youth Outcomes," *Journal of Community Psychology* 31, no. 1 (2003); J. A. Fredericks and J. S. Eccles, "Is Extracurricular Participation Associated with Beneficial Outcomes? Concurrent and Longitudinal Relations," *Developmental Psychology* 42, no. 4 (2006).
4. S. Dillon, "Failing Grades on Civics Exam Called a 'Crisis,'" *New York Times*, May 4, 2011.
5. P. Levine, *What the NAEP Civics Assessment Measures and How Students Perform* (Medford, MA: CIRCLE, 2013).
6. R. Pondiscio, "Let's Set a National Standard for Our Students—A Really Low One," *Atlantic*, April 9, 2013, http://www.theatlantic.com/national/archive/2013/04/lets-set-a-national-standard-for-our-students-a-really-low-one/274808/.
7. K. Kawashima-Ginsberg and P. Levine, "Policy Effects on Informed Political Engagement," *American Behavioral Scientist* 58, no. 5 (2014).
8. D. E. Campbell, *Putting Civics to the Test: The Impact of State-Level Civics Assessments on Civic Knowledge* (Washington, DC: American Enterprise Institute, 2014).
9. P. Levine, *We Are the Ones We Have Been Waiting For: The Promise of Civic Renewal in America* (New York: Oxford University Press, 2013).

10. J. Kahne and E. Middaugh, *Democracy for Some: The Civic Opportunity Gap in High School* (Medford, MA: CIRCLE, 2009).

11. K. Kawashima-Ginsberg, *Do Discussion, Debate, and Simulations Boost NAEP Civics Performance?* (Medford, MA: CIRCLE, 2013).

12. Commission on Youth Voting and Civic Knowledge, *All Together Now: Collaboration and Innovation for Youth Engagement* (Medford, MA: CIRCLE, 2013).

13. D. E. Hess, "Controversies About Controversial Issues in Democratic Education," *PS: Political Science and Politics* 37, no. 2 (2004); D. E. Hess and P. McAvoy, *The Political Classroom: Ethics and Evidence in Democratic Education* (New York: Routledge, 2014).

14. E. C. Hope and R. J. Jagers, "The Role of Sociopolitical Attitudes and Civic Education in the Civic Engagement of Black Youth," *Journal of Research on Adolescents* 24, no. 3 (2014).

15. A. W. Brown, *The Improvement of Civics Instruction in Junior and Senior High Schools* (Ypsilanti, MI: Standard Printing, 1929).

16. R. G. Niemi and J. Smith, "Enrollments in High School Government Classes: Are We Short-Changing Both Citizenship and Political Science Training?," *PS: Political Science and Politics* 34, no. 2 (2001).

17. In fact, high school students earn more credits in the social studies than in previous decades, not to mention that more Americans now complete high school. M. H. Lopez, K. B. Marcelo, and P. Levine, *Getting Narrower at the Base: The American Curriculum After NCLB* (Medford, MA: CIRCLE, 2008).

18. Niemi and Smith, "Enrollments in High School Government Classes."

19. National Task Force on Civic Learning and Democratic Engagement, *Crucible Moment: College Learning and Democracy's Future* (Washington, DC: Association of American Colleges and Universities, 2012).

20. Commission on Youth Voting and Civic Knowledge, *All Together Now*.

21. U.S. Department of Education, *Advancing Civic Learning and Engagement in Democracy: A Road Map and Call to Action* (Washington, DC: U.S. Department of Education, 2012).

22. S. Godsay et al., *State Civic Education Requirements* (Medford, MA: CIRCLE, 2012).

23. Commission on Youth Voting and Civic Knowledge, *All Together Now*.

24. Kawashima-Ginsberg, *Do Discussion, Debate, and Simulations Boost NAEP Civics Performance?*

25. M. West, "Testing, Learning, and Teaching: The Effects of Test-Based Accountability on Student Achievement and Instructional Time in Core Academic Subjects," in *Beyond the Basics: Achieving a Liberal Education for All Children*, ed. C. E. Finn and D. Ravitch (Washington, DC: Fordham Institute, 2007).

26. J. Stoddard, "The Need for Media Education in Democratic Education," *Democracy & Education* 22, no. 1 (2014).

27. C. J. Cohen et al., *Participatory Politics: New Media and Youth Political Action* (Oakland, CA: Mills College, 2012).

28. National Conference on Citizenship, *America's Civic Health Index: Civic Health in Hard Times* (Washington, DC: National Conference on Citizenship, 2009).

29. Pew Research Center, "July 16–Aug. 7, 2012—Civic Engagement," http://www.pewinternet.org/datasets/august-2012-civic-engagement.

30. Cohen et al., *Participatory Politics*.

31. D. W. Shaffer, *How Computer Games Help Children Learn* (New York: Palgrave, 2007).

32. Pew Research Center, "Political Polarization in the American Public," June 12, 2014, http://www.people-press.org/2014/06/12/political-polarization-in-the-american-public.

33. Pew Research Center, *Trends in Political Values and Core Attitudes: 1987–2007* (Washington, DC: Pew Research Center, 2007).

34. N. Eliasoph, *Avoiding Politics: How Americans Produce Apathy in Everyday Life* (New York: Cambridge University Press, 1998).

35. Commission on Youth Voting and Civic Knowledge, *All Together Now*.

36. K. Kawashima-Ginsberg and P. Levine, "Diversity in Classrooms: The Relationship Between Deliberative and Associative Opportunities in School and Later Electoral Engagement," *Analyses of Social Issues and Public Policy* 14, no. 1 (2014).

37. CIRCLE and Carnegie Corporation of New York, *The Civic Mission of Schools* (New York: Carnegie Corporation of New York, 2003).

38. W. Damon, *Failing Liberty 101: How We Are Leaving Young Americans Unprepared for Citizenship in a Free Society* (Palo Alto, CA: Hoover Institution Press, 2011); Pondiscio, "Let's Set a National Standard for Our Students—A Really Low One"; D. J. Feith, *Teaching America: The Case for Civic Education* (Lanham, MD: Rowman & Littlefield, 2011).

39. A. Hartry and K. Porter, *We the People Curriculum: Results of a Pilot Test* (Alexandria, VA: MPR Associates, 2004); Educational Testing Service, *A Comparison of the Impact of the* We the People . . . *Curricular Materials on High School Students Compared to University Students* (Pasadena, CA: Educational Testing Service, 1991).

40. M. Levinson, *No Citizen Left Behind* (Cambridge, MA: Harvard University Press, 2012); National Action Civics Collaborative home page, http://actioncivicscollaborative.org.

41. G. Graff, *Beyond the Culture Wars: How Teaching the Conflicts Can Revitalize American Education* (New York: W. W. Norton, 1993).

42. G. Graff, "President's Column: Argument over Information," *MLA Newsletter* 40, no. 3 (2008).

43. CIRCLE and Carnegie Corporation of New York, *The Civic Mission of Schools.*

44. We note also that civic learning can occur outside of the traditional classroom settings. For example, some researchers argue that extracurricular activities provide young people with a chance to develop social capital, agency skills, and hands-on experience with community problem solving (e.g., K. Kawashima-Ginsberg, *Harry, Hermione, Ron, and Neville—Portraits of American Teenagers' Extracurricular Involvement, and Implications for Educational Interventions* [Medford, MA: CIRCLE, 2014]). And out-of-school programs such as YouthBuild appear to provide meaningful opportunities to develop personal and civic leadership for young people who have dropped out of the formal educational system.

45. See summary in P. Levine, *The Future of Democracy: Developing the Next Generation of American Citizens* (Medford, MA: Tufts University Press, 2007).

46. K. Kawashima-Ginsberg and P. Levine, "Policy Effects on Informed Political Engagement," *American Behavioral Scientist* 58, no. 5 (2014).

47. J. E. Kahne and S. E. Sporte, "Developing Citizens: The Impact of Civic Learning Opportunities on Students' Commitment to Civic Participation," *American Educational Research Journal* 45, no. 3 (2008).

48. D. E. Campbell, "Voice in the Classroom: How an Open Classroom Climate Fosters Political Engagement Among Adolescents," *Political Behavior* 30, no. 4 (2008); M. McDevitt and S. Kiousis, *Education for Deliberative Democracy: The Long-Term Influence of Kids Voting* (College Park, MD: CIRCLE, 2004); Hess and McAvoy, *The Political Classroom*; E. S. Smith, "The Effects of Investment in the Social Capital of Youth on Political and Civic Behavior in Young Adulthood: A Longitudinal Analysis," *Political Psychology* 20, no. 3 (1999); D. A. McFarland and R. J. Thomas, "Bowling Young: How Youth Voluntary Associations Influence Adult Political Participation," *American Sociological Review* 71, no. 3 (2006); E. C. Metz and J. Youniss, "Longitudinal Gains in Civic Development Through School-Based Required Service," *Political Psychology* 26, no. 3 (2005); D. Hart et al., "High School Community Service as a Predictor of Adult Voting and Volunteering," *American Educational Research Journal* 44, no. 1 (2007).

49. S. Billig, S. Root, and D. Jesse, *The Impact of Participation in Service-Learning on High School Students' Civic Engagement* (College Park, MD: CIRCLE, 2005).

50. Kawashima-Ginsberg, *Do Discussion, Debate, and Simulations Boost NAEP Civics Performance?*

51. H. Rosing, "Understanding Student Complaints in the Service Learning Pedagogy," *American Journal of Community Psychology* 46, no. 3 (2010).

52. J. H. Scott, "The Intersection of Moral Growth and Service-Learning," in *Facilitating the Moral Growth of College Students*, ed. D. L. Liddell and D. L. Cooper (San Francisco, CA: Jossey-Bass, 2012).

53. Larson and Angus, "Adolescents' Development of Skills."

54. W. C. Parker et al., "Beyond Breadth-Speed-Test: Toward Deeper Knowing and Engagement in an Advanced Placement Course," *American Educational Research Journal* 50, no. 6 (2013).

55. National Council for the Social Studies, *College, Career, and Civic Life (C3) Framework for Social Studies State Standards* (Silver Springs, MD: National Council for the Social Studies, 2013).

56. CIRCLE, *Recent Civic Education Policy Changes* (Medford, MA: CIRCLE, 2014).

57. Levinson, *No Citizen Left Behind.*

58. Well-known programs include Generation Citizen, Mikva Challenge, and Earthforce. See the National Action Civics Collaborative, http://actioncivics collaborative.org.

59. N. C. Chesler et al., "Design of a Professional Practice Simulator for Educating and Motivating First-Year Engineering Students," *Advances in Engineering Education* 3, no. 3 (2013).

60. K. Kawashima-Ginsberg, *Summary of Findings from the Evaluation of iCivics' Drafting Board Intervention* (Medford, MA: CIRCLE, 2012).

61. CIRCLE, *Pathways into Leadership: A Study of YouthBuild Graduates* (Medford, MA: CIRCLE, 2012).

62. B. Mezuk and S. Anderson, "New Findings from the Chicago Debate League Study," Presentation at the NAUDL National Debate Championship, April 19, 2013, http://urbandebate.org/Portals/0/EmergingResearch/Mezuk%20Studies .pdf.

Chapter 4

1. W. Au, "High-Stakes Testing and Curricular Control: A Qualitative Metasynthesis," *Educational Researcher* 36, no. 5 (2007); J. McMurrer, *Choices, Changes, and Challenges: Curriculum and Instruction in the NCLB Era* (Washington, DC: Center on Education Policy, 2007).

2. Civil Rights Project, "UCLA Report Finds Changing U.S. Demographics Transform School Segregation Landscape 60 Years After Brown v. Board of

Education," May 15, 2014, https://civilrightsproject.ucla.edu/news/press-releases/2014-press-releases/ucla-report-finds-changing-u.s.-demographics-transform-school-segregation-landscape-60-years-after-brown-v-board-of-education.

3. R. Balfanz, V. Byrnes, and J. Fox, *Sent Home and Put Off-Track: The Antecedents, Disproportionalities, and Consequences of Being Suspended in the Ninth Grade* (Washington, DC: Center for Civil Rights Remedies and the Research-to-Practice Collaborative, National Conference on Race and Gender Disparities in Discipline, 2012).

4. The Equity and Excellence Commission, *For Each and Every Child—A Strategy for Education Equity and Excellence* (Washington, DC: U.S. Department of Education, 2013).

5. L. Darling-Hammond, M. B. Zielezinski, and S. Goldman, *Using Technology to Support At-Risk Students' Learning* (Washington, DC: Alliance for Excellent Education, 2014).

6. Coalition of Essential Schools, "Common Principles," http://essentialschools.org/common-principles/.

7. J. Mehta, "Deeper Learning Has a Race Problem," *Education Week*, June 20, 2014, http://blogs.edweek.org/edweek/learning_deeply/2014/06/deeper_learning_has_a_race_problem.html.

8. K. Yuan and V. Le, "Estimating the Percentage of Students Who Were Tested on Cognitively Demanding Items Through the State Achievement Test" (working paper, RAND Corporation, November 2012).

9. D. T. Conley, *Deeper Learning Research Series: A New Era for Educational Assessment* (Boston, MA: Jobs for the Future, 2014).

10. R. Rothstein, *Class and Schools: Using Social, Economic, and Educational Reform to Close the Black-White Achievement Gap* (Washington, DC: Economic Policy Institute, 2004).

11. J. S. Coleman et al., *Equality of Educational Opportunity* (Washington, DC: U.S. Department of Health, Education and Welfare, Office of Education, 1966); C. Jencks, *Inequality: A Reassessment of the Effect of Family and Schooling in America* (New York: Basic Books, 1972); C. Jencks and M. Phillips, *The Black-White Test Score Gap* (Washington, DC: Brookings Institution Press, 1998); R. Kahlenberg, "Socioeconomic School Integration: Preliminary Lessons from More Than 80 Districts," in *Integrating Schools in a Changing Society: New Policies and Legal Options for a Multiracial Generation*, ed. E. Frankenberg and E. Debray (Chapel Hill, NC: University of North Carolina Press, 2011), 167–86.

12. National Center for Education Statistics, *Early Childhood Longitudinal Study* (Washington, DC: U.S. Department of Education, 2004).

13. A. Lareau, *Unequal Childhoods: Class, Race, and Family Life* (Berkeley and Los Angeles, CA: University of California Press, 2003).

14. H. S. Adelman and L. Taylor, "Mental Health in Schools and System Restructuring," *Clinical Psychological Review* 19, no. 2 (1999); S. L. Syme, "Social Determinants of Health: The Community as Empowered Partner," *Preventing Chronic Disease: Public Health Research, Practice, and Policy* 1, no. 1 (2004); R. Rothstein, *Class and Schools*; J. S. Eccles and J. Gootman, *Community Programs to Promote Youth Development* (Washington, DC: National Academies Press, 2002); P. Noguera and L. Wells, "The Politics of School Reform: A Broader and Bolder Approach for Newark," *Berkeley Review of Education* 2, no. 1 (2011).

15. P. Barton and R. Coley, *The Black-White Achievement Gap: When Progress Stopped* (Princeton, NJ: Educational Testing Service, 2010).

16. UNICEF Office of Research, *Child Well-Being in Rich Countries: A Comparative Overview* (Florence, Italy: UNICEF Office of Research, 2013).

17. B. Hart and T. R. Risley, *Meaningful Differences in the Everyday Experience of Young American Children* (Baltimore, MD: Paul H. Brookes Publishing, 1995).

18. The research on early literacy learning suggests that it is an urgent priority to expand access to high-quality preschool, but investing in early childhood education alone will not be sufficient to ensure students' later success. Several studies on federally funded Head Start programs have shown that the benefits of such programs are often undermined when children do not receive ongoing support, both within and outside of school, after they enter kindergarten. K. L. Bierman et al., "Helping Head Start Parents Promote Their Children's Kindergarten Adjustment: The Research-Based Developmentally Informed Parent Program," *Child Development* 86, no. 6 (2015): 1877–91; L. A. Karoly, M. R. Kilburn, and J. S. Cannon, *Proven Benefits of Early Childhood Interventions* (Santa Monica, CA: RAND Corporation, 2005); K. Denton and J. West, *Children's Reading and Mathematics Achievement in Kindergarten and First Grade* (Washington, DC: National Center for Education Statistics, 2002).

19. Adelman and Taylor, "Mental Health in Schools and System Restructuring"; P. Noguera, *City Schools and the American Dream: Reclaiming the Promise of Public Education* (New York: Teachers College Press, 2003); C. Payne, *So Much Reform, So Little Change: The Persistence of Failure in Urban Schools* (Cambridge, MA: Harvard Education Press, 2008); R. Rothstein, *Class and Schools*; A. S. Bryk, *Organizing Schools for Improvement: Lessons from Chicago* (Chicago, IL: University of Chicago Press, 2010).

20. The Equity and Excellence Commission, *For Each and Every Child*; B. Baker et al., "Adjusted Poverty Measures and the Distribution of Title I Aid: Does Title I Really Make the Rich States Richer?" *Education Finance and Policy* 8, no. 3 (2013): 394–417; L. Darling-Hammond, *The Flat World and Education: How America's Commitment to Equity Will Determine Our Future* (New York: Teachers College Press, 2010).

21. C. K. Jackson, R. C. Johnson, and C. Persico, *The Effect of School Finance Reforms on the Distribution of Spending, Academic Achievement, and Adult Outcomes* (Cambridge, MA: National Bureau of Economic Research, 2014).

22. *Study of Deeper Learning: Opportunities and Outcomes* (Palo Alto, CA: American Institutes for Research, 2014); L. Darling-Hammond, J. Ancess, and S. Ort, "Reinventing High School: Outcomes of the Coalition Campus Schools Project," *American Educational Research Journal* 39, no. 3 (2002); D. Friedlaender et al., *High Schools for Equity: Policy Supports for Student Learning in Communities of Color* (Stanford, CA: School Redesign Network at Stanford University, 2007); D. Friedlaender et al., *Student-Centered Schools: Closing the Opportunity Gap* (Stanford, CA: Stanford Center for Opportunity Policy in Education, 2014); M. Martinez and D. McGrath, *Deeper Learning: How Eight Innovative Public Schools Are Transforming Education in the Twenty-First Century* (New York: New Press, 2014); P. Wasley et al., *Small Schools: Great Strides. A Study of New Small Schools in Chicago* (New York: Bank Street College of Education, 2000).

23. American Institutes for Research, *Study of Deeper Learning*.

24. The examples in this section are from Friedlaender et al., *Student-Centered Schools*.

25. D. Edelson, D. N. Gordin, and R. D. Pea, "Addressing the Challenges of Inquiry Learning Through Technology and Curriculum Design," *Journal of the Learning Sciences* 8, nos. 3, 4 (1999).

26. For a review, see L. Darling-Hammond et al., *Powerful Learning: What We Know About Teaching for Understanding* (San Francisco, CA: Jossey-Bass, 2008).

27. B. Barron, "Achieving Coordination in Collaborative Problem-Solving Groups," *Journal of the Learning Sciences* 9, no. 4 (2000): 403–36, doi: 10.1207/S15327809JLS0904_2; B. Barron, "When Smart Groups Fail," *Journal of the Learning Sciences* 12, no. 3 (2003): 307–59, doi: 10.1207/S15327809JLS1203_1.

28. Darling-Hammond et al., *Powerful Learning*.

29. L. Darling-Hammond and F. Adamson, *Beyond Basic Skills: The Role of Performance Assessment in Achieving 21st Century Standards of Learning* (Stanford, CA: Stanford University, Stanford Center for Opportunity Policy in Education, 2010), 7–8.

30. P. Noguera and J. Y. Wing, *Unfinished Business: Closing the Racial Achievement Gap in Our Schools* (San Francisco, CA: Jossey-Bass, 2006).

31. G. H. Gregory and C. Chapman, *Differentiated Instructional Strategies: One Size Doesn't Fit All* (Thousand Oaks, CA: Corwin Press, 2013); D. Lawrence-Brown, "Differentiated Instruction: Inclusive Strategies for Standards-Based Learning that Benefit the Whole Class," *American Secondary Education* 32, no. 3 (2004).

32. The organization Engaging Schools (formerly Educators for Social Responsibility) has published materials that provide helpful guidance in this area. See http://engagingschools.org.

33. National Commission on Equity and Excellence, *For Each and Every Child*.

34. Jackson, Johnson, and Persico, *Effect of School Finance Reforms*.

35. J. Guryan, *Does Money Matter? Regression-Discontinuity Estimates from Education Finance Reform in Massachusetts* (Cambridge, MA: National Bureau of Economic Research, 2001).

36. OECD, *Education at a Glance 2013: OECD Indicators* (Paris: OECD Publishing, 2013).

37. L. Darling-Hammond, *Getting Teacher Evaluation Right: What Really Matters for Improvement and Effectiveness* (New York: Teachers College Press, 2013).

38. See Learning Forward, https://learningforward.org/.

39. M. Fullan and M. Langworthy, *A Rich Seam: How New Pedagogies Find Deep Learning* (London: Pearson, 2014).

Chapter 5

1. This figure refers to the 2012–13 school year, the most recent year for which figures were available. The total of more than six million students includes children with disabilities ages three through five who attended public preschool that year. T. D. Snyder, C. de Brey, and S. A. Dillow, "Table 204.40. Children 3 to 21 Years Old Served Under Individuals with Disabilities Education Act (IDEA), Part B, by Race/Ethnicity and Age Group: 2000–01 Through 2012–13," in *Digest of Education Statistics 2014* (Washington, DC: National Center for Education Statistics, Institute of Education Sciences, U.S. Department of Education, 2016), http://nces.ed.gov/pubs2016/2016006.pdf.

2. This figure refers only to students ages six to twenty-one. T. D. Snyder, C. de Brey, and S. A. Dillow, "Table 204.60. Percentage Distribution of Students 6 to 21 Years Old Served Under Individuals with Disabilities Education Act (IDEA), Part B, by Educational Environment and Type of Disability: Selected Years, Fall 1989 Through Fall 2012," in *Digest of Education Statistics 2014*

(Washington, DC: National Center for Education Statistics, Institute of Education Sciences, U.S. Department of Education, 2016).

3. These figures include children with disabilities ages three through five who attended public preschool, as well as children ages six through twenty-one who attended elementary and secondary schools. Snyder, de Brey, and Dillow, "Table 204.40."

4. The William and Flora Hewlett Foundation, *Deeper Learning Defined* (Menlo Park, CA: William and Flora Hewlett Foundation, 2013).

5. L. S. Fuchs et al., "Intensive Intervention for Students with Mathematics Disabilities: Seven Principles of Effective Practice," *Learning Disability Quarterly* 31 (2008); K. R. Harris, S. Graham, and L. H. Mason, "Improving the Writing, Knowledge, and Motivation of Struggling Young Writers: Effects of Self-Regulated Strategy Development with and without Peer Support," *American Educational Research Journal* 43, no. 2 (2006).

6. L. S. Fuchs et al., "Intensive Intervention for Students with Mathematics Disabilities"; R. Gersten et al., *Mathematics Instruction for Students with Learning Disabilities or Difficulty Learning Mathematics: A Synthesis of the Intervention Research* (Portsmouth, NH: Center on Instruction, RMC Research Corporation, 2008); S. Vaughn et al., "Response to Early Reading Interventions: Examining Higher Responders and Lower Responders," *Exceptional Children* 75 (2012).

7. M. Wagner et al., *After High School: A First Look at the Postschool Experiences of Youth with Disabilities* (Menlo Park, CA: SRI International, 2005).

8. National Center for Education Statistics, *National Assessment of Educational Progress* (Washington, DC: Institute of Education Sciences, U.S. Department of Education, 2015).

9. S. Vaughn and J. Wanzek, "Intensive Interventions in Reading for Students with Reading Disabilities: Meaningful Impacts," *Learning Disabilities Research and Practice* 2, no. 92 (2014).

10. L. S. Fuchs et al., "Inclusion Versus Specialized Intervention for Very-Low-Performing Students: What Does Access Mean in an Era of Academic Challenge?" *Exceptional Children* 81, no. 2 (2015); E. Swanson et al., "Improving Reading Comprehension and Social Studies Knowledge Among Middle School Students with Disabilities," *Exceptional Children* 81, no. 4 (2015): 426–42.

11. National Center on Intensive Intervention, *Implementing Intensive Intervention: Lessons Learned from the Field* (Washington, DC: U.S. Department of Education and Office of Special Education Programs, 2013).

12. R. McIntosh et al., "Observations of Students with Learning Disabilities in General Education Classrooms," *Exceptional Children* 60, no. 3 (1994); N.

Jones and M. Brownell, "Examining the Use of Classroom Observations in the Evaluation of Special Education Teachers," *Journal of Assessment for Effective Instruction* 39, no. 2 (2014).

13. J. Harr-Robins et al., *The Inclusion of Students with Disabilities in School Accountability Systems* (Washington, DC: National Center for Education Evaluation and Regional Assistance, Institute of Education Sciences, and U.S. Department of Education, 2012).

14. D. Conley, *A New Era for Educational Assessment* (Boston, MA: Jobs for the Future, 2014).

15. Vaughn et al., "Response to Early Reading Interventions."

16. J. W. Pellegrino and M. L. Hilton, *Education for Life and Work: Developing Transferable Knowledge and Skills in the 21st Century* (Washington, DC: National Academies Press, 2012).

17. R. Gersten et al., *Assisting Students Struggling with Reading: Response to Intervention and Multi-Tier Intervention for Reading in the Primary Grades. A Practice Guide* (Washington, DC: National Center for Education Evaluation and Regional Assistance, Institute of Education Sciences, and U.S. Department of Education, 2009).

18. S. Vaughn et al., "Improving Reading Comprehension and Social Studies Knowledge in Middle School," *Reading Research Quarterly* 48, no. 1 (2013); S. Vaughn et al., "Improving Middle-School Students' Knowledge and Comprehension in Social Studies: A Replication," *Educational Psychology Review* 27 (2014).

19. J. Wanzek et al., "The Effects of Team-Based Learning on Social Studies Knowledge Acquisition in High School," *Journal of Research on Educational Effectiveness* 7, no. 2 (2014).

20. Swanson et al., "Improving Reading Comprehension."

21. A growing research base associates executive functions with learning in (1) reading: see J. Booth, J. Boyle, and S. Kelly, "Do Tasks Make a Difference? Accounting for Heterogeneity of Performance of Children with Reading Difficulties on Tasks of Executive Function: Findings from a Meta-Analysis," *British Journal of Developmental Psychology* 28, no. 1 (2010): 133–76; L. Cutting et al., "Effects of Fluency, Oral Language, and Executive Function on Reading Comprehension Performance," *Annals of Dyslexia* 59, no. 1 (2009); G. Locascio et al., "Executive Dysfunction Among Children with Reading Comprehension Deficits," *Journal of Learning Disabilities* 43, no. 5 (2010); E. Souvignier and J. Mokhlesgerami, "Using Self-Regulation as a Framework for Implementing Strategy Instruction to Foster Reading Comprehension," *Learning and*

Instruction 16 (2006); H. Swanson and M. Howell, "Working Memory, Short-Term Memory, and Speech Rate as Predictors of Children's Reading Performance at Different Ages," *Journal of Educational Psychology* 93 (2001); C. Was and D. Woltz, "Re-Examining the Relationship Between Working Memory and Comprehension: The Role of Available Long-Term Memory," *Journal of Memory and Language* 56 (2007); (2) mathematics: see R. Bull et al., "Short-Term Memory, Working Memory, and Executive Functioning in Preschoolers: Longitudinal Predictors of Mathematical Achievement at Age 7 Years," *Developmental Neuropsychology* 33 (2008); R. Bull and G. Scerif, "Executive Functioning as a Predictor of Children's Mathematics Ability: Inhibition, Switching, and Working Memory," *Developmental Neuropsychology* 19 (2001); P. Cirino, "The Interrelationships of Mathematical Precursors in Kindergarten," *Journal of Experimental Child Psychology* 108 (2011); P. Cirino et al., "Cognitive Arithmetic Differences in Learning Disabled Groups and the Role of Behavioral Inattention," *Learning Disabilities Research & Practice* 22, no. 1 (2007); P. Cirino et al., "Neuropsychological Concomitants of Calculation Skills in College Students Referred for Learning Difficulties," *Developmental Neuropsychology* 21, no. 2 (2002); L. S. Fuchs et al., "Do Different Types of School Mathematics Development Depend on Different Constellations of Numerical versus General Cognitive Abilities?" *Developmental Psychology* 46 (2010); D. C. Geary, "Mathematics and Learning Disabilities," *Journal of Learning Disabilities* 37 (2004); S. van der Sluis et al., "Executive Functioning in Children, and Its Relations with Reasoning, Reading, and Arithmetic," *Intelligence* 35 (2007); and (3) writing: see L. Altemeier et al., "Executive Functions for Reading and Writing in Typical Literacy Development and Dyslexia," *Journal of Clinical and Experimental Neuropsychology* 30, no. 5 (2008); S. Hooper et al., "Aptitude-Treatment Interactions Revisited: Effect of Metacognitive Intervention on Subtypes of Written Expression in Elementary School Students," *Developmental Neuropsychology* 29 (2006); S. Hooper et al., "Executive Functions in Elementary School Children With and Without Problems in Written Expression," *Journal of Learning Disabilities* 36 (2002); T. Santangelo et al., "Self-Regulated Strategy Development: A Validated Model to Support Students Who Struggle with Writing," *Learning Disabilities: A Contemporary Journal* 5, no. 1 (2007).

Research also suggests that executive functions influence general academic outcomes. See W. Barnett et al., "Educational Effects of the Tools of the Mind Curriculum: A Randomized Trial," *Early Childhood Research Quarterly* 23 (2008); C. Blair, "School Readiness: Integrating Cognition and Emotion in a

Neurobiological Conceptualization of Children's Functioning at School Entry," *American Psychologist* 57 (2002); C. Blair and R. Razza, "Relating Effortful Control, Executive Function, and False Belief Understanding to Emerging Math and Literacy Ability in Kindergarten," *Child Development* 78 (2007); A. Diamond et al., "Preschool Program Improves Cognitive Control," *Science* 318 (2007).

22. K. Cain and J. Oakhill, "Profiles of Children with Specific Reading Comprehension Difficulties," *British Journal of Developmental Psychology* 76, no. 4 (2006): 683–96; K. Cain, J. Oakhill, and P. Bryant, "Children's Reading Comprehension Ability: Concurrent Prediction by Working Memory, Verbal Ability, and Component Skills," *Journal of Educational Psychology* 96, no. 1 (2004): 31.

23. H. Swanson and R. O'Connor, "The Role of Working Memory and Fluency Practice on Reading Comprehension of Students Who Are Dysfluent Readers," *Journal of Learning Disabilities* 42, no. 6 (2009): 548–75; H. Swanson et al., "Working Memory, Short-Term Memory, and Reading Disabilities: A Selective Meta-Analysis of the Literature," *Journal of Learning Disabilities* 42 (2009).

24. L. Mann, *On the Trail of Process* (New York: Grune & Stratton, 1979).

25. Mann, *On the Trail of Process*; P. Pintrich, "Understanding Self-Regulated Learning," in *New Directions for Teaching and Learning*, vol. 63, ed. R. J. Menges and M. D. Svinicki (San Francisco, CA: Jossey-Bass, 1995); B. Zimmerman, "A Social Cognitive View of Self-Regulated Academic Learning," *Journal of Educational Psychology* 81, no. 3 (1989); G. R. Lyon, "Identification and Remediation of Learning Disability Sub-Types: Preliminary Findings," *Learning Disabilities Research & Practice* 1 (1985).

26. L. S. Fuchs et al., "Remediating Number Combination and Word Problem Deficits Among Students with Mathematics Difficulties: A Randomized Control Trial," *Journal of Educational Psychology* 101 (2009).

27. J. Boyle, "Strategic Note-Taking for Middle-School Students with Learning Disabilities in Science Classes," *Learning Disability Quarterly* 33 (2010); A. Kim, "Graphic Organizers and Their Effects on the Reading Comprehension of Students with LD: A Synthesis of the Research," *Journal of Learning Disabilities* 37, no. 2 (2004).

28. M. Dembo and M. Eaton, "Self-Regulation of Academic Learning in Middle-Level Schools," *Elementary School Journal* 100, no. 5 (2000); J. Krouse and H. Krouse, "Toward a Multimodal Theory of Academic Achievement," *Educational Psychologist* 16 (1981).

29. Zimmerman, "Social Cognitive View"; B. Zimmerman and A. Bandura, "Impact of Self-Regulatory Influences on Writing Course Attainment," *American*

Educational Research Journal 31, no. 4 (1994); B. Zimmerman et al., *Developing Self-Regulated Learners: Beyond Achievement to Self-Efficacy* (Washington, DC: American Psychological Association, 1996); B. Zimmerman and R. Risemberg, "Becoming a Self-Regulated Writer: A Social Cognitive Perspective," *Contemporary Educational Psychology* 22 (1997).

30. S. Berkeley et al., "Implementation of Response to Intervention: A Snapshot of Progress," *Journal of Learning Disabilities* 42 (2011); J. Borkowski et al., "Components of Children's Metamemory: Implications for Strategy Generalization," in *Memory Development: Individual Differences and Universal Changes*, ed. F. Weinert and M. Perlmutter (Hillsdale, NJ: Lawrence Erlbaum, 1988); M. Carr and J. Borkowski, "Attributional Training and the Generalization of Reading Strategies with Underachieving Students," *Learning and Individual Differences* 1 (1989); L. Chan, "Combined Strategy and Attributional Training for Seventh-Grade Average and Poor Readers," *Journal of Research in Reading* 19 (1996).

31. H. Swanson et al., "Cognitive Processing Deficits in Poor Readers with Symptoms of Reading Disabilities and ADHD: More Alike Than Different?," *Journal of Educational Psychology* 91 (1999).

32. D. Fuchs et al., "Responsiveness-to-Intervention: Definitions, Evidence, and Implications for the Learning Disabilities Construct," *Learning Disabilities Research and Practice* 18 (2003); S. Baker et al., "A Synthesis of Empirical Research on Teaching Mathematics to Low-Achieving Students," *Elementary School Journal* 103 (2002); G. Biancarosa and C. Snow, *Reading Next: A Vision for Action and Research in Middle and High School Literacy; A Report to Carnegie Corporation of New York* (Washington, DC: Alliance for Excellence in Education, 2004); Gersten et al., *Assisting Students Struggling with Reading*; H. Swanson, "Searching for the Best Cognitive Model for Instructing Students with Learning Disabilities: A Component and Composite Analysis," *Educational and Child Psychology* 17, no. 3 (2000).

33. J. Hattie and H. Timperley, "The Power of Feedback," *Review of Educational Research* 77, no. 1 (2007); S. Vaughn, R. Gersten, and D. J. Chard, "The Underlying Message in LD Intervention Research: Findings from Research Syntheses," *Exceptional Children* 67, no. 1 (2000): 99–114.

34. J. K. Torgesen, "Individual Differences in Response to Early Interventions in Reading: The Lingering Problem of Treatment Resisters," *Learning Disabilities Research & Practice* 15, no. 1 (2000): 55–64.

35. J. Wanzek and S. Vaughn, "Response to Varying Amounts of Time in Reading Intervention for Students with Low Response to Intervention," *Journal of*

Learning Disabilities 41, no. 2 (2008).

36. B. Elbaum et al., "Grouping Practices and Reading Outcomes for Students with Disabilities," *Exceptional Children* 65 (1999).

37. National Center on Intensive Intervention, *Data-Based Individualization: A Framework for Intensive Intervention* (Washington, DC: Office of Special Education and U.S. Department of Education, 2013); S. L. Deno and P. K. Mirkin, *Data-Based Program Modification: A Manual* (Minneapolis, MN: Leadership Training Institute/Special Education, 1977); L. S. Fuchs, S. L. Deno, and P. L. Mirkin, "The Effects of Curriculum-Based Measurement Evaluation on Pedagogy, Student Achievement, and Student Awareness of Learning," *American Educational Research Journal* 21 (1984).

Chapter 6

1. M. Martinez and D. McGrath, *Deeper Learning: How Eight Innovative Public Schools Are Transforming Education in the Twenty-First Century* (New York: New Press, 2014).

2. S. Schneider, *Revolution, Reaction or Reform? The 1974 Bilingual Education Act* (New York: Las Americas, 1976), 22.

3. The 1960s was a period of historically low immigration, and recognition of speakers of languages other than English—to the extent that they were acknowledged at all—was generally limited to the pockets of Spanish speakers mostly clustered in the Southwest and the Miami area.

4. N. Mehlman Petrzela, "Before the Federal Bilingual Education Act: Legislation and Lived Experience in California," *Peabody Journal of Education* 85, no. 4 (2010).

5. R. Moran, "The Politics of Discretion: Federal Intervention in Bilingual Education," *California Law Review* 76, no. 6 (1988): 1273.

6. D. Pompa, *New Education Legislation Includes Important Policies for English Learners, Potential Pitfalls for Their Advocates* (Washington, DC: Migration Policy Institute, 2015).

7. C. Ryan, *Language Use in the United States: American Community Survey Reports* (Washington, DC: U.S. Census Bureau, 2013).

8. The 2013 figures are the most recent available, as of this writing. J. Zong and J. Batalova, *Frequently Requested Statistics on Immigrants and Immigration in the United States* (Washington, DC: Migration Policy Institute, 2015).

9. Ibid.

10. Ibid.

11. N. Lakhani, "'Lost' in Spanish," *Los Angeles Times*, March 9, 2015, http://www

.pressreader.com/usa/los-angeles-times/20150309/281479274884014/TextView.

12. A. Ruiz Soto, S. Hooker, and J. Batalova, *Fact Sheet: Top Languages Spoken by English Language Learners Nationally and by State* (Washington, DC: Migration Policy Institute, 2015).

13. E. Jensen, "China Replaces Mexico as the Top Sending Country for Immigrants to the United States," *Research Matters* (blog), U.S. Census Bureau, May 1, 2015, http://researchmatters.blogs.census.gov/2015/05/01/china-replaces-mexico-as-the-top-sending-country-for-immigrants-to-the-united-states.

14. A. Terrazas, *Immigrants in New Destination States* (Washington, DC: Migration Policy Institute, 2011).

15. W. Cornelius, "Mass Public Responses to the 'New' Latin Immigration to the United States," in *Latinos Remaking America*, ed. M. Suárez-Orozco and M. Paez (Berkeley, CA: University of California Press, 2002).

16. R. M. Callahan, "Tracking and High School English Learners: Limiting Opportunity to Learn," *American Educational Research Journal* 42 (2005); R. M. Callahan and P. Gándara, *On Nobody's Agenda: English Learners and Postsecondary Education* (Cambridge, MA: Harvard Education Press, 2004).

17. M. Martinez-Wenzl, K. Pérez, and P. Gándara, "Is Arizona's Approach to Educating Its English Learners Superior to Other Forms of Instruction?" *Teachers College Record* 114 (2012).

18. T. B. Parrish et al., *Effects of the Implementation of Proposition 227 on the Education of English Learners, K–12: Findings from a Five-Year Evaluation* (Washington, DC: American Institutes of Research; San Francisco, CA: WestEd, 2006), http://www.wested.org/online_pubs/227YR5_Report.pdf.

19. L. Hill, M. Weston, and J. Hayes, *Reclassification of English Learner Students in California* (San Francisco, CA: Public Policy Institute of California, 2014).

20. F. López, E. McEnearney, and M. Weistat, "Language Instruction Educational Programs and Academic Achievement of Latino English Learners: Considerations for States with Changing Demographics," *American Journal of Education* 121 (2015); R. Rumberger and L. Tran, "State Language Policies, School Language Practices, and the English Learner Achievement Gap," in *English Learners and Restrictive Language Policies*, ed. P. Gándara and M. Hopkins (New York: Teachers College Press, 2010).

21. K. Lillie et al., "Separate and Not Equal: The Implementation of Structured English Immersion in Arizona's Classrooms," *Teachers College Record* 114, no. 9 (2012); P. Gándara and R. Rumberger, "Immigration, Language, and Education: How Does Language Policy Structure Opportunity?" *Teachers College Record* 111 (2008).

22. The *Lau v. Nichols* 1974 decision was based on Title VI of the Civil Rights Act, which found that not providing English learners with access to the same curriculum that all other students receive is a violation of the nondiscrimination clause regarding national origin (and interpreted to include language). The court did not provide a specific remedy, only affirming that the ELL students needed to be provided with a means to access the regular curriculum as quickly as possible.

23. National Assessment of Educational Progress, *The Nation's Report Card: 2013 Report* (Washington, DC: U.S. Department of Education), http://www.nationsreportcard.gov/reading_math_2013/#/student-groups.

24. See, for example, H. Hopkins et al., "Fully Accounting for English Learner Performance: A Key Issue in ESEA Reauthorization," *Educational Researcher* 20 (2013).

25. D. Berliner, "Our Impoverished View of Education Reform," *Teachers College Record* 108 (2006); P. Carter and K. Welner, *Closing the Opportunity Gap: What America Must Do to Give Every Child an Even Chance* (New York: Oxford University Press, 2013).

26. Berliner, "Our Impoverished View of Education Reform."

27. D. Lichter, S. Sanders, and K. Johnson, "Hispanics at the Starting Line: Poverty Among Newborn Infants in Established Gateways and New Destinations," *Social Forces* (2015).

28. C. DeNavas-Walt and B. D. Proctor, *U.S. Census Bureau, Current Population Reports, P60-252, Income and Poverty in the United States: 2014* (Washington, DC: U.S. Government Printing Office, 2015).

29. Zong and Batalova, *Frequently Requested Statistics on Immigrants and Immigration in the United States.*

30. J. Hagan and N. Rodriguez, "Resurrecting Exclusion: The Effects of 1996 Immigration Reform on Communities and Families," in *Latinos Remaking America,* ed. M. Suárez-Orozco and M. Páez (Berkeley, CA: University of California Press, 2002).

31. D. Murphey, L. Guzman, and A. Torres, *America's Hispanic Children: Gaining Ground, Looking Forward* (Washington, DC: ChildTrends, 2014).

32. R. M. Callahan, *The English Learner Dropout Dilemma: Multiple Risks and Multiple Resources* (Santa Barbara, CA: California Dropout Research Project, 2013).

33. P. Gándara and F. Contreras, *The Latino Education Crisis: The Consequences of Failed Social Policy* (Cambridge, MA: Harvard University Press, 2009).

34. M. Martinez-Wenzl, *¿Listo para el Colegio? Examining College Readiness Among Latino Newcomer Immigrants* (Los Angeles, CA: University of California, Los Angeles, 2014).

35. M. Huelsman, *The Debt Divide: The Racial and Class Bias Behind the "New Normal" of Student Borrowing* (New York: Demos, 2015).

36. C. Falicov, "Ambiguous Loss: Risk and Resilience in Latino Immigrant Families," in *Latinos: Remaking America*, ed. M. Suárez Orozco and M. Paez (Berkeley, CA: University of California Press, 2002); C. Suárez-Orozco and M. Suárez-Orozco, *Children of Immigration* (Cambridge, MA: Harvard University Press, 2001).

37. G. Orfield, *Latinos in Education: Recent Trends* (Cambridge, MA: Harvard University, Graduate School of Education, 1995); G. Orfield and J. Yun, *Resegregation in American Schools* (Cambridge, MA: Civil Rights Project at Harvard University, 1999).

38. R. Ream, *Uprooting Children: Mobility, Social Capital, and Mexican American Underachievement* (New York: LFB Scholarly Publishing, 2005).

39. D. J. Hernandez, "Immigrant Youth in the United States," in *Youth Activism: An International Encyclopedia*, ed. L. Sherrod et al. (Westport, CT: Greenwood Press, 2006), 336–40.

40. J. Lee and M. Zhou, "The Success Frame and Achievement Paradox: The Costs and Consequences for Asian Americans," *Race and Social Problems* 6 (2014).

41. R. Gonzales, "Learning to Be Illegal: Undocumented Youth and Shifting Legal Contexts in the Transition to Adulthood," *American Sociological Review* 76, no. 4 (2011).

42. J. Kasperkevic, "The High Cost of Being a Legal Immigrant in the U.S.: $465," *Guardian*, January 8, 2014, https://www.theguardian.com/money/2014/jan/08/undocumented-dreamers-immigration-daca-cost-fee.

43. C. García Coll and A. K. Marks, eds., *The Immigrant Paradox in Children and Adolescents: Is Becoming American a Developmental Risk?* (Washington, DC: American Psychological Association, 2012).

44. E. Bialystok, *Bilingualism in Development: Language, Literacy, and Cognition* (New York: Cambridge University Press, 2001).

45. Ibid.

46. G. Valdés, *Expanding Definitions of Giftedness: The Case of Young Interpreters from Immigrant Communities* (New York: Routledge, 2003).

47. L. Santibañez and M. E. Zárate, "Bilinguals in the United States and College Enrollment," in *The Bilingual Advantage: Language, Literacy and the U.S. Labor Market*, ed. R. Callahan and P. Gándara (Bristol, UK: Multilingual Matters, 2014).

48. R. Rumbaut, "English Plus: Exploring the Socio-economic Benefits of Bilingualism in Southern California," in *The Bilingual Advantage*, ed. Callahan and Gándara; A. Portes and L. Hao, "The Price of Uniformity: Language, Family,

and Personality Adjustment in the Immigrant Second Generation," *Ethnic and Racial Studies* 25 (2002).

49. Bialystok, *Bilingualism in Development*.
50. R. Sternberg, ed., *Handbook of Creativity* (Cambridge, UK: Cambridge University Press, 1999).
51. S. Page, *The Difference: How the Power of Diversity Creates Better Groups, Firms, Schools and Societies* (Princeton, NJ: Princeton University Press, 2008).
52. F. Genesee and P. Gándara, "Bilingual Education Programs: A Cross-National Perspective," *Journal of Social Issues* 55 (1999); J. P. Rubin, *Reducing the Impact of Language Barriers* (New York: Forbes, 2011), http://www.forbes.com/forbesinsights/language_study_reg/.
53. J. Meltzer and E. Hamann, *Meeting the Literacy Development Needs of Adolescent English Language Learners Through Content Area Learning. Part I: Focus on Motivation and Engagement* (Providence, RI: Education Alliance at Brown University, 2004).
54. G. Kao and M. Tienda, "Optimism and Achievement: The Educational Performance of Immigrant Youth," *Social Science Quarterly* 76 (1995).
55. E. E. Telles and V. Ortiz, *Generations of Exclusion: Mexican Americans, Assimilation, and Race* (New York: Russell Sage Foundation, 2009).
56. C. Suárez-Orozco and M. Suárez-Orozco, *Transformations: Immigration, Family Life, and Achievement Motivation Among Latino Adolescents* (Stanford, CA: Stanford University Press, 1995).
57. A. Duckworth et al., "Grit: Perseverance and Passion for Long-Term Goals," *Journal of Personality and Social Psychology* 92 (2007).
58. B. Leyendecker and M. Lamb, "Latino Families," in *Parenting and Child Development in Non-Traditional Families*, ed. M. Lamb (East Sussex, UK: Psychology Press, 1998), 251.
59. R. Asera, *Calculus and Community: A History of the Emerging Scholars Program* (New York: College Board, 2001).
60. G. P. Knight, M. E. Bernal, and G. Carlo, "Socialization and the Development of Cooperative, Competitive, and Individualistic Behaviors Among Mexican American Children," in *Meeting the Challenge of Linguistic and Cultural Diversity in Early Childhood Education*, ed. E. E. García and B. McLaughlin (New York: Teachers College Press, 1995).
61. Leyendecker and Lamb, "Latino Families."
62. See, for example, M. Rutter, "Protective Factors in Children's Responses to Stress and Disadvantage," in *Primary Prevention of Psychopathology*, ed. M. W. Kent and J. E. Rolf (Hanover, NH: University Press of New England, 1979); E.

Werner, "Resilience in Development," *Current Directions in Psychological Science* 4 (1995); A. Masten, "Ordinary Magic: Resilience Processes in Development," *American Psychologist* 56 (2001).

63. S. Luthar, D. Cicchetti, and B. Becker, "The Construct of Resilience: A Critical Evaluation and Guidelines for Future Work," *Child Development* 71 (2000): 543.

64. M. Tienda and F. Mitchell, eds., *Multiple Origins, Uncertain Destinies: Hispanics and the American Future* (Washington, DC: National Academies Press, 2006).

65. B. Benard, *Resiliency: What We Have Learned* (San Francisco, CA: WestEd, 2004).

66. Suárez-Orozco and Suárez-Orozco, *Transformations*.

67. G. W. Allport, *The Nature of Prejudice* (Garden City, NY: Doubleday, 1954).

68. E. O. Cohen, *Designing Group Work: Strategies for Heterogeneous Classrooms* (New York: Teachers College Press, 1986).

69. Martinez-Wenzl, Pérez, and Gándara, "Is Arizona's Approach to Educating Its English Learners Superior to Other Forms of Instruction?"

70. F. Genesee et al., *Educating English Learners: A Synthesis of Research Evidence* (New York: Cambridge University Press, 2006), 201.

71. I. Umansky and S. Reardon, "Reclassification Patterns Among Latino English Learner Students in Bilingual, Dual Immersion, and English Immersion Classrooms," *American Educational Research Journal* 51, no. 5 (2014); R. Valentino and S. Reardon, "Effectiveness of Four Instructional Programs Designed to Serve English Language Learners: Variation by Ethnicity and Initial English Proficiency," *Educational Evaluation and Policy Analysis* 37, no. 4 (2014).

72. Genesee et al., *Educating English Learners*.

73. Umansky and Reardon, "Reclassification Patterns Among Latino English Learner Students."

74. Santibañez and Zárate, "Bilinguals in the United States."

75. Agirdag used National Education Longitudinal Study data. O. Agirdag, "The Literal Cost of Language Assimilation for the Children of Immigration: The Effects of Bilingualism on Labor Market Outcomes," in *The Bilingual Advantage*, eds. Callahan and Gándara.

76. Rumbaut, "English Plus."

77. Portes and Hao, "The Price of Uniformity."

78. Callahan, "Tracking and High School English Learners."

79. U. Aldana and A. Mayer, "The International Baccalaureate: A College-Preparatory Pathway for Heritage Language Speakers and Immigrant Youth," in *The Bilingual Advantage*, ed. Callahan and Gándara.

80. P. Gándara, *Project SOL: Preparing Secondary English Learners for Graduation and College* (Los Angeles, CA: Civil Rights Project/Proyecto Derechos Civiles, UCLA, 2013).

81. Zong and Batalova, *Frequently Requested Statistics on Immigrants and Immigration in the United States.*

82. L. Maxwell, "Arne Duncan Touts Advantages of Bilingualism," *Education Week*, May 30, 2013, http://blogs. edweek.org/edweek/learning-the-language/2013/05/arne_ duncan_touts_advantages_o.html.

83. J. King, "The Importance of Bilingual Education," March 25, 2016, transcript, speech before the California Association of Bilingual Educators, http://www.ed.gov/news/speeches/importance-bilingual-education?utm_content=&utm_medium=email&utm_name=&utm_source=govdelivery&utm_term=.

84. Moran, "The Politics of Discretion."

85. C. Ovando and V. Collier, *Bilingual and ESL Classrooms* (New York: McGraw-Hill, 1985).

86. As I wrote this chapter, California voters were considering a ballot question that would reverse the ban and make it easier to create bilingual programs. On November 8, 2016, the measure passed with overwhelming support. See Corey Mitchell, "California Voters Repeal Ban on Bilingual Education," *Education Week*, November 8, 2016, http://blogs.edweek.org/edweek/learning-the-language/2016/11/fate_of_californias_propositio.html?qs=california+bilingual+inmeta:Cover_year%3D2016.

87. A. Zehler et al., *Descriptive Study of Services to LEP Students and LEP Students with Disabilities* (Washington, DC: Development Associates, 2003.

Chapter 7

1. D. K. Cohen, *Teaching and Its Predicaments* (Cambridge, MA: Harvard University Press, 2011), 4.

2. J. Mehta and S. Fine, *The Why, What, Where, and How of Deeper Learning in American Secondary Schools* (Boston, MA: Jobs for the Future, 2015); P. Cusick, *The Egalitarian Ideal and the American High School: Studies of Three Schools* (New York: Longman, 1983); G. Graff, *Clueless in Academe: How Schooling Obscures the Life of the Mind* (New Haven, CT: Yale University Press, 2003).

3. J. Jennings, *Reflections on a Half-Century of School Reform: Why Have We Fallen Short and Where Do We Go from Here?* (Washington, DC: Center on Education Policy, 2012); G. Cawelti, "The Side Effects of NCLB," *Educational Leadership* 64, no. 3 (2006).

4. The William and Flora Hewlett Foundation, *Deeper Learning Defined* (Menlo Park, CA: Hewlett Foundation, 2013); Cohen, *Teaching and Its Predicaments*.

5. Hewlett Foundation, *Deeper Learning Defined*.

6. A. Sfard, *Thinking as Communicating: Human Development, the Growth of Discourses, and Mathematizing* (New York: Cambridge University Press, 2008).

7. K. Weick and R. McDaniel, "How Professional Organizations Work: Implications for School Organization and Management," in *Schooling for Tomorrow: Directing Reforms to Issues That Count*, ed. T. J. Sergiovanni and J. H. Moore (Rockleigh, NJ: Allyn & Bacon, 1989); E. Wenger, *Communities of Practice: Learning, Meaning, and Identity* (Cambridge, MA: Cambridge University Press, 1998); B. Rogoff et al., "Development Through Participation in Sociocultural Activity," *New Directions for Child Development* 67 (1995).

8. Hewlett Foundation, *Deeper Learning Defined*.

9. Ibid.

10. R. Roeser, J. Eccles, and A. Sameroff, "School as a Context of Early Adolescents' Academic and Social-Emotional Development: A Summary of Research Findings," *Elementary School Journal* 100, no. 5 (2000); S. E. Wortham, "The Interdependence of Social Identification and Learning," *American Educational Research Journal* 41, no. 3 (2004); E. W. Gordon, *Pedagogy and the Development of Intellective Competence* (New York: College Board National Forum, 2000); J. G. Greeno, *Students with Competence, Authority and Accountability: Affording Intellective Identities in Classrooms* (New York: College Board, 2001).

11. Students move toward an identity that psychologist James Greeno calls "intellective." See J. Boaler and J. G. Greeno, "Identity, Agency, and Knowing in Mathematics Worlds," in *Multiple Perspectives on Mathematics Teaching and Learning*, ed. J. Boaler (Stamford, CT: Elsevier Science, 2000).

12. P. Eckert, *Jocks and Burnouts: Social Categories and Identity in the High School* (New York: Teachers College Press, 1989); P. Eckert, "Adolescent Social Categories, Information and Science Learning," in *Toward a Scientific Practice of Science Education*, ed. M. Gardner et al. (Hillsdale, NJ: Lawrence Erlbaum, 1990).

13. E. Yazzie-Mintz, *Charting the Path from Engagement to Achievement: A Report on the 2009 High School Survey of Student Engagement* (Bloomington, IN: Center for Evaluation and Education Policy at Indiana University, 2010).

14. D. K. Cohen, *Teaching Practice: Plus Que Ça Change* (East Lansing, MI: Michigan State University, National Center for Research on Teacher Education, 1988); Cohen, *Teaching and Its Predicaments*; L. Cuban, *How Teachers Taught: Constancy and Change in American Classrooms, 1890–1990* (New York: Teachers College Press, 1993).

15. The descriptions of teaching in this section are based on my observations of high school mathematics lessons. Ms. A, the first teacher, is an archetype, not a real person. The lesson I describe is a composite of the many lessons of this sort I have observed in high schools over the last six years. Ms. B, the second teacher, is a real person. The lesson we see was planned by two residents in the Boston Teacher Residency program (Clarissa Gore and Meaghan Provencher) and taught by one of them (Provencher). The activities, materials, and dialogue presented here were recorded during my observations in her classroom during the 2014–15 school year.

16. Mehta and Fine, *Why, What, Where, and How of Deeper Learning*; Cusick, *The Egalitarian Ideal and the American High School*; P. Cusick, *Inside High School: The Student's World* (New York: Holt, Rinehart, and Winston, 1973); Graff, *Clueless in Academe*.

17. Cohen, *Teaching and Its Predicaments*; M. Lampert and F. Graziani, "Instructional Activities as a Tool for Teachers' and Teacher Educators' Learning," *Elementary School Journal* 109, no. 5 (2009); F. Newman et al., *Authentic Achievement: Restructuring Schools for Intellectual Quality* (San Francisco, CA: Jossey-Bass, 1996).

18. Philip Jackson, Willard Waller, and Dan Lortie were early identifiers of these patterns in the practice of teaching. See P. Jackson, *Life in Classrooms* (New York: Holt, Rinehart, and Winston, 1968); W. Waller, *The Sociology of Teaching* (New York: John Wiley & Sons, 1932); D. C. Lortie, *Schoolteacher* (Chicago, IL: University of Chicago Press, 1975).

19. L. Sims, "Look Who's Talking: Differences in Math Talk in U.S. and Chinese Classrooms," *Teaching Children Mathematics* 15, no. 2 (2008); J. Holt, *The Underachieving School* (New York: Pitman, 1969).

20. A. Powell, E. Farrar, and D. K. Cohen, *The Shopping Mall High School* (Boston, MA: Houghton Mifflin, 1985); Cuban, *How Teachers Taught*; Mehta and Fine, *Why, What, Where, and How of Deeper Learning*.

21. Lortie, *Schoolteacher*; L. C. Sam and P. Ernest, "A Survey of Public Images of Mathematics," *Research in Mathematics Education* 2, no. 1 (2000); A. Barkatsas and J. Malone, "A Typology of Mathematics Teachers' Beliefs About Teaching and Learning Mathematics and Instructional Practices," *Mathematics Education Research Journal* 17, no. 2 (2005).

22. T. E. Deal and K. D. Peterson, *Shaping School Culture: The Heart of Leadership* (San Francisco, CA: Jossey-Bass, 1999); T. E. Deal and K. D. Peterson, *Shaping School Culture: Pitfalls, Paradoxes, and Promises* (San Francisco, CA: Jossey-Bass, 2009).

23. R. Moses and C. Cobb, *Radical Equations: Civil Rights from Mississippi to the*

Algebra Project (Boston, MA: Beacon Press, 2001).

24. In the Common Core State Standards for Mathematics (2010), what students need to learn about rate of change and slope are connected thus: "Construct a function to model a linear relationship between two quantities. Determine the rate of change and initial value of the function from a description of a relationship or from two (x, y) values, including reading these from a table or from a graph. Interpret the rate of change and initial value of a linear function in terms of the situation it models, and in terms of its graph or a table of values" (8.F.B.4). They are also expected to "Use similar triangles to *explain why* the slope m is the same between any two distinct points on a non-vertical line in the coordinate plane; *derive* the equation $y = mx$ for a line through the origin and the equation $y = mx + b$ for a line intercepting the vertical axis at b" (8.EE.B.6; emphases mine).

25. For example, options traders study the relationship between the rate of change in the price of an option relative to a small change in the price of the underlying asset, known as an options delta; mapmakers decide on scale depending on what they want to highlight for the user; and coaches train long-distance runners based on knowledge of when it makes sense to slow down or speed up in a race.

26. On this kind of graph, there is a unique pair of numbers associated with every point on an infinitely large flat surface (its *coordinates*). The coordinates describe where that point is in relation to a reference point called the *origin*: How far left or right of the origin is the point? How far above or below? Invented in the seventeenth century by Descartes, this representation caused a revolutionary leap in the growth of mathematics because it made possible a link between the two separate fields of algebra and geometry. It allowed an easy visual comparison between functions. It played a crucial role in the invention of calculus.

27. K. Asante, "Secondary Students' Attitudes Towards Mathematics," *IFE Psychology* 20, no. 1 (2012); K. Sanchez, B. Zimmerman, and R. Ye, "Secondary Students' Attitudes Toward Mathematics," *Academic Exchange Quarterly* 8, no. 2 (2004); A. Lipnevich et al., "Mathematics Attitudes and Mathematics Outcomes of U.S. and Belarusian Middle School Students," *Journal of Educational Psychology* 103, no. 1 (2011).

28. J. Hiebert et al., *Teaching Mathematics in Seven Countries: Results from the TIMSS 1999 Video Study* (Washington, DC: National Center for Education Statistics, 2003).

29. A. Arcavi, "The Role of Visual Representations in the Learning of Mathematics," *Educational Studies in Mathematics* 52, no. 3 (2003): 215–41.

30. J. Bransford, A. Brown, and R. Cocking, eds., *How People Learn: Brain, Mind, Experience, and School* (Washington, DC: National Academy Press, 1999).

31. These figures are taken from the Massachusetts Department of Elementary and Secondary Education's 2015 summary of data for Ms. B's school.

32. National Center for Education Statistics, *The Condition of Education 2012* (Washington, DC: National Center for Education Statistics, U.S. Department of Education, 2012); S. Ginder et al., *2013–14 Integrated Postsecondary Education Data System (IPEDS) Methodology Report* (Washington, DC: National Center for Education Statistics, U.S. Department of Education, 2014), https://nces.ed.gov/pubsearch/pubsinfo.asp?pubid=2014067; National Center for Education Statistics, "Public High School Graduation Rates" (Washington, DC: National Center for Education Statistics, U.S. Department of Education, 2012), http://nces.ed.gov/programs/coe/indicator_coi.asp.

33. The ways that functions are represented (graphs, verbal descriptions, tables, and equations) and how the elements of these representations are connected are at the heart of the "core" mathematics in this domain. See G. Leinhardt, O. Zaslavsky, and M. Stein, "Functions, Graphs, and Graphing: Tasks, Learning, and Teaching," *Review of Educational Research* 60, no. 1 (1990).

34. Megan Staples identifies such co-construction as an essential learning practice in secondary mathematics classrooms that seek to promote students' mathematical understanding and engagement. See M. Staples, "Supporting Whole-Class Collaborative Inquiry in a Secondary Mathematics Classroom," *Cognition and Instruction* 25, no. 2–3 (2007): 161–217.

35. E. Fennema and T. P. Carpenter, "A Longitudinal Study of Learning to Use Children's Thinking in Mathematics Instruction," *Journal for Research in Mathematics Education* 27, no. 4 (1996).

36. Boaler and Greeno, "Identity, Agency, and Knowing in Mathematics Worlds."

37. C. Dweck, *Mindset: The New Psychology of Success: How We Can Learn to Fulfill Our Potential* (New York: Ballantine Books, 2007).

38. "Look for and make use of structure" is one of the eight mathematical practices that the Common Core State Standards require teaching throughout grades K–12. But it has long been identified as a key to doing mathematics of all sorts. See, for example, M. Kline, *Mathematical Thought from Ancient to Modern Times* (New York: Oxford University Press, 1972).

39. The design Ms. B is enacting is based on a protocol created by Grace Kelemanik and Amy Lucenta for the Boston Teacher Residency.

40. They are learning to communicate in what has been called "the mathematics register" by M. A. K. Halliday, *Language as Social Semiotic* (London: Edward

Arnold, 1978), describing "the discipline-specific use of language employed in mathematics education." It should be noted that this does not refer solely to specific vocabulary but also to meanings, styles, and modes of argument.

41. Individual development toward these competencies cannot be understood without reference to the social context within which they are embedded. See, for example, J. Wertsch, *Vygotsky and the Social Formation of Mind* (Cambridge, MA: Harvard University Press, 1988); J. Wertsch, ed., *Culture, Communication, and Cognition: Vygotskian Perspectives* (New York: Cambridge University Press, 1985); B. Rogoff, *Apprenticeship in Thinking: Cognitive Development in Social Context* (New York: Oxford University Press, 1990); Sfard, *Thinking as Communicating*.

42. A. Powell, E. Farrar, and D. Cohen, *The Shopping Mall High School* (Boston, MA: Houghton Mifflin, 1985).

43. M. Staples, J. Bartlo, and E. Thanheiser, "Justification as a Teaching and Learning Practice: Its (Potential) Multifaceted Role in Middle Grades Mathematics Classrooms," *Journal of Mathematical Behavior* 31 (2012); M. Blanton and J. Kaput, "Teaching and Learning a New Algebra," in *Mathematics Classrooms That Promote Understanding*, ed. E. Fennema and T. Romberg (Mahwah, NJ: Lawrence Erlbaum, 2005); J. Kaput, "Algebra and Technology: New Semiotic Continuities and Referential Connectivity," in *Proceedings of the Twenty-first Annual Meeting of the North American Chapter of the International Group for the Psychology of Mathematics Education*, ed. F. Hitt and M. Santos (Columbus, OH: ERIC Clearinghouse for Science, Mathematics, and Environmental Education, 1999).

44. S. Chapin and C. O'Connor, "Academically Productive Talk: Supporting Students' Learning in Mathematics," in *The Learning of Mathematics, Sixty-Ninth Yearbook*, ed. W. G. Martin, M. Strutchenns, and P. Elliott (Reston, VA: National Council of Teachers of Mathematics, 2007); M. Smith and M. K. Stein, *Five Practices for Orchestrating Productive Mathematics Discussions* (Reston, VA: National Council of Teachers of Mathematics, 2011).

45. Student names are pseudonyms.

46. M. Lampert, *Teaching Problems and the Problems of Teaching* (New Haven, CT: Yale University Press, 2001).

47. R. Stevens and R. Hall, "Disciplined Perception: Learning to See in Technoscience," in *Talking Mathematics in School*, ed. M. Lampert and M. Blunk (New York: Cambridge University Press, 1998).

48. Cohen, *Teaching Practice: Plus Que Ça Change*; Cohen, *Teaching and Its Predicaments*; D. K. Cohen and J. Spillane, "Policy and Practice: The Relations Between

Governance and Instruction," *Review of Research in Education* 18 (1992).

49. Personal correspondence.

50. Bransford, Brown, and Cocking, *How People Learn*.

51. See also C. Bereiter and M. Scardamalia, "Cognitive Coping and the Problem of Inert Knowledge," in *Thinking and Learning Skills: Volume 2, Research and Open Questions*, ed. S. Chipman, J. Segal, and R. Glaser (Mahwah, NJ: Lawrence Erlbaum, 1985).

52. A. N. Whitehead, "The Aims of Education," *Daedalus* 88, no. 1 (1959): 192–205.

53. Hewlett Foundation, *Deeper Learning Defined*.

54. G. Leinhardt, O. Zaslavsky, and M. Stein, "Functions, Graphs, and Graphing: Tasks, Learning, and Teaching," *Review of Educational Research* 60, no. 1 (1990).

55. This short summary of the knowledge, skill, and commitments needed for deeper teaching is similar in content to the list of Mathematics Teaching Practices issued by the National Council of Teachers of Mathematics (2014) to align instruction with the learning goals in the Common Core State Standards (Principles to Actions) and the Design Principles for Instruction underlying the lesson guides issued by the Mathematics Resource Assessment project as part of the Math Design Collaborative initiated by the Bill and Melinda Gates Foundation.

56. M. Lampert, T. Boerst, and F. Graziani, "Organizational Assets in the Service of School-Wide Ambitious Teaching Practice," *Teachers College Record* 113, no. 7 (2011).

57. S. Loucks-Horsley and C. Matsumoto, "Research on Professional Development for Teachers of Mathematics and Science: The State of the Scene," *School Science and Mathematics* 99, no. 5 (1999); D. L. Ball and D. K. Cohen, "Developing Practice, Developing Practitioners: Toward a Practice-Based Theory of Professional Education," in *Teaching as the Learning Profession: Handbook of Policy and Practice* (San Francisco, CA: Jossey-Bass, 1999); D. K. Cohen and H. C. Hill, *Learning Policy* (New Haven, CT: Yale University Press, 2001).

58. M. McDonald, E. Kazemmi, and S. Kavanagh, "Core Practices and Pedagogies of Teacher Education: A Call for a Common Language and Collective Activity," *Journal of Teacher Education* 64 (2013).

59. See, for example, I. C. Fountas and G. S. Pinnell, *Guided Reading: Good First Teaching for All Children* (Portsmouth, NH: Heinemann, 1996). Some of the instructional activities in use across subjects and grade levels are collected on a website called Teacher Education by Design. They can be viewed at www.TEDD.org.

60. The use of instructional activity protocols to enable teachers to teach mathematics ambitiously is based on research conducted by the Learning Teaching Practice project. See Lampert and Graziani, "Instructional Activities as a Tool"; M. Lampert et al., "Using Designed Instructional Activities to Enable Novices to Manage Ambitious Mathematics Teaching," in *Instructional Explanations in the Disciplines*, ed. M. K. Stein and L. Kucan (New York: Springer, 2010).

61. This derives from Aristotelian ethics and psychological research on the acquisition of habits. For a contemporary perspective on this argument, see I. Horn, *Strength in Numbers: Collaborative Learning in Secondary Mathematics* (Reston, VA: National Council of Teachers of Mathematics, 2012).

62. D. Wiliam, "Content Then Process: Teacher Learning Communities in the Service of Formative Assessment," in *Ahead of the Curve: The Power of Assessment to Transform Teaching and Learning*, ed. D. Reeves (Bloomington, IN: Solution Tree Press, 2007); E. Kazemi, "School Development as a Means to Improve Mathematics Teaching and Learning: Towards Multidirectional Analyses of Learning Across Contexts," in *Participants in Mathematics Teacher Education: Individuals, Teams, Communities, and Networks*, ed. K. Krainer and T. Wood (Rotterdam, The Netherlands: Sense Publishers, 2008); J. W. Stigler and B. Thompson, "Thoughts on Creating, Accumulating, and Utilizing Shareable Knowledge to Improve Teaching," *Elementary School Journal* 109, no. 5 (2009).

63. D. K. Cohen et al., *Improvement by Design: The Promise of Better Schools* (Chicago, IL: University of Chicago Press, 2013); Smith and Stein, *Five Practices for Orchestrating Productive Mathematics Discussions*.

Chapter 8

1. See, for example, M. Berends, S. J. Bodilly, and S. M. Kirby, "The Future of Whole School Designs: Conclusions, Observations, and Policy Implications," in *Facing the Challenges of Whole School Reform: New American Schools After a Decade*, ed. M. Berends, S. J. Bodilly, and S. M. Kirby (Santa Monica, CA: RAND Education, 2002); B. Malen, R. T. Ogawa, and J. Kranz, "What Do We Know About School-Based Management? A Case Study of the Literature—A Call for Research," in *Choice and Control in American Schools* (Philadelphia, PA: Falmer, 1990); S. C. Purkey and M. S. Smith, "School Reform: The District Policy Implications of the Effective Schools Literature," *Elementary School Journal* 85, no. 3 (1985).

2. Center on Education Policy, *From the Capital to the Classroom: Year 2 of the No Child Left Behind Act* (Washington, DC: Center on Education Policy, 2004); S. Fuhrman, *The New Accountability* (Philadelphia, PA: Consortium for Policy

Research in Education, 1999); S. Fuhrman and R. Elmore, "Understanding Local Control in the Wake of State Education Reform," *Educational Evaluation and Policy Analysis* 12, no. 1 (1990); L. Hamilton et al., *Standards-Based Accountability Under No Child Left Behind: Experiences of Teachers and Administrators in Three States* (Santa Monica, CA: RAND Education, 2007); M. Kirst, *Accountability: Implications for State and Local Policymakers* (Washington, DC: Office of Educational Research and Improvement, U.S. Department of Education, 1990); N. Kober, J. Jennings, and J. Peltason, *Better Federal Policies Leading to Better Schools* (Washington, DC: Center on Education Policy, 2010); National Governors Association, Council of Chief State School Officers, and Achieve, Inc., *Benchmarking for Success: Ensuring U.S. Students Receive a World-Class Education* (Washington, DC: National Governors Association, 2008).

3. The William and Flora Hewlett Foundation, *Deeper Learning Defined* (Menlo Park, CA: Hewlett Foundation, 2013); Huberman et al., *The Shape of Deeper Learning: Strategies, Structures, and Cultures in Deeper Learning Network High Schools* (Washington, DC: American Institutes for Research, 2014); National Research Council, *Education for Life and Work: Developing Transferable Knowledge and Skills in the 21st Century* (Washington, DC: National Academies Press, 2012).

4. D. Goldhaber, D. Brewer, and D. Anderson, "A Three-Way Error Components Analysis of Educational Productivity," *Education Economics* 7, no. 3 (1999); J. Grissom, S. Loeb, and B. Master, "Effective Instructional Time Use for School Leaders: Longitudinal Evidence from Observations of Principals," *Educational Researcher* 42, no. 8 (2013); S. G. Rivkin, E. A. Hanushek, and J. F. Kain, "Teachers, Schools, and Academic Achievement," *Econometrica* 73, no. 2 (2005); J. Rockoff, "The Impact of Individual Teachers on Student Achievement: Evidence from Panel Data," *American Economic Review* 94, no. 2 (2004); V. M. J. Robinson, C. A. Lloyd, and K. J. Rowe, "The Impact of Leadership on Student Outcomes: An Analysis of the Differential Effects of Leadership Types," *Educational Administration Quarterly* 44, no. 5 (2008); J. Sebastian and E. Allensworth, "The Influence of Principal Leadership on Classroom Instruction and Student Learning: A Study of Mediated Pathways to Learning," *Educational Administration Quarterly* 48, no. 4 (2012); J. Supovitz, P. Sirinides, and H. May, "How Principals and Peers Influence Teaching and Learning," *Educational Administration Quarterly* 46, no. 1 (2011).

5. E. A. Hanushek, "The Trade-Off Between Child Quantity and Quality," *Journal of Political Economy* 100, no. 1 (1992).

6. Grissom, Loeb, and Master, "Effective Instructional Time Use for School Leaders"; Sebastian and Allensworth, "Influence of Principal Leadership."

7. M. S. Knapp et al., *Learning-Focused Leadership and Leadership Support: Meaning and Practice in Urban Systems* (Seattle, WA: University of Washington, Center for the Study of Teaching and Policy, 2010); M. McLaughlin and J. Talbert, *Reforming Districts: How Districts Support School Reform* (Seattle, WA: University of Washington, Center for the Study of Teaching and Policy, 2003).

8. A. Odden, *Strategic Management of Human Capital: Improving Instructional Practice and Student Learning in Schools* (New York: Routledge, 2011).

9. Berends, Bodilly, and Kirby, "Future of Whole School Designs"; Malen, Ogawa, and Kranz, "What Do We Know About School-Based Management?"; Purkey and Smith, "School Reform."

10. See, for example, W. Togneri and S. E. Anderson, *Beyond Islands of Excellence: What Districts Can Do to Improve Instruction and Achievement in All Schools—A Leadership Brief* (Washington, DC: Learning First Alliance, 2003).

11. J. P. Spillane, "State Policy and the Non-Monolithic Nature of the Local School District: Organizational and Professional Considerations," *American Educational Research Journal* 35, no. 1 (1998).

12. T. Corcoran, S. H. Fuhrman, and C. L. Belcher, "The District Role in Instructional Improvement," *Phi Delta Kappan* 83, no. 1 (2001): 78–84.

13. "Issues," Education Commission of the States, http://www.ecs.org/research-reports/issues/.

14. M. Busch et al., *The National School District and Network Grants Program: Year 2 Evaluation Report* (Washington, DC: American Institutes for Research, 2004); S. Yatsko et al., *Tinkering Toward Transformation: A Look at Federal School Improvement Grant Implementation* (Seattle, WA: Center on Reinventing Public Education, University of Washington, 2012).

15. J. Mirel, "Progressive School Reform in Comparative Perspective," in *Southern Cities, Southern Schools: Public Education in the Urban South*, ed. D. Plank and R. Ginsberg (New York: Greenwood Press, 1990); T. Steffes, "Solving the 'Rural School Problem': New State Aid, Standards, and Supervision of Local Schools, 1900–1933," *History of Education Quarterly* 48, no. 2 (2008).

16. L. G. Bjork and T. J. Kowalski, eds., *The Contemporary Superintendent: Preparation, Practice, and Development* (Thousand Oaks, CA: Corwin Press, 2005).

17. J. Marsh, *Connecting Districts to the Policy Dialogue: A Review of Literature on the Relationship of Districts with States, Schools, and Communities* (Seattle, WA: University of Washington, Center for the Study of Teaching and Policy, 2000).

18. M. I. Honig, "Where's the 'Up' in Bottom-Up Reform?," *Educational Policy* 18, no. 4 (2004): 527–61; Spillane, "State Policy"; J. P. Spillane, "Cognition and Policy Implementation: District Policymakers and the Reform of Mathematics Education," *Cognition and Instruction* 18, no. 2 (2000).

19. L. Hubbard, H. Mehan, and M. K. Stein, *Reform as Learning: When School Reform Collides with School Culture and Community Politics* (New York: Routledge, 2006).

20. We use the title "curriculum and instruction" to refer to the central office department charged with supporting the curricular and instructional needs of a district's teaching staff—for example, by adopting curricular materials and providing professional development. Other common titles for this department include "instructional services" and "teaching and learning." Very small districts tend not to have full C&I departments but still have a person or a subset of administrators handling those functions.

21. M. I. Honig, *From Tinkering to Transformation: Strengthening School District Central Office Performance* (Washington, DC: American Enterprise Institute, 2013); M. I. Honig and L. R. Rainey, "Central Office Leadership in Principal Professional Learning Communities: The Practice Beneath the Policy," *Teachers College Record* 116, no. 4 (2014).

22. M. I. Honig et al., "Research Use as Learning: The Case of Fundamental Change in School District Central Offices," *American Educational Research Journal*, under review.

23. Honig, *From Tinkering to Transformation.*

24. Our study of central office transformation involved three urban districts between August 2007 and July 2008. Our study of research use as learning involved six districts—one midsized urban district, two midsized suburban districts, and three small rural districts—between January 2011 and June 2012. M. I. Honig et al., *Central Office Transformation for District-Wide Teaching and Learning Improvement* (Seattle, WA: University of Washington, Center for the Study of Teaching and Policy, 2010); Honig et al., "Research Use as Learning."

25. Our seventeen partner districts include midsized and large, urban and suburban districts, from September 2011 to the present.

26. See, for example, Honig et al., *Central Office Transformation*; M. I. Honig, "District Central Office Leadership as Teaching: How Central Office Administrators Support Principals' Development as Instructional Leaders," *Educational Administration Quarterly* 48, no. 4 (2012); Honig, *From Tinkering to Transformation;* Honig and Rainey, "Central Office Leadership"; Honig et al., "Research Use as Learning."

27. A. M. Collins, J. S. Brown, and A. Holum, "Cognitive Apprenticeship: Making Thinking Visible," *The Principles of Learning: Study Tools for Educators* (Pittsburgh, PA: Institute for Learning, University of Pittsburgh, 2003).

28. See, for example, B. Turnbull, D. Riley, and J. MacFarlane, *Districts Taking Charge of the Principal Pipeline* (Washington, DC: Policy Studies Associates, 2015); Honig et al., *Central Office Transformation*; Honig, *From Tinkering to Transformation*.

29. Odden, *Strategic Management of Human Capital*.

30. Grissom, Loeb, and Master, "Effective Instructional Time Use for School Leaders"; Honig et al., *Central Office Transformation*.

31. N. Venkateswaran, *When Principals Lead for Improved Teaching: The Importance of Principal-Teacher Interactions* (Seattle, WA: University of Washington, 2015).

32. M. L. Franke, E. Kazemi, and D. Battey, "Understanding Teaching and Classroom Practice in Mathematics," in *Second Handbook of Research on Mathematics Teaching and Learning*, ed. F. K. Lester (Greenwich, CT: Information Age Publishers, 2007); M. Windschitl et al., "The Beginner's Repertoire: Proposing a Core Set of Instructional Practices for Teachers of Science," *Science Education* 96, no. 5 (2012).

33. B. Portin et al., *Leading for Learning Improvement in Urban Schools* (Seattle, WA: University of Washington, Center for the Study of Teaching and Policy, 2009).

34. Honig et al., *Central Office Transformation*; L. R. Rainey and M. I. Honig, *From Procedures to Partnership: Redesigning Principal Supervision to Help Principals Lead for High-Quality Teaching and Learning* (Seattle, WA: University of Washington, Center for Educational Leadership and District Leadership Design Lab, 2015).

35. Honig et al., "Research Use as Learning."

36. Honig et al., *Central Office Transformation;* Honig, "District Central Office Leadership as Teaching"; Honig and Rainey, "Central Office Leadership"; Rainey and Honig, *From Procedures to Partnership*. For a summary of research findings on principal supervision showing an association with improved performance, see "Principal Supervisor Performance Standards (PSPS)," District Leadership Design Lab, University of Washington, http://www.dl2uw.org/principal-supervisor-performance-standards.html.

37. Honig et al., *Central Office Transformation*.

38. Rainey and Honig, *From Procedures to Partnership*.

39. Honig, *From Tinkering to Transformation*.

40. Honig et al., "Research Use as Learning."

41. Honig, *From Tinkering to Transformation*; Honig et al., *Central Office Transformation*.

42. Honig et al., *Central Office Transformation*.

43. M. Plecki et al., *How Leaders Invest Staffing Resources for Learning Improvement* (Seattle, WA: University of Washington, Center for the Study of Teaching and Policy, 2009).

44. Odden, *Strategic Management of Human Capital*.

45. M. I. Honig, "No Small Thing: School District Central Office Bureaucracies and the Implementation of New Small Autonomous Schools Initiatives," *American Educational Research Journal* 46, no. 2 (2009).

46. Honig et al., *Central Office Transformation*.

47. Honig, *From Tinkering to Transformation*.

Chapter 9

1. National Research Council, *Incentives and Test-Based Accountability in Education* (Washington, DC: National Academies Press, 2011).

2. C. Gewertz, "Opting Out of Testing: A Rising Tide for States and Districts?," *Education Week*, March 3, 2014, http://blogs.edweek.org/edweek/curriculum/2014/03/opting_out_of_testing.html?qs=parents+common+core+testing.

3. R. L. Linn, *Test-Based Accountability* (Princeton, NJ: Gordon Commission on the Future of Assessment in Education, n.d.); R. L. Linn, "Educational Accountability Systems," in *The Future of Test-Based Educational Accountability*, ed. K. E. Ryan and L. A. Shepard (New York: Routledge, 2008), 3–24.

4. D. T. Conley, *Getting Ready for College, Careers, and the Common Core: What Every Educator Needs to Know* (San Francisco, CA: Jossey-Bass, 2014); Jobs for the Future, *Education and Skills for the 21st Century: An Agenda for Action* (Boston, MA: Jobs for the Future, 2005); Secretary's Commission on Achieving Necessary Skills, *What Work Requires of Schools: A SCANS Report for America 2000* (Washington, DC: U.S. Department of Labor, 1991).

5. It's always worth noting that only one of the "three Rs" actually begins with the letter *r*.

6. C. Gewertz, "Teacher's Union President: Halt All High Stakes Linked to Common Core," *Education Week*, April 30, 2013, http://blogs.edweek.org/edweek/curriculum/2013/04/halt_high_stakes_linked_to_common_core.html?cmp=ENL-EU-NEWS2; C. Gewertz, "Opting Out of Testing: A Rising Tide for States and Districts?" *Education Week*, March 3, 2014, http://blogs.edweek.org/edweek/curriculum/2014/03/opting_out_of_testing.html; S. Sawchuk, "New York Union Encourages Districts to Boycott Field Tests," *Education*

Week, May 30, 2014, http://blogs.edweek.org/edweek/teacherbeat/2014/05/
new_york_union_encourages_dist.html.

7. M. S. Tucker, *Fixing our National Accountability System* (Washington, DC: National Center on Education and the Economy, 2014).

8. J. D. Bransford, A. L. Brown, and R. R. Cocking, eds., *How People Learn: Brain, Mind, Experience, and School* (Washington, DC: National Academy Press, 2000); J. Pellegrino and M. Hilton, eds., *Education for Life and Work: Developing Transferable Knowledge and Skills in the 21st Century* (Washington, DC: National Academies Press, 2012); Achieve, Education Trust, and Thomas B. Fordham Foundation, *Ready or Not: Creating a High School Diploma That Counts* (Washington, DC: Achieve, 2004); "ACT College and Career Readiness Standards," ACT, http://www.act.org/standard/; D. T. Conley, *Understanding University Success* (Eugene, OR: Center for Educational Policy Research, University of Oregon, 2013); D. T. Conley et al., *College Board Advanced Placement Best Practices Course Study* (Eugene, OR: Center for Educational Policy Research, 2006); D. T. Conley and R. Brown, "Analyzing State High School Assessments to Determine Their Relationship to University Expectations for a Well-Prepared Student" (paper presented at the American Educational Research Association, Chicago, IL, 2003); "ThinkReady: An Innovative, Formative Assessment of Students' Cognitive Abilities," Educational Policy Improvement Center, 2015, https://collegereadyinfo.epiconline.org/thinkready/; M. Seburn, S. Frain, and D. T. Conley, *Job Training Programs Curriculum Study* (Washington, DC: National Assessment Governing Board, WestEd, Educational Policy Improvement Center, 2013); Texas Higher Education Coordinating Board and Texas Education Agency Division of Curriculum, *Texas College and Career Readiness Standards* (Austin, TX: Educational Policy Improvement Center, 2009); College Board, *Standards for College Success* (New York: College Board, 2006).

9. G. Robinson, "A Remarkable Feat in Education: The Every Student Succeeds Act Puts a Stop to the Department of Education's Decades-Long Stranglehold on Education Policy," *U.S. News & World Report*, January 4, 2016, http://www.usnews.com/opinion/knowledge-bank/articles/2016-01-04/the-every-student-succeeds-act-loosens-the-federal-grip-on-education.

10. D. T. Conley and L. Darling-Hammond, "Building Systems of Assessment for Deeper Learning," in *Beyond the Bubble Test: How Performance Assessments Support 21st Century Learning*, ed. L. Darling-Hammond and F. Adamson (San Francisco, CA: Jossey-Bass, 2014), 277–310; D. T. Conley, *A New Era for Educational Assessment* (Boston, MA: Jobs for the Future, 2014).

11. American Educational Research Association (AERA), American Psychological Association, and National Council for Measurement in Education, *The Standards for Educational and Psychological Testing* (Washington, DC: AERA, 2014).

12. The 2014 version of the *Standards for Educational and Psychological Testing* takes up the issue of validity in greater depth, but test-development practices for the most part have not yet changed dramatically to reflect a greater sensitivity to validity issues.

13. "High-Stakes Testing and Effects on Instruction: Research Review," Center for Public Education, March 30, 2006, http://www.centerforpubliceducation .org/Main-Menu/Instruction/High-stakes-testing-and-effects-on-instruction- At-a-glance/High-stakes-testing-and-effects-on-instruction-Research-review .html.

14. W. J. Popham, "Teaching to the Test," *Educational Leadership* 58, no. 6 (2001): 16–20.

15. N. Lemann, *The Big Test: The Secret History of the American Meritocracy* (New York: Farrar, Straus, Giroux, 1999).

16. K. Cherry, "History of Intelligence Testing: The History and Development of Modern IQ Testing," *Verywell,* last modified August 27, 2016, https://www .verywell.com/history-of-intelligence-testing-2795581.

17. D. B. Tyack, *The One Best System: A History of American Urban Education* (Cambridge, MA: Harvard University Press, 1974).

18. J. Oakes, *Keeping Track: How Schools Structure Inequality* (New Haven, CT: Yale University Press, 1985).

19. See "Structural Inequality in Education," *Wikipedia,* http://en.wikipedia.org/ wiki/Structural_inequality_in_education.

20. D. Koretz, "Limitations in the Use of Achievement Tests as Measures of Educators' Productivity," *Journal of Human Resources* 37, no. 4 (2002): 752–77.

21. J. Goodlad and J. Oakes, "We Must Offer Equal Access to Knowledge," *Educational Leadership* 45, no. 5 (1988); J. Oakes, *Keeping Track: How Schools Structure Inequality* (New Haven, CT: Yale University Press, 1985).

22. See "Criterion-Referenced Test," Glossary of Education Reform, last modified April 30, 2014, http://edglossary.org/criterion-referenced-test/.

23. J. H. Block, *Mastery Learning: Theory and Practice* (New York: Holt, Rinehart, & Winston, 1971); B. Bloom, *Mastery Learning* (New York: Holt, Rinehart, & Winston, 1971); T. R. Guskey, "Mastery Learning: Applying the Theory," *Theory into Practice* 19, no. 2 (1980): 104–11; T. R. Guskey, "What Is Mastery Learning? And Why Do Educators Have Such Hopes for It?" *Instructor* 90, no. 3 (1980): 80; T. R. Guskey, "Individualizing Within the Group-Centered

Classroom: The Mastery Learning Model," *Teacher Education and Special Education* 3 no. 4 (1980): 47–54.

24. L. Horton, "Mastery Learning: Sound in Theory, But . . . ," *Educational Leadership* 37, no. 2 (1979).

25. Horton, "Mastery Learning."

26. R. E. Slavin, "Mastery Learning Reconsidered," *Review of Educational Research* 57 (1987).

27. R. Brandt, "On Outcome-Based Education: A Conversation with Bill Spady," *Educational Leadership* 50, no. 4 (1992/1993).

28. R. K. Hambleton, et al., *Psychometric Review of the Maryland School Performance Assessment Program* (Annapolis, MD: Maryland State Department of Education, 2000).

29. R. Rothman, "The Certificate of Initial Mastery," *Educational Leadership* 52, no. 8 (1995).

30. D. Koretz, B. Stecher, and E. Deibert, *The Reliability of Scores from the 1992 Vermont Portfolio Assessment Program* (Santa Monica, CA: Center for the Study of Evaluation, University of California, Los Angeles, 1993).

31. M. Dudley, "The Rise and Fall of a Statewide Assessment System," *English Journal* 86, no. 1 (1997); M. W. Kirst and C. Mazzeo, "The Rise, Fall, and Rise of State Assessment in California, 1993–96," *Phi Delta Kappan* 78, no. 4 (1996).

32. R. L. Linn, E. L. Baker, and D. W. Betenbenner, *Accountability Systems: Implications of Requirements of the No Child Left Behind Act of 2001* (Los Angeles, CA: Center for the Study of Evaluation; National Center for Research on Evaluation, Standards, and Student Testing; and University of California, Los Angeles, 2002); U.S. Department of Education, *No Child Left Behind* (Washington, DC: U.S. Department of Education, 2001).

33. R. L. Linn, "Conflicting Demands of No Child Left Behind and State Systems: Mixed Messages About School Performance," *Education Policy Analysis Archives* 13, no. 33 (2005); H. Mintrop and G. L. Sunderman, "Predictable Failure of Federal Sanctions-Driven Accountability for School Improvement—and Why We May Retain It Anyway," *Educational Researcher* 38, no. 5 (2009).

34. J. Jennings and D. S. Rentner, "Ten Big Effects of the No Child Left Behind Act on Public Schools," *Phi Delta Kappan* 82, no. 2 (2006).

35. G. Cawelti, "The Side Effects of NCLB," *Educational Leadership* 64, no. 3 (2006).

36. These methods are still widely used, particularly by colleges themselves.

37. R. S. Brown and D. T. Conley, "Comparing State High School Assessments

to Standards for Success in Entry-Level University Courses," *Journal of Education Assessment* 12, no. 2 (2007); D. T. Conley, *Understanding University Success* (Eugene, OR: Center for Educational Policy Research, University of Oregon, 2003); D. T. Conley, *The Texas College and Career Readiness Initiative: Overview & Summary Report* (Eugene, OR: Educational Policy Improvement Center—EPIC, 2011); D. T. Conley, *Getting Ready for College, Careers, and the Common Core: What Every Educator Needs to Know* (San Francisco, CA: Jossey-Bass, 2014); D. T. Conley, K. Aspengren, and O. Stout, *Advanced Placement Best Practices Study: Biology, Chemistry, Environmental Science, Physics, European History, US History, World History* (Eugene, OR: EPIC, 2006); D. T. Conley et al., *College Board Validity Study for Math* (New York: College Board, 2006); D. T. Conley et al., *College Board Validity Study for Science* (New York: College Board, 2006); D. T. Conley et al., *Reaching the Goal: The Applicability and Importance of the Common Core State Standards to College and Career Readiness* (Eugene, OR: EPIC, 2011); D. T. Conley et al., *Texas Career and Technical Education Career Pathways Analysis Study* (Eugene, OR: EPIC, 2009); D. T. Conley et al., *Validation Study III: Alignment of the Texas College and Career Readiness Standards with Courses in Two Career Pathways* (Eugene, OR: EPIC, 2009); D. T. Conley et al., *Texas College and Career Readiness Initiative: Texas Career and Technical Education Phase I Alignment Analysis Report* (Eugene, OR: EPIC, 2009); D. T. Conley, *Texas College and Career Readiness Initiative Phase II: Examining the Alignment Between the Texas College and Career Readiness Standards and Entry-Level College Courses at Texas Postsecondary Institutions* (Eugene, OR: EPIC, 2008); "ThinkReady: An Innovative, Formative Assessment of Students' Cognitive Abilities"; M. Seburn, S. Frain, and D. T. Conley, *Job Training Programs Curriculum Study* (Washington, DC: National Assessment Governing Board, WestEd, Educational Policy Improvement Center, 2013); *Texas College and Career Readiness Standards* (Austin, TX: Texas Higher Education Coordinating Board and Educational Policy Improvement Center, 2009).

38. C. Hinton, K. W. Fischer, and C. Glennon, *Mind, Brain, and Education* (Boston, MA: Jobs for the Future, 2012).

39. C. S. Dweck, G. M. Walton, and G. L. Cohen, *Academic Tenacity: Mindsets and Skills That Promote Long-Term Learning* (Seattle, WA: Bill & Melinda Gates Foundation, 2011).

40. M. S. Donovan, J. D. Bransford, and J. W. Pellegrino, eds., *How People Learn: Bridging Research and Practice* (Washington, DC: National Academy Press, 1999); Pellegrino and Hilton, eds., *Education for Life and Work*.

41. J. Medina, *Brain Rules: 12 Principles for Surviving and Thriving at Work, Home, and School* (Seattle, WA: Pear Press, 2008).

42. National Research Council, *Learning and Understanding: Improving Advanced Study of Mathematics and Science in U.S. High Schools* (Washington, DC: National Academies Press, 2002).

43. D. Knecht, "The Consortium and the Commissioner: A Grass Roots Tale of Fighting High Stakes Graduation Testing in New York," *Urban Review: Issues and Ideas in Public Education* 39, no. 1 (2007).

44. M. Baldwin, M. Seburn, and D. T. Conley, *External Validity of the College-Readiness Performance Assessment System (C-PAS)* (paper presented at the 2011 American Educational Research Association Annual Conference, New Orleans, LA, 2011); D. T. Conley, *The College-Readiness Performance Assessment System* (Eugene, OR: EPIC, 2007); D. T. Conley et al., *College-Readiness Performance Assessment System (C-PAS) Conceptual Model* (Eugene, OR: EPIC, 2007).

45. See http://education.ohio.gov/Topics/Ohios-Learning-Standards/Ohio-Performance-Assessment-Pilot-Project-OPAPP.

46. "NH Performance Assessment Network," New Hampshire Department of Education, http://www.education.nh.gov/assessment-systems/.

47. Ibid.

48. "Career Pathways Collaborative Offers New Assessments for Career and Technical Education," Center for Educational Testing & Evaluation, http://careerpathways.us/news/career-pathways-collaborative-offers-new-assessments-career-and-technical-education.

49. J. Soland, L. S. Hamilton, and B. M. Stecher, *Measuring 21st Century Competencies: Guidance for Educators* (New York: Asia Society/RAND Corporation, 2013).

50. "Envision Schools College Success Portfolio," Stanford Center for Assessment Learning and Equity, https://scale.stanford.edu/content/envision-schools-college-success-portfolio.

51. G. Reyes, et al., *Examining High Leverage Instructional Practices That Support Equitable Use of Performance Assessment at Summit Public Schools* (Stanford, CA: Stanford Center for Assessment, Learning, and Equity, 2015).

52. D. T. Conley, "Proficiency-Based Admissions," in *Choosing Students: Higher Education Admission Tools for the 21st Century*, ed. W. Camara and E. Kimmell (Mahwah, NJ: Lawrence Erlbaum, 2005); Oregon State Department of Education, *Career-Related Learning Standards and Extended Application Standard: Guide for Schools to Build Relevant and Rigorous Collections of Evidence* (Salem, OR: Oregon State Department of Education, 2005).

53. B. M. Stecher et al., *Using Alternative Assessments in Vocational Education: Appendix B: Kentucky Instructional Results Information System* (Berkeley, CA: National Center for Research in Vocational Education, 1997).

54. Soland, Hamilton, and Stecher, *Measuring 21st Century Competencies*.

55. *Take the Test: Sample Questions from OECD's PISA Assessments* (Paris: OECD Publishing, 2009); D. Kastberg et al., *Technical Report and User Guide for the Program for International Student Assessment (PISA)* (Washington, DC: U.S. Department of Education, 2014).

56. "Compare SAT Specifications," College Board, https://collegereadiness.college board.org/sat/inside-the-test/compare-old-new-specifications.

57. "About Us," ACT Aspire, http://www.discoveractaspire.org/in-a-nutshell.html.

58. "Take the SAT," College Board, https://collegereadiness.collegeboard.org/.

59. D. T. Conley, *Learning Strategies as Metacognitive Factors: A Critical Review* (Eugene, OR: EPIC, 2014).

60. M. R. West, *The Limitations of Self-Report Measures of Non-cognitive Skills* (Washington, DC: Brookings Institution, 2014).

61. A. L. Duckworth and C. Peterson, "Grit: Perseverance and Passion for Long-Term Goals," *Journal of Personality and Social Psychology* 92, no. 6 (2007); C. MacCann, A. L. Duckworth, and R. D. Roberts, "Empirical Identification of the Major Facets of Conscientiousness," *Learning and Individual Differences* 19, no. 4 (2009); P. Tough, *How Children Succeed: Grit, Curiosity, and the Hidden Power of Character* (New York: Houghton Mifflin Harcourt, 2012).

62. C. A. Farrington, *Academic Mindsets as a Critical Component of Deeper Learning* (Chicago, IL: University of Chicago, 2013).

63. P. C. Kyllonen, *The Case for Noncognitive Assessments* (Princeton, NJ: Educational Testing Service Research & Development, 2005).

64. "Angela Duckworth: Research," Angela Duckworth, http://angeladuckworth .com/research/.

65. A. L. Duckworth and D. S. Yeager, "Measurement Matters: Assessing Personal Qualities Other Than Cognitive Ability for Educational Purposes," *Educational Researcher* 44, no. 4 (2015): 237–51.

66. See www.mindsetworks.com/Science.

67. See www.epiconline.org/projects/campusready.

68. "Homepage," CORE Districts, http://coredistricts.org.

69. M. R. West, *Should Non-Cognitive Skills Be Included in School Accountability Systems? Preliminary Evidence from California's CORE Districts* (Washington, DC: Brookings Institution, 2016).

70. Kyllonen, *The Case for Noncognitive Assessments*.
71. Portions of this section are excerpted or adapted from D. T. Conley and L. Darling-Hammond, *Creating Systems of Assessment for Deeper Learning* (Stanford, CA: Stanford Center for Opportunity Policy in Education, 2013).
72. Conley and Darling-Hammond, "Building Systems of Assessment for Deeper Learning."

ABOUT THE
EDITORS

RAFAEL HELLER, PhD, is the managing editor of *Kappan* magazine. He was previously the principal policy analyst at Jobs for the Future, where he led efforts to synthesize new ideas and research in secondary education and explore their implications for policy and practice. Prior to joining JFF in 2014, Dr. Heller was an independent consultant for many years, serving as a writer, editor, and strategic counsel to numerous education advocacy groups, foundations, associations, and other organizations. He has worked as a senior policy associate at the Alliance for Excellent Education, directing a range of projects focused on improving literacy instruction in the nation's middle and high schools, and he has been an editor at the Association of American Colleges and Universities. Earlier in his career, he spent several years teaching writing, rhetoric, and English, including a stint as professor and English department chair at the Universidad San Francisco de Quito, Ecuador.

ADRIA STEINBERG, EdM, brings decades of experience leading and writing about program and policy development efforts to improve the educational options and prospects of young people who have traditionally been underserved by our educational and workforce systems. As senior adviser to the Students at the Center initiative at Jobs for the Future, she helps to guide policy, strategy, and framework development and to translate research into action-oriented tools. She also has coauthored and served as developmental editor of numerous papers produced or commissioned by JFF on student-centered approaches to learning and on the educational reforms necessary to achieve deeper learning. As senior adviser to JFF's Back on Track initiative, she helps to guide strategy development in creating and scaling up high-quality pathways to family-supporting careers and postsecondary credentials for off-track and disconnected youth.

REBECCA E. WOLFE, PhD, is a senior director at Jobs for the Future, where she oversees the Students at the Center initiative. Students at the Center is at the forefront of national efforts to leverage knowledge and research on student-centered approaches that lead to deeper learning in order to effect meaningful change at scale—especially for our most vulnerable youth. Dr. Wolfe has authored or coauthored numerous publications on topics related to student-centered and deeper learning. Recent selections include *Effective Schools for Deeper Learning: An Exploratory Study* and *Anytime, Anywhere: Student-Centered Learning for Schools and Teachers*. Prior to joining JFF, Dr. Wolfe was the education director at the Fairfield County Community Foundation, a middle school site coordinator for GEAR UP, and an educator in several college readiness efforts for low-income youth.

ABOUT THE
CONTRIBUTORS

DAVID T. CONLEY, PhD, is founder and president of EdImagine, an educational strategy consulting company, and professor of educational policy and leadership at the University of Oregon, where he directs the Center for Educational Policy Research. He is also a senior fellow for deeper learning under the sponsorship of the Hewlett Foundation. Dr. Conley's research has focused on college and career readiness, systems of assessment, and models of educational accountability. He writes extensively on what it takes for students to be prepared to succeed in college and careers, including his most recent book, *Getting Ready for College, Careers, and the Common Core: What Every Educator Needs to Know.*

LOUIS DANIELSON, PhD, is a managing director at the American Institutes for Research and for over three decades has been involved in programs that improve results for students with disabilities. Until recently, he held leadership roles in the U.S. Department of Education's Office for Special Education Programs and was responsible for the Individuals with Disabilities Education Act national activities programs. A frequent contributor to professional journals, Dr. Danielson has published extensively and is a frequent speaker at national and international conferences and events focusing on special education.

LINDA DARLING-HAMMOND, EdD, is president of the Learning Policy Institute and Charles E. Ducommun Professor of Education Emeritus at Stanford University, where she is faculty director of the Stanford Center for Opportunity Policy in Education. She is former president of the American Educational Research Association and a member of the National Academy of Education and the American Academy of Arts and Sciences. Her research and policy work focus on educational equity, teaching quality, and school reform. She began her career as a public high school teacher, has helped to start several schools, and advises school leaders and policy makers at the local, state, and federal levels. Her most recent book is *Beyond the Bubble Test: How Performance Assessments Support 21st Century Learning.*

SARAH FINE is an advanced doctoral candidate at the Harvard Graduate School of Education as well as a visiting scholar at the High Tech High Graduate School of Education. Prior to starting her doctoral studies, she worked as a teacher, department chair, and instructional coach at a high school in the District of Columbia, and as a freelance education journalist. Her dissertation focuses on the intersection of deeper learning and restorative justice in the context of school change. Her work has appeared in a diverse array of publications, including the *Washington Post, Education Week*, and the *Harvard Educational Review.*

DIANE FRIEDLAENDER, PhD, is a senior associate at the Stanford Center for Opportunity Policy in Education (SCOPE), where she oversees research and professional development efforts. At SCOPE, Dr. Friedlaender has led qualitative research of schools that are effectively preparing low-income students and students of color for college, career, and life, including *Student-Centered Schools: Closing the Opportunity Gap* and *High Schools for Equity: Policy Supports for Student Learning in Communities of Color*, coauthored with Linda Darling-Hammond. She also conducts research at the school district level. Her areas of expertise include educational equity, urban education, secondary school transformation, arts integration, and qualitative research methods.

PATRICIA GÁNDARA, PhD, is a research professor and codirector of the Civil Rights Project at the University of California, Los Angeles. She is also a member of the National Academy of Education and a fellow of the American Educational Research Association, the Rockefeller Foundation Bellagio Center in Italy, the French-American Association at Sciences Po Graduate Institute, Paris, and an Educational Testing Service fellow in Princeton, New Jersey. Her most recent books are *Forbidden Language: English Learners and Restrictive Language Policies*, with Megan Hopkins, and *The Bilingual Advantage: Language, Literacy, and the U.S. Labor Market*, with Rebecca Callahan.

NANCY HOFFMAN, PhD, is senior adviser at Jobs for the Future, a national nonprofit in Boston focused on improving educational and workforce outcomes for low-income youth and adults. Dr. Hoffman is cofounder of the Pathways to Prosperity Network, a collaboration of JFF, the Harvard Graduate School of Education, and states and regions focused on ensuring that many more young people complete high school and attain a post-secondary credential with currency in the labor market. Her most recent book is *Schooling in the Workplace: How Six of the World's Best Vocational Education Systems Prepare Young People for Jobs and Life*. Her current work includes coauthoring a book with Bob Schwartz on the career pathways movement. She serves on the Massachusetts Board of Higher Education.

LYNN HOLDHEIDE, EdM, is a principal technical assistance consultant for the American Institutes for Research. She has more than ten years of experience in providing responsive technical assistance of the highest quality to state education agencies, educator preparation programs, and regional comprehensive centers. With experience as a special education teacher at the Indiana State Department of Education and Vanderbilt University, she is well positioned to advance coherence and alignment in instructional expectations across general and special education so that all teachers are prepared to support the learning of students with disabilities.

MEREDITH I. HONIG, PhD, is an associate professor of educational policy, organizations, and leadership and director of the District Leadership

Design Lab (DL2) at the University of Washington, Seattle. She founded DL2 in 2013 to help improve the quality of knowledge and support available to school district central office leaders across the country interested in pursuing major performance improvements. Her publications on central office leadership and change have appeared in various publications, including the *American Educational Research Journal* and *The School Administrator.*

KEI KAWASHIMA-GINSBERG, PhD, is the director of the Center for Information and Research on Civic Learning and Engagement (CIRCLE) at the Jonathan M. Tisch College of Civic Life at Tufts University. She and her team conduct original research and produce resources for educators and public audiences on a wide range of topics related to civic learning opportunities and experiences of young people. With a background in positive youth development and interest in diverse and marginalized youth, she sees research as a powerful tool to address educational inequity.

MAGDALENE LAMPERT, PhD, is the senior adviser to New Visions for Public Schools in New York City for its curriculum and teacher development project in high school mathematics, and was previously coordinator of documentation, design, and development for teaching and learning at the Boston Plan for Excellence. She has taught elementary and high school mathematics, preservice and inservice teacher education, and doctoral courses for aspiring teacher educators. She has written extensively about teaching practice, including the book *Teaching Problems and the Problems of Teaching.* Dr. Lampert is professor emerita in the University of Michigan School of Education. She received the 2014 Outstanding Contribution to Education Award from the Harvard Graduate School of Education and was elected to the American Academy of Arts and Sciences in 2016.

PETER LEVINE, PhD, is associate dean for research and a professor of citizenship and public affairs in the Jonathan M. Tisch College of Civic Life at Tufts University. Levine is the author of *We Are the Ones We Have Been Waiting For: The Promise of Civic Renewal in America* and five other books on philosophy and politics. Previously, he was a member of the Institute for

Philosophy & Public Policy in the University of Maryland's School of Public Policy and deputy director of the National Commission on Civic Renewal.

JAL MEHTA, PhD, is an associate professor of education at the Harvard Graduate School of Education. His primary research interest is in understanding what it would take to create high-quality schooling at scale, with a particular interest in the professionalization of teaching. He is the author of *The Allure of Order: High Hopes, Dashed Expectations, and the Troubled Quest to Remake American Schooling* and coeditor of *The Futures of School Reform*. He is currently working with Sarah Fine on a book, *In Search of Deeper Learning*, a contemporary study of schools, systems, and nations that are seeking to produce ambitious instruction.

PEDRO NOGUERA, PhD, is a distinguished professor of education at the Graduate School of Education and Information Studies at the University of California, Los Angeles. His research focuses on the ways in which schools are influenced by social and economic conditions, as well as by demographic trends in local, regional, and global contexts. He is the author of twelve books and over two hundred articles and monographs. Prior to joining the faculty at UCLA, he served as a professor at New York University, Harvard University, and the University of California, Berkeley. In 2014 he was elected to the National Academy of Education.

LYDIA R. RAINEY, PhD, is research director at the District Leadership Design Lab (DL2) at the University of Washington, Seattle, where she leads the DL2's knowledge-building efforts related to district central office performance improvement. For over ten years, Dr. Rainey has participated in numerous studies of how school systems, including school districts and charter management organizations, design and implement policies to improve their performance.

SHARON VAUGHN, PhD, is the Manuel J. Justiz Endowed Chair and executive director of the Meadows Center for Preventing Educational Risk at the University of Texas College of Education. She is the author of numerous books and research articles that address the reading and social outcomes of students with learning difficulties. She has served as the editor-in-chief of the *Journal of Learning Disabilities* and the coeditor of *Learning Disabilities Research & Practice*. Dr. Vaughn is the recipient of the American Educational Research Association's Special Interest Group distinguished researcher award and the University of Texas distinguished faculty award.

REBECCA ZUMETA EDMONDS, PhD, is a principal researcher at the American Institutes for Research, where she serves as project director for an Investing in Innovation Fund (i3) Development Grant, and as codirector of the National Center on Intensive Intervention. Previously, Dr. Zumeta Edmonds coordinated technical assistance for the National Center on Response to Intervention and worked for the Washington State Department of Special Education. She chairs the Professional Development Standards and Ethics Committee of the Council for Exceptional Children's Division for Learning Disabilities, and she has taught special education in public and private lab schools in the Seattle area.

INDEX

293